Chapter Thirty Three
After Seven Years

Sir Francis, as I afterwards learned, did not insist upon the matter, but the very next day, as I was in the peach-house, I heard the door open, and I felt anything but comfortable as I saw Courtenay enter the place and come slowly up to me.

I was prepared for anything, but I had no cause for expecting war. He had come in peace.

"We're going away directly after lunch," he said in a low, surly tone, as if he resented what he was saying. "I'll—, I'll—there! I'll try—to be different when I come back again."

He turned and went hurriedly out of the place, and he had not been gone long when the door at the other end clicked, and I found, as soon as he who entered had come round into sight, that it was Philip.

He came up to me in a quick, impetuous way, as if eager to get his task over, and as our eyes met I could see that he had evidently been suffering a good deal.

"I'm going away this afternoon," he said quickly. "I wish I hadn't said and done all I have. I beg—"

He could not finish, but burst into a passionate fit of sobbing, and turned away his face.

"Good-bye!" I said. "I shall not think about it any more."

"Then we'll shake hands," he cried—"some day—next time we meet."

We did shake hands next time we met, but when Philip Dalton said those words he did not know it would be seven years first. But so it was.

I never knew exactly how it happened, but I believe one of my uncles was influenced to take some part in the affair, and Sir Francis did all the rest. What I do know is that about three months after the young Daltons had gone I was on my way to a clergyman's house, where I stayed a year, being prepared for my future career; and when I had been with the Reverend Hartley Dallas a year I was able to join the Military College at Woolwich, where I went through the regular course, and in due time obtained my commission in the artillery.

I had not long been in the service before the Crimean war broke out, and our battery was one of the first despatched to the seat of war, where, in company with my comrades, I went through that terrible period of misery and privation.

One night I was in charge of a couple of guns in a rather dangerous position near the Redan, and after repairing damages under fire my lads had contrived to patch up a pretty secure shelter with sand-bag and gabion, ready for knocking down next day, but it kept off the rain, and where we huddled together there was no mud under our feet, though it was inches deep in the trench.

It was a bitter night, and the tiny bit of fire that we had ventured to make in the hole we had scooped underground hardly kept the chill from our half-frozen limbs. Food was not plentiful, luxuries we had none, and in place of the dashing-looking artillerymen in blue and gold people are accustomed to see on parade, anyone who had looked upon us would have seen a set of mud-stained, ragged scarecrows, blackened with powder, grim looking, but hard and full of fight.

I was seated on an upturned barrel, hugging my sheepskin-lined greatcoat closer to me, and drawing it down over my high boots, as I made room for a couple of my wet, shivering men, and I felt ashamed to be the owner of so warm a coat as I looked at their well-worn service covering, when my sergeant put in his head and said:

"Captain of the company of foot, sir, would be glad if you could give him a taste of the fire and a drop of brandy; he's half dead with the cold."

"Bring him in," I said; and I waited, thinking about home and the old garden at Isleworth and then of that at Hampton; I didn't know why, but I did. And then I was thinking to myself that it was a good job that we had the stern, manly feeling to comfort us of our hard work being our duty, when I heard the *slush, slush, slush, slush,* sound of feet coming along the trenches, and then my sergeant said:

"You'll have to stoop very low to get in, sir, but you'll find it warm and dry. The lieutenant's inside."

"Yes, come in," I said; and my men drew back to let the fresh corner get a bit of the fire.

"It's awfully kind of you," he said, as he knelt down, took off his dripping gloves, and held his blue fingers to the flame. "What a night! It isn't fit for a dog to be out in. 'Pon my soul, gunner, I feel ashamed to come in and get shelter, and leave my poor boys in the trench."

"Get a good warm then, and let's thaw and dry one of them at a time. I'm going to turn out soon."

"Sorry for you," he said. "Brandy—thanks. It's worth anything a night like this. I've got some cigars in my breast-pocket, as soon as my fingers will let me get at them."

He had taken off his shako, and the light shone full upon his face, which I recognised directly, though he did not know me, as he looked up and said again:

"It's awfully kind of you, gunner."

"Oh! it's nothing," I said, "Captain Dalton—Philip Dalton, is it not?"

"Yes," he said; "you know me?"

"To be sure," I replied; "but you said that next time we met we'd shake hands."

He sank back and his jaw dropped.

"You remember me—Grant? How is Sir Francis?"

"Remember you!" he said, seizing my hand, "Oh! I say, what a young beast I was!"

I learned more than once that he and his brother turned out fine, manly soldiers, and did their duty well in that hard-fought campaign. I tried also to do mine, and came back one of the last to leave the Crimea, another grade higher in my rank.

During my college life I often used to go over and see the brothers Brownsmith, to be warmly welcomed at every visit; and if ever he got to know that I was going to Isleworth to spend Sunday, Ike used to walk over, straighten his back and draw himself up to attention, and salute me, looking as serious as if in uniform. He did not approve of my going into the artillery, though.

"It's wrong," he used to say; and in these days he was back at Isleworth, for Mr Solomon had entered into partnership with his brother, and both Ike and Shock had elected to follow him back to the old place.

"Yes," he would say, "it's wrong, Mars Grant, I was always drew to you because your father had been a sojer; but what would he have said to you if he had lived to know as you turned gunner?"

"What would you have had me, then? You must have artillerymen."

"Yes, of course, sir; but what are they? You ought to have been a hoozoar: —

"'Oh, them as with jackets go flying,
Oh, they are the gallant hoozoars,'"

he sang — at least he tried to sing; but I went into the artillery.

By the way, I did not tell you the name of the sergeant who ushered Philip Dalton into my shelter that night. His name was John Hampton, as fine a soldier as ever stepped. He joined the artillery when I got my commission. Poor Shock, for I knew him better by that name; he followed me with the fidelity of a dog; he always contrived something hot for me when we were almost starving, and any day he would have gone without that I might eat. And I believe that he would have fought for me to the death.

Poor Shock! The night when I was told that he could not live, after being struck down by a piece of shell, I knelt by him in the mud and held his hand. He just looked up in my face and said softly:

"Remember being shut up in the sand-pit, sir, and how you prayed? If you wouldn't mind, sir — once again?"

I bent down lower and lower, and at last — soldier — hardened by horrors — grown stern by the life I led — I felt as if I had lost in that rough, true man the best of friends, and I cried over him like a child!

The Rule of S. Benet.

Agents for the sale of the Early English Text Society's
Publications.

DUBLIN: WILLIAM M^cGEE, 18 Nassau Street.

EDINBURGH: T. G. STEVENSON, 22 South Frederick Street.

GLASGOW: OGLE & Co., 1 Royal Exchange Square.

BERLIN: ASHER & Co., Unter den Linden 20.

NEW YORK: C. SCRIBNER & Co., LEYPOLDT & HOLT.

PHILADELPHIA: J. B. LIPPINCOTT & Co.

The Rule of S. Benet.

LATIN AND ANGLO-SAXON

INTERLINEAR VERSION.

EDITED, WITH AN INTRODUCTION AND NOTES

BY

DR. H. LOGEMAN.

LONDON:

PUBLISHED FOR THE EARLY ENGLISH TEXT SOCIETY

BY N. TRÜBNER AND CO., 57 AND 59 LUDGATE HILL.

MDCCCLXXXVIII.

Unaltered reprint 2000
ISBN 0 85991 848 3
Distributed for the Early English Text Society by
Boydell & Brewer Ltd, PO Box 9, Woodbridge, Suffolk IP12 3DF
and Boydell & Brewer Inc, PO Box 41026, Rochester, NY 14604-4126
Printed and bound in Great Britain by Antony Rowe Ltd, Chippenham, Wiltshire

ON some pages of the Introduction to this volume, and also in the Notes at the end, I have had to mention gratefully the help I have received from various quarters.

But apart from the aid specified there, I must here give the names of two gentlemen, whose assistance to me has been very valuable. First and foremost my thanks are due to Dr. Furnivall, who with great kindness has facilitated the publishing of this book, both as my doctoral dissertation, to be presented to the Faculty of Letters at the Utrecht University, and as one of the issues for the Early English Text Society. I must also thank him heartily for the trouble he has taken in correcting my necessarily faulty English. Secondly to my brother, Mr. W. S. Logeman, who volunteered to extract by far the greater part of the text for lexicographical purposes. I need hardly say that this labour has been of material service to me, and I gladly take this opportunity of publicly acknowledging my obligations.

H. LOGEMAN.

CONTENTS.

INTRODUCTION.

TEXT.

[1] Those showing the order or sequence of the A.-Saxon words in construing the Latin.

[2] Part of a word put for the whole of it, as *pra* for *prarost*.

[1] A Roman liquid measure.

INTRODUCTION.

I. Outlines of the History of Benedictinism in England until the Reformation.

THE Latin convent rule, known under the name of the Rule of S. Benet, was written by that Saint about the year 516 A.D.[1] Saint Benedict was not the first who found it necessary to lay down rules for monks to live by. He wrote only for those 'qui regulas *nigris monachis* ediderunt' (i.e. those that were afterwards called Black Friars, and Benedictines). Dugdale, on the page cited below, enumerates some six and more fathers who were the authors of Rules. Of these we may especially mention S. Basilius, and refer the reader to page 118[2] infra, where Benedictus of Nursia himself speaks of the Regula sanctis patris nostri Basilii, as 'bene viventium et oboedientium monachorum instituta virtutum.'

According to the commonly accepted idea, Pope Gregory the Great introduced Benedictinism, along with Christianity, into England in the year 596, when Augustine, prior of the Monastery of S. Andrew at Rome, came across with several

---

[1] See Dugdale's Monasticon, ed. 1817 and 1846, I, p. xxiii. S. Benedictus pater noster . . . . regulam monachorum edidit circa annum Christi 516.

[2] I here give the translation from the Durham MS., Bb. 1. 6 (see Wanley, p. 298), a collation of which was not given by Professor Schröer: 'Eac swylce þæra haligra fædera lif. 7 heora drohtnunga. 7 se regol ures halgan fæder basilii hwæt is hit elles butan ge timbrunga haligra manna. 7 ðæra muneca þ (read þe) wel 7 rihte libbað, 7 ge hersume synd.' See A. Schröer, Die Angelsächsischen Prosabearbeitungen der Benediktinerregel, Kassel, 1885-1888, p. 133. I may here thankfully mention the service rendered me by the Rev. Canon D. Greenwell, Librarian to the Dean and Chapter of Durham Cathedral, who, on my applying for the loan of the MS., volunteered to transcribe the whole of the Ben. Rule contained in it, and who, assisted by the Rev. J. T. Fowler, Librarian to the University of Durham, did so entirely as 'a labour of love.' Let me here publicly thank the reverend gentlemen for this extraordinary kindness.

2

other Benedictine monks [1]. Hook adds that 'Before Dunstan's time we may doubt the existence anywhere in England of the Benedictine Rule in its completeness.' Lingard [2] argues against this. According to this learned historian, Benedictine writers have unsuccessfully tried to establish and maintain that S. Gregory was a Benedictine himself. According to him, it was not until Wilfrid's time (latter half of the seventh century) that the monks of Britain got acquainted with the Rule of S. Benedict. Be this as it may [3], all are agreed in attributing a high character and a great authority to the Rule in England when once introduced.

A few notes on the fate of the Benedictines in England may be convenient to the reader. Dugdale, in his great collection of materials for the study of Monasticism in England, says [4] :—

' Tres autem apud nos celebres fuerunt monachismi veteris reformationes. . . . Altera sub Dunstano fuit, in consilio Wintoniensi anno 965 regnante Edgaro, magnificentissimo coenobiorum instauratore. Tunc primum monachis praescripta fuit constitutio generalis tam ex Benedicti Regula quam ex veteribus consuetudinibus contexta quae dicta est Regularis Concordia Anglicae nationis [5].'

If this 'Regularis Concordia' is not Dunstan's, it owes its origin at least to his mind, which pervades the time in which he lived. His was the age of the revival of monasticism. It is Dunstan's mind that speaks through Eadgar's mouth when the latter prompts Aethelwold to a translation of the Benedictine Rule [6]. What Dunstan aimed at, was to lead back monastic life to its original purity and severe discipline in accordance with the Rule of S. Benet, and to infuse the spirit of monasticism into the whole of the English Church. When, after sundry vicissitudes, Dunstan came to power shortly after Eadgar's accession, the reforms sadly wanted

---

[1] See Smith and Cheetham, Dict. of Christ. Antiquities ; and Hook, Church Dictionary, in voce.

[2] Alterthümer der Angelsächsischen Kirche. Deutsch von Dr. F. H., in Rom. Breslau, 1847. When writing, I had not the English ed. at my disposal.

[3] This is not the place for further investigations of the matter. I refer to Lingard, pp. 64, 70, and 72.

[4] Monasticon Anglicanum, I, p. xiii.

[5] See infra, Ch. II of this Introduction, sub I.

[6] See Schröer, Die Prosabearbeitungen, pp. xiii–xviii ; infra, p. xxxiv.

were carried into effect. And his faithful friend Aethelwold followed in his footsteps [1].

The institution of several affiliated congregations, as those of the Cistercian and Cluniac monks, shows on the one hand great interest in Benedict's Regulations; on the other hand, however, the fact that this revival was deemed necessary, clearly indicates that here and there the observance of the Rule had gradually become laxer. The same may be said with regard to the Councils held every now and then at London, and in other places. When we find one synod revive an enactment that no meat shall be eaten, it is a sure sign that for some time this precept had not been observed [2]. About the year 1421 we find that degeneration had again set in, and that a reform was contemplated. At a meeting in Westminster Abbey between King Henry V and the Abbots and prelates of the Order of Black Monks, more than 360 in number, a reform was decided upon [3].

Coming a hundred years down, we now approach Henry the Eighth's time, the age of the decline of monasticism, the time when monasteries were to be dissolved, along with the ties that had bound Henry VIII to Rome. That corruption had set in, is a fact recognised alike by both Roman Catholic and Protestant writers. 'It is not pretended that every single community of the very numerous houses in England,' says Weldon [4], 'where the Rule of S. Benet was followed, was at the time of its dispersion in the highest state of regular discipline,' and [5] :—

---

[1] I cannot but refer to B. ten Brink's words on this subject, which are very characteristic (Engl. Litt. Geschichte, 1877, I, p. 129); to Cockayne, Leechdoms, III, p. 412; and Bishop Stubbs, Memorials of S. Dunstan, Introduction, passim, but especially pp. cv and cviii.

[2] 'Sana de constitutione quam paulo ante concilium fecerant abbates ordinis Sancti Benedicti per Angliam constituti de carnibus non comedendis sacro approbante concilio his verbis diffinitum est.' Luard, Annales Monastici, II, 318; Annales de Waverleia, MCCXXXVII. For other councils, see ib., IV, 547-550.

[3] See Dom. Bennet Weldon, a Chronicle of the English Bened. Monks, etc., preface, p. vii, who quotes Thomas Walsingham, Historia Anglicana, ed. 1864, II, p. 337.

[4] Ib., p. xii.

[5] Liber Monasterii de Hyde, by E. Edwards. Preface, p. lxiii.

'The complaints'—against the inmates, as will be seen, of not a very serious nature—'relate for the most part to certain anticipations by some of the more youthful monks of the teachings of what has lately been called muscular Christianity, as shown in their addiction to the practice of long-bow archery in the Hyde meadows, and to that of keeping late hours, sitting for long discussions, sometimes to the hour of eight in the evening and even beyond it (and, it is much to be feared, occasionally over a potation to freshen their talk), instead of betaking themselves to bed immediately after supper, according to the good wont of their predecessors.'

And now a complaint on the part of the Roman Catholics, which is at the same time a serious accusation :—

'In estimating the case with which so many venerable monasteries were overthrown, it must be borne in mind that for some years previous to their final suppression, many steps had been taken by those in power to render that suppression more easy. One of these, and perhaps the chief, was the appointment by the Court of compliant and suborned men, already apostates at heart, to highest positions in the religious houses. No one was more prominent in this disgraceful intrigue than the highest ecclesiastical authority in the kingdom, the primate Cranmer.'

As a proof of this, D. Weldon [1] instances the case of a man who was recommended for a vacancy, and who was—in an introductory letter quoted—said to be 'very tractable, and as ready to set forward his prince's causes as no man more of his coat' (1538). And the late Professor Brewer, a Protestant historian of Henry VIII [2], has an admission bearing on this subject, when he says: (Nothing) . . . . 'warrant(s) us in believing that the era preceding the Reformation was more corrupt than that which succeeded it.'

We now understand the preamble of the Act 27 Henry VIII, intitled ' An act concerning the suppression or Dissolution of certain Religious houses and geven to the Kings Highness and to his Heirs for ever.

'For as much as manifest sinne, vycyous carnal and abominable living ys daily used and cōmitted in such littell and small abbayes and priories and other religious houses of monkes chanons and nonnes where the congregation is under the number of XII'[3], etc.

How the new hope to which Mary's accession gave birth

---

[1] Weldon, pref., p. xiii.

[2] The Reign of Henry VIII, from his accession to the death of Wolsey, by the late J. S. Brewer, M.A., ed. by James Gairdner, of the Public Record Office, I, 1884 ; see p. 600.

[3] Monasticon Anglicanum, Appendix to Vol. VIII, p. 1654.

was cut short with the end of her brief reign, and the succession of the Protestant Elizabeth, who undid all, and how the Benedictines fared unto this very day, all this and more the curious may pursue in the works I have cited in the foot-notes. I may fitly close this section of the introduction by two more passages from Professor Brewer's book, which are worth quoting :—

'The greater monasteries were necessarily modified by the circumstances of the times, and their religious characters impaired. They admitted a number of lay inmates, or, at least, kept open house for persons not connected with their foundations' (I, p. 50) and (ib., p. 51):

'That in so large a body of men, so widely dispersed, seated for so many centuries in the richest and fairest estates of England, for which they were mainly indebted to their own skill, perseverance, and industry, discreditable members were to be found (and what literary chiffonier, raking in the scandalous annals of any profession, cannot find filth and corruption) is likely enough, but that the corruption was either so black or so general as party spirit would make us believe, is contrary to all analogy, and is unsupported by impartial and contemporary evidence[1].'

II. Bibliography of the various treatises, found in the Cottonian MS., Tib. A. 3.

The manuscript from which the present copy of the Benedictine Rule is taken, is the Cotton MS., Tiberius A. 3. It is described by Wanley on pp. 193[2]-199 of his catalogue. The MS. is slightly injured, but has been rebound and beautifully pasted up. At p. 198, section LXI, Wanley records the very gaps that I have noted below (on p. 1, ll. 1, 2, etc.), so that these injuries must be anterior to him, and therefore also to the fire of 1731.

The MS. is a miscellaneous one, containing a varied col-

---

[1] Just now a notice reaches me of a book only recently published, 'Henry VIII and the English Monasteries ; an attempt to illustrate the History of their Suppression.' By Francis Aidan Gasquet. Vol. I. The book, which lays blame on Protestants as well as on Roman Catholics, is characterised as being 'most conscientiously fair.' For a full statement of the case against the monasteries, I refer the reader to Ch. V of R. W. Dixon's History of the Church of England. Vol. I, 1878 (London : Smith, Elder, and Co.).

[2] Wanley, by a misprint, 793.

lection of interlinear versions, prayers, confessions, and other treatises. The authorities of the great public libraries are not, so far as I know, keeping registers of the MSS. published or transcribed. The work in arrear is of course enormous; but an inverted Wanley to begin with,—to which the present is a humble contribution—would be an invaluable boon to students of the Oldest English, and would be a foundation for librarians to work upon. I therefore proceed to give notes of where the various pieces in the MS. Tiberius A. 3 are printed, if they have been edited at all; and I hope that all who have ever turned over the leaves of MSS. to hunt for unpublished matter, will be glad of my attempt; especially those who have diligently copied out page after page, only to find that this had been already done by some one else. Since Wanley's time the pagination of the MS. has been slightly altered, and my statements refer to this new pagination.

That some one will take this work up for all MSS. is a consummation devoutly to be wished.

The greater part of the MS. was copied out by Junius (see below, p. xxxii, on the value of these transcriptions), and his copies are kept in the Bodleian Library, at Oxford. It is to the various MSS. of this collection that the words 'MS. Junius' (infra) refer.

Contents of the MS. Tiberius A. 3.

No. I (fo. 3). Regularis Concordia Anglicae Nationis Monachorum Sanctimonialiumque.

MSS. Jun. 52. 109 (now = No. 46). Wanley, pp. 92 and 99. VII.

Of this, the Latin text has been printed in full at least twice: (a) in R. P. Clem. Reyneri Apostolatus Benedictinorum, and (b) in the later editions of the Monasticon Anglicanum, see edd. 1817, 1846, I, p. xxvii. The Anglo-Saxon text has never been printed in full. Besides the smaller quotations given from it by Wanley himself, other extracts have been put in type several times. Selden printed the prologue and the greater part of the epilogue in his notes to Eadmer. See his Works, ed. 1726, II (tomus 2), pp. 1612–1621 (see MS. Junius, 18; Wanley, p. 103). Selden, in accordance with the usage of his time, 'edits'[1] the MS., and though he does not mention the MS. from which his text is taken, it is highly probable that our MS. is the one. Th. Wright, in his Biographia Litt.

---

[1] See Skeat, Preface to the Gospel of S. Matthew, p. viii.

Brit., Anglo-Saxon period (I), p. 459, prints the 11th chapter by way of specimen. Quite recently the prologue and part of the first chapter have been published—critically edited, as the title page says—by Dr. Edward Breck, 'Fragment of Aelfric's translation of Aethelwold's De consuetudine Monachorum,' etc., Leipsic. W. Drugulin's printing office, 1887. An edition of the whole text is preparing by Mr. W. S. Logeman. I may here add that the work is generally supposed to be one of Dunstan's, but it has been attributed also to Aelfric, whilst of late, independently of each other, Professor A. Ebert (Allgemeine Gesch. der Litt. des Mittelalters III, p. 506), and the above-named Dr. Breck, have fathered it upon Aethelwold, Abbot of Abingdon, and afterwards Bishop of Winchester.

II–XVII, inclusive, are all of a nature that makes us turn to Cockayne's Leechdoms (London, 1864–1866) to see if any are printed in it. As a matter of fact, I find the following state of affairs :—

No. II (fo. 27 b). Leechdoms, III, 198.
MS. Jun. 43. Wanley, p. 88.

No. III (fo. 32 b). Leechdoms, III, 184 (without the Latin text).
MS. Jun. 44. Wanley, p. 89 (imperfect? Wanley).

No. IV (fo. 35 b). Unprinted[1] (but copied by me for publication).
MS. Jun. 43. Wanley, p. 88.

No. V (fo. 36). Unprinted.

No. VI (fo. 36 b). Unprinted.

No. VII (fo. 36 b). Leechdoms, III, 150.
MS. Jun. 44. Wanley, p. 89.

No. VIII (fo. 37). Unprinted, but copied for publication.
MS. Jun. 44. Wanley, p. 89, sub VIII.

No. IX (fo. 37 b). Leechdoms, III, 154 and 168.
MS. Jun. 43. Wanley, p. 88, sub II and V. There is, however, a discrepancy in the two concluding passages of the texts. Having at the moment of writing no access to either MS., I am unable to solve the difficulty, which was perhaps also felt by Wanley. At least, he says, very prudently; 'Idem Codex, inquit, ch. Junius,' etc.

No. X (fo. 39 b). Leechdoms, III, 176.
MS. Jun. 44. Wanley, p. 89, sub V.

---

[1] I consulted Professor Napier on this subject. He was so kind as to put his bibliographical knowledge at my disposal whenever I wished to draw upon it.

No. XI (fo. 40).   Leechdoms, III, 180.
MS. Jun. 44. Wanley, p. 89, sub IX.

No. XII (fo. 40 b).   Leechdoms, III, 180.
MS. Jun. 44. Wanley, p. 89, sub VII.

No. XIII (fo. 40 b).   Leechdoms, III, 146.
MS. Jun. 41, sub II. Wanley, p. 87.

No. XIV (fo. 41).   Leechdoms, III, 156.

No. XV (fo. 41 b).   Unprinted (copied).
MS. Jun. 44. Wanley, pp. 89 and 90, sub XI.

No. XVI (fo. 42).   Unprinted (copied).

No. XVII (fo. 42 b).   Leechdoms, III, 144.
MS. Jun. 41. Wanley, p. 87.

Nos. XVIII–XX, and Nos. XXIII, XXIV inclusive, (ff. 43–44), are small tracts, very short notes, in fact ('Notulae' Wanley), on Adam, Noah, Fasting, the Virgin's Age, and on Crime. They are shortly to appear in the Anglia XI.

No. XVIII.
MS. Jun. 44. Wanley, p. 90, sub XIV.

No. XXI is Latin (fo. 43 b).

No. XXII (fo. 44).   Leechdoms, III, 228 (partly, only, and from the MS. Caligula A. XV).

No. XXIII.
MS. Jun. 44. Wanley, p. 90, sub XIV.

No. XXV (ff. 44–57). A collection of confessions and prayers as yet unprinted. They will shortly appear in the Anglia. Only the latter part (Wanley, p. 196), beginning : 'Dæt sceal geþencan,' also appearing in an Oxford MS. (Wanley, p. 51), was used by Thorpe in Ancient Laws, II, 260.
MS. Jun. 63. Wanley, p. 93.

No. XXVI (ff. 57–60 b).   'Missa, cum rubricis Saxonice.' I am not aware that it has been printed.

No. XXVII (fo. 60 b) has been published several times; see Wülker's Grundrisz, p. 476 (III, § 568).
MS. Jun. 66. Wanley, p. 95. Zupitza (Zeitschr. f. D. Alt. 31. 28 ff.) has recently treated of the relation of the two MSS. known to exist. I must here mention a note in the preface to Wanley's Catalogue. Amongst some books that used to be in the library of Christ Church, Canterbury, he names (p. 8) a 'Locutio Latina glosata Anglice, ad instruendos pueros (forte Aelfric Bata).' I have no means of de-

termining whether this is the identical copy that is now in the Cottonian Library. It would seem not, from the fact that it is mentioned as a separate book, whereas both the Oxford and the London copies are part of a collection of treatises. The query rises, were they always so? The Oxford MS. is to be published by Zupitza.

Nos. XXVIII–XXXI (fo. 65). Latin.

No. XXXII (fo. 65 b). Leechdoms, III, 238 (here, as in some of the cases quoted before, only as ' variae lectiones ').

> MS. Jun. 41. Wanley p. 87. See Wülker's Grundrisz, III, § 571; Anglia X, p. 457 ff.
>
> The notae that Wanley mentions on p. 196 b of his catalogue (Nota de Archa noe, de S. Petri Ecclesia, et de Templo Salomonis, Saxonice, fo. 73 a, b) have not yet been printed, but I presume they are shortly to appear in the Anglia (xi). MS. Jun. 44. Wanley, p. 90, sub XIV.

No. XXXIII (fo. 73 b). Cockayne's Narratiunculae, p. 39; cf. Wülker's Grundrisz, § 602.

No. XXXIV (fo. 77 b). Aelfric's Homilies (ed. Thorpe), II, 240.

No. XXXV (fo. 83). Is in Napier's ed. of Wulfstan's Homilies.

> MS. Jun. 69. Wanley, p. 95.

No. XXXVI (fo. 87). Kemble's Salomon and Saturn, p. 84.

> MS. Jun. 69. Wanley, p. 96. It will be included in Professor Napier's first volume of Homilies, to be edited for the Early English Text Society.

Nos. XXXVII–XLVIII (fo. 88 b), inclusive, will all be found in Professor Napier's Wulfstan.

No. XLIX (fo. 93 b). Latin.

No. L (fo. 94 b). I. Edited in Thorpe's Anc. Laws, II, 260. Nos. 2–6 inclusive are also to be found there, but printed from other MSS. See above, under No. 25.

> MS. Jun. 59. Wanley, p. 93.

No. LI (fo. 97). Printed by Kluge, Internationale Zeitschrift für Vergl. Sprachforschung, ed. Techmer, II, 118.

> MS. Jun. 52. Wanley, p. 92.

Nos. LII and LIII (fo. 101 b). So far as I know, unprinted. One would expect these to be included in Cockayne's Leechdoms.

No. LIV (fo. 102). See Kluge, E. Stud., VIII, 472. It contains a reminiscence of the A.-S. poem, the Seafarer.

No. LV (fo. 103). 'Que sunt instrumenta Bonorum,
Latine et eadem Saxonice. Sectio excerpta ex Regula
S. Benedicti,' says Wanley. It is a copy of chapter four,
of the work which, as I have said above (p. xv) and below
(p. xxxi), has been edited, with some variae lectiones, by
Professor A. Schröer ; but he has not given a collation of this
Tiberius MS.

Nos. LVI, LVII (fo. 105). These will probably be included
in Professor Napier's collection of Homilies.

    MS. Jun. 48 (by a misprint in Wanley: 47). Wanley, p. 90 (for No.
    LVII).

No. LVIII (fo. 106). Leechdoms, III. p. 286. See
Wanley, p. 110 (C. C. C. C. L. 12).

No. LIX (fo. 106). See Wülker's Grundrisz, §§ 564-566,
p. 475.

No. LX (fo. 107 b). 'Votiva Laus.' Latin.

No. LXI (fo. 118). This is our Benedictine Rule. See
below, sections III and IV.

    MS. Jun. 92. Wanley, p. 103. Junius copied only part of the gloss
    into a printed text : ' Regula S. Benedicti Latine Duaci impressa, A. D.
    1611, Saxonice per Junium glossata ex Cottoniano codice qui inscri-
    bitur, Tiberius A. 3.' When preparing my text for the press, I was not
    in a position to compare Junius's copy.

No. LXII (fo. 163 b) Regulae S. Fulgentii Latine, cum
interlineata versione Saxonice.'

    MS. Jun. 52. Wanley, pp. 91, 92. Wanley, in bestowing this name on
    this collection of monastic precepts, evidently followed Junius, who,
    at the beginning of his copy, says : Benedicti regulam interlineatam,
    quam habet Cottonianus codex qui inscribitur, Tiberius A. 3, mox
    excipiunt S. Fulgentii regulae, similiter interlineatae.

The Precepts, as in the present MS., begin thus :—

'DICEBAT VERO SANCTUS FULGENTIUS.

' Juxta[1] regulam patrum vivere semper stude ; maxime autem secundum
  sancti confessoris tui benedicti ; Non declines ab ea in quoquam : nec
  illi addas quippiam, nec minuas ; Totum enim quod sufficit habet, et
  nusquam minus habet ; cujus verba atque imperia sectatores suos per-
  ducunt ad celi palatia ;' and then follows immediately—

' A KALENDIS AUTEM OCTOBRIS USQUE IN PASCHA

' hora nona hoc faciunt,' etc.

These words : 'A kalendis autem Octobris,' etc., to the end of our

---

[1] I leave out the interlinear gloss, and here tacitly correct the Latin. These
rules will be printed separately elsewhere.

so-called Regulae S. Fulgentii, at fo. 168 b, form part of a treatise printed in Migne's Patrol. Cursus completus, Vol. 66, p. 938, where it is headed: Ordo Monasticus S. P. Benedicto attributus. It is this fact that makes it all but necessary for me to say a word on the subject. The reason why these Precepts have been ascribed to S. Benet seems to be this. A monk at S. Germain du Pré[1] stated that they were found in a 'vetus quoddam MS. Cassinense,' which enjoys a high reputation for genuineness.

This circumstance seems to have been sufficient reason for Arnoldus Wion to print the Precepts with the edition of the Benedictine Rule in 1593 at Venice, and thus silently[2] sanction S. Benet's authorship. The argument is, however, a very shallow one, and so long as no other proofs are adduced, ' hoc opusculum non pro vero fetu magni S. Benedicti vendere praesumimus ' (Migne, Vol. 66, p. 938).

The words at the beginning: *Juxta regulam* to *celi palatia*, headed by *Dicebat vero sanctus Fulgentius*, and especially the latter, must have given rise to Junius's error.

Nos. LXIII and LXIV (fo. 168 b) are Latin monastic precepts which, *variis lectionibus*, also occur in MS. Titus A. 4, ff. 107 and 117.

No. LXV (fo. 174). ' Aethelwoldus de consuetudine mona-chorum Saxonice.' It has been printed by A. Schröer, Englische Studien, IX, 291. See E. Breck, as quoted *supra*, passim.

 MS. Jun. 52. Wanley, p. 91.

No. LXVI (fo. 177) is a Latin fragment, and, I think, unprinted.

No. LXVII (fo. 178). This did not originally belong to the MS. It most probably belonged to MS. Tib. A. 6. See Wanley's note, and Prof. Earle's ed. of the two parallel Chronicles, p. xxv (Oxford, 1865). See Wanley, p. 84 (MS. Laud, G. 36, II).

 MS. Jun. 66. Wanley, p. 95. It appears from Wanley's note that in his time it belonged to MS. Tib. A. 3.

No. LXVIII (fo. 179). See Leechdoms, III, 218.

No. LXIX (fo. 179 b). Latin, and, so far as I know, not printed.

---

[1] R. P. Jacobus du Brevil monachus S. Germani a Pratis; see Migne, Vol. 66, note at the end of the treatise there, p. 942.
[2] I have not seen this edition, but presume that Wion does not expressly attribute the Precepts to S. Benet.

III. The Latin Text. Nineteenth-century Editions.

Manner of Editing.

WE have already seen (p. xv) that S. Benedict of Nursia wrote his Rule about the year 516. No earlier writers have yet been pointed out as his sources. It is quite probable that he had none [1]. The Rule no doub t originated in the saint's desire to provide his own followers with a code of laws to live by. However much he venerated his *foregengan*, as the conditions under which his monks lived differed from those of his predecessors, he must have been mainly, if not quite, original in the choice of his precepts. No doubt, his reading the works of a S. Basil and others may have made him feel the desirability of writing regulations of his own. But I should be surprised to hear that after-search had established a definite and direct relationship of matter between our Rule and any one of the works whose key-note it has more or less struck [2]. The number of commentaries that our Rule has called forth would seem to be legion. This Introduction is hardly the place for their enumeration. Neither can we allow ourselves to copy out the encomia of which S. Benedict and his followers can boast. Suffice it to refer for these to Migne, (see below) volume 66, which contains the greater part of these encomia, and references to more works on the subject.

Our Latin text has been edited several times. Apart from the older editions, such as the one of 1593 (printed at Venice by Fr. Arnoldus Wion), I here enumerate those nineteenth century edd. that have come to my knowledge:—

(*a*) MIGNE. Patrologiae Cursus Completus, vol. 66, p. 215 ff., Regula S. Benedicti cum commentariis.

These commentaries make the edition a very useful one. However, the work is very difficult to be got at, its enormous bulk—over 200 volumes—makes few persons care to buy it.

---

[1] See Guéranger, as quoted infra, 'sanctus spiritus per beatum Benedictum . . . Regulam Monachorum edidit' (p. vi).

[2] See however: Concordia Regularum, auctore S. Benedicto, . . . auctore Fr. Hugone Menardo . . . Parisiis, 1638.

(*b*) *Guéranger*. Enchiridion Benedictinum, complectens Regulam vitam et Laudes sanctissimi occidentalium monachorum Patriarchae, accedunt Exercitia S. Gertrudis Magnae et Blosii speculum. Andegavi. Typis Cosnier et Lachese. MDCCCLXII, contains page I, ff. Regula S. Patris Benedicti Juxta exemplar Cassinense.

(*c*) Pax. Monastic Gleanings. No. I.

The Rule of Our most holy Father S. Benedict, patriarch of monks ; in Latin and English. Translated by A Monk of S. Augustine's Monastery, Ramsgate. London, Burns & Oates, 1872.

(*d*) Regula Sancti Patris Benedicti juxta antiquissimos codices recognita, a P(atre) Edmundo Schmidt. Cum Permissu Superiorum. MDCCCLXXX. Ratisbonae, Neo Eboraci et Cincinnatii. Sumptibus, Chartis et Typis Friderici Pristet, S. Sedis Apostolicae Typographi.

This contains twenty-two pages of Prolegomena, in which the author treats of the relations of the MSS., and in which he wishes to establish that S. Benet prepared *two* drafts of his Rule. The work appears to be printed privately. At my request, however, the author kindly placed a copy at my disposal, for which I here beg to thank him most heartily.

(*e*) The Rule of our Most Holy Father Saint Benedict. Edited, with an English translation and Explanatory Notes by A Monk of S. Benedict's Abbey, Fort-Augustus. Jussu Superiorum. London, Burns & Oates, 1886.

(*f*) ' Die Winteney Version der Regula S. Benedicti, lateinisch und englisch zum erstenmale herausgegeben ' has just appeared at Halle (M. Niemeyer), with a most interesting Preface. Before the work was published, the editor, Herr Dr. A. Schröer, professor at the University of Freiburg, presented me with a copy of the advance sheets of the text. For this courteous act I here express my sincere gratitude, as well as for other kindnesses received at that gentleman's hands.

The English work is a thirteenth century text, taken from the MS. Cott. Claud. D. III, whence the Latin text is also transcribed.

Herr Schmidt used fifteen Latin texts for his edition ;
Professor Schröer only those four of which he published the
Anglo-Saxon version [1]. As Herr Schmidt used a collation of
our codex (Schmidt = F) as well as one of the MS. Tib. A. IV
(= Schröer's T, Schmidt's G), the total number of Latin codices
to which I shall subsequently have occasion to refer to is
nineteen. I designate them as follows :—

A. Cod. Tegernseensis.   Royal Libr., Munich (clm. 19408).
B.   „   Mondseensis.   R. and Imp. Libr., Vienna (2332).
C.   „   Fuldensis.   Bibl. Fuld. (D. 3).
D.   „   Parisiensis.   Nat. Libr. (4208).
E.   „   Frisingensis.   Royal Libr., Munich (clm. 6255).
F.   ,,   Londinensis I.   Cott. Libr., Tib. (A. 3).
G.   ,,   Londinensis II.   Cott. Libr., Tit. (A. 4).
H.   „   Veronensis I.   City Library.
I.   „   Bruxellensis.   Library of the Dukes of Burgundy (8305).
K.   ,,   Romanus.   Vatican Cod. Lat. 5949.
L.   „   Einsidlensis, No. 236.
O.   „   Oxoniensis.   Bodl. Libr., Hatton MS.
P.   ,,   Faucensis.   Library of the Cathedral Chapter at Augsburg.
Q.   „   Veronensis II.   Library of the Cath. Ch. at Verona.
R.   ,,   Sangallensis.   Chapter Library, 916.
S. is Schröer's C Winteney Version.   MS. Cott. Claud. D. III.   Cf. p. xxvii.
T.   „   A. (MS. C. C. C. C. 178).   Schröer, Prosa Bearb., p. xix
           (Anglia, vi. 430).
U.   „   O. (MS. C. C. C. O. 197).   Schröer, ib., p. xxi.
W.   ,,   Wells fragment, belonging to the Dean and Chapter of Wells
           Cathedral.   Schröer, ib., p. xxv.

For further particulars about MSS. A–R, the few privileged
persons who possess the book may be referred to Schmidt's
Preface, pp. xii–xv, from which part of the above has been ab-
stracted. For G, see also Schröer, Die Prosabearbeitungen,
p. xxiii. For F, see supra, Ch. II. The collation of our text,
undertaken for Herr Schmidt by a friend, appears to be rather
incorrect.

It must not be supposed that there are no more Latin
texts than those enumerated. I have casually come across
others in the Library of Durham Cathedral, in the Lambeth
Palace Library, in the Phillips Library at Cheltenham, and

---

[1] See A. Schröer, Die Prosabearbeitungen der B. R., p. xxvi, and now the
above-mentioned preface, p. xi.

(of the fourth chapter only) in MS. Tib. A. 3, fo. 103 (see above, p. xxiv).

In the MS. Tib. A. 3 (fo. 118, above, p. xxiv), our Latin text occurs in an exceedingly corrupt state. 'Scatetque mendis,' justly observes Schmidt (p. xiii). Guéranger, Schmidt, Migne, etc., have, in their editions, largely deviated from the MS. readings. Lower down in this Introduction, in §§ 7 and 8 of No. V, some remarks will be found bearing on the edition of the Latin text, to which I beg to refer the reader. It will be seen from those, what my position is with regard to hitherto prevalent modes of editing Latin texts. The principles there stated have led me to deviate as little as possible from the MS. readings, nay, I have tried to keep to them always, except in cases where their spelling would make the text absolutely unintelligible to the ordinary reader. No one will for a moment feel doubts as to the meaning of *debead, prospiciad, habbatis*, etc., but I deem it possible that the spelling *medicetur*, as lemma to *he smæge* (96. 2), might throw those off the track who did not at the moment think of the phenomenon which will be found discussed, infra, No. V, § 63. Hence, such spellings have been banished from the text, but I have been careful to mark these divergencies in the foot-notes, whereas the spelling differences whose meaning was obvious, I have put in the text itself.

I have adhered to the paragraphs of the MS., as well as to its peculiar [1] punctuation. The contractions have all been expanded [2], and to denote them, the letters not actually found in the MS. are printed in Roman type, whereas the rest of the Latin text is in italics.

In the first few pages of this Rule, some gaps occur; see the Text, p. 1 ff., passim. The Latin letters, so far as they may be supposed to have disappeared, are added in brackets. The headings of the chapters are almost always majuscules in

---

[1] So peculiar that I afterwards, but too late, wished I had adopted a less embarrassing plan.

[2] I am unable to agree with E. Kölbing, E. Stud., III, 469 note, in so far as he says that it is unnecessary to denote these contractions.

black ink, but mostly tinged with red. The first line, or part of it, of the Latin text in each chapter is usually also in capital black letters, no red ink being applied here. In this edition they have been denoted by small capitals. The illuminated capitals found in the MS. at the beginning of the chapters are mostly of a red, green, or blue colour ; once or twice they have been forgotten. The glossator or glossators has or have sometimes added Latin words in the line of the gloss above the Latin[1]. These additions are sometimes words that also occur in other Latin texts, so that we may suppose the then glossator to have copied these from another Latin text. In this case the added word has been inserted in the text, and in the *Latin* foot-notes attention has been drawn to this by the words : *added* or *supplied* by glossator. Of a different nature are the words that are scribbled over the Latin text, without being at all found in the other texts. They may be termed Latin glosses, and though comparatively rare, are found, e.g. where the word *debere* or *debemus* (see text, CAP. IV, passim) is added to explain the infinitive used as an imperative. Of this nature is the gloss *i plane* to *sane* (78. 17). These words, although Latin, are always put in the line above, as partaking of the nature of glosses. They, too, may be due to more than one scribe, but they are now found in the MS. in the characteristic handwriting of the Anglo-Saxon scribe. Attention has mostly been drawn to these additions in the Anglo-Saxon foot-notes.

IV. The Anglo-Saxon Text. Manner of Editing.
The ' Paving Letters.'

THE prose paraphrases of the Rule of S. Benet in Anglo-Saxon that have been edited by A. Schröer[2] have no connection

---

[1] Our MS. is a copy ; so that if more than one glossator has been at work— which I have every reason to believe—the external traces of their work are effaced. The reader will see that the existence of more than one glossator must be assumed, by referring to the work, and especially the notes (e. g. note to 10. 7, p. 121 ; and 47. 3, etc.)

[2] (a) Bibliothek der Angelsächsischen Prosa, von C. W. M. Grein, fortgesetzt von R. P. Wülker, Zweiter Band : Die Angelsächsischen Prosabearbeitungen

whatever with the present interlinear text. Of course, some words are the same, both in the interlinear and paraphrastical translations, but the greater number of them are different. This constitutes the principal claim of our text to a separate edition. It would be an interesting task to compare the vocabulary of the two versions together. There is no doubt that where the meaning of an Anglo-Saxon word can be demonstrated from glosses, there is a chance of its being the correct one. But still the glossator may have misunderstood his Latin[1], a fact of very frequent occurrence; and in some cases, through lack of other instances, we may be unable to control his rendering, which, of course, is not checked by any context. But in the case of a running text, the translation, even if corresponding word for word, is free, and we cannot always depend on the translated word being an exact equivalent of the original. Where we have an interlinear translation—a sort of crib—as well as a paraphrase, we may be certain that those words which occur in both translations are accurate renderings.

So far as I am aware, the thirty-ninth chapter, which Thomas Wright published in his 'Biographia Britannica Literaria' (I, p. 442, Latin and gloss), is the only part of the present Benedictine Rule that has been edited, excepting, of course, the few specimen lines that may be found in Wanley's and in other catalogues. But the MS. appears to have been extracted from for lexicographical purposes, and consequently words and phraseological quotations from it are to be found in the various A.-S. dictionaries. Part of the glossing was copied into a Latin printed text by the indefatigable Junius. His texts, however useful they may be to the student of literature, should not be used for linguistic purposes. Junius

---

der Benedictiner Regel. Herausgegeben von A. Schröer. Kassel, 1885–1888. (b) Die Winteney-Version der Regula S. Benedicti, Lateinisch und English. Mit Einleitung Anmerkungen, Glossar und einem Facsimile zum ersten Male herausgegeben von Dr. M. M. Arnold Schröer. Halle a.-S. Max Niemeyer, 1888. See supra, p. xxvii.

[1] It seems like biting sarcasm when in the historical tract in MS. Faustina, A. 10 we read of the 'scearpþanclan witan þe . . . þisse engliscan geþeodnesse ne behofien' (Cockayne, Leechdoms, III, 440; i. e. the keen-witted sages that . . . do not need this English translation.)

appears to enjoy the reputation of being a faithful copyist, but when collating his copy of the so-called 'Regulae S. Fulgentii' (above, p. xxiv) with the MS., I observed that this reputation was entirely unfounded [1]. He adds words not in his MSS. He leaves out words found in his original, or transposes them. He does not distinguish between ð and þ, which he consequently uses indiscriminately [2]. He entirely disregards the punctuation of the MS., and he adds numbers of chapters after his own pleasure or notions of how they ought to have been. Lastly, he corrects his text without giving the reading of the MS.

The convent to which this MS. belonged is not known. Nor is there any author on whom we have reason to father our version. The likelihood indeed is that this interlinear version *gradually* developed, so that it cannot be assigned to any one person.

The object of this edition is to furnish the student with a text as it is found in the manuscript, with all its gaps, imperfections, and absurdities. I am of opinion that however stupidly a scribe may have mangled his original, the reading of the MS. is still the only thing of which we are sure. I have tampered so little with the MS. that I have left even the most palpable errors unchanged ; here, however, I have followed the example set by former editors, and starred the forms which without doubt are merely clerical errors. It need hardly be said that I should not have followed this plan, were this text destined for the use of those desirous of learning the rudiments of Anglo-Saxon. Moreover, if the present were the only version extant, I might have taken into consideration the wants of those students who wished to read this text for the 'realia,' and I should thus

---

[1] See H. Sweet, Introduction to Gregory's Pastoral Care, p. xix, whose sole blame is that Junius 'sometimes swerved from the path of literal accuracy in a few unimportant particulars.' See, on the contrary, Zupitza, Zeitschrift für Deutsches Altertum, 31. 2 ; Breck, Fragment, etc. (supra, p. xxi), p. 5. MacLean, Anglia, 6. 448.

[2] It is generally assumed that the scribes themselves did not distinguish between the ð and þ, and used them promiscuously. But if even any distinction is to be found, editors should take care not to obscure this find by not adhering strictly to the writing of the MSS.

have been compelled to make a more or less readable text of
it. But for this there is, of course, no occasion. Those who
wish to read S. Benet's precepts for the sake of their contents
will find their wishes gratified in the present volume by
looking up the Latin text; and if any one desires to read it in
Anglo-Saxon, the very handy editions of Professor Schröer are
now available. There can be no doubt, to my thinking, that
it must be the aim of an editor to give the text as the
manuscript records it. Of course he may then set to work
and, by dint of exterior and interior criticism, try to eliminate
some mistakes, but—in the case of an edition like the present
—I am of opinion that this should be done in foot-notes.
Nothing can be gained by imprudently introducing one's own
—if I may so express it—one's own Anglo-Saxon amidst the
language—though a corrupted specimen of it—of our fore-
fathers. Indeed a great deal may be lost—unity.

Now, doubtless, it may be objected that when, e. g. the
word *gebetrode* is found in the MS. as *gebeorode,* there can be no
doubt that this was not a mistake, but simply a *blunder,* and
that therefore no purpose is served by retaining it in the text.
True, partly! But even here there is this consideration, that
to watch the mistakes of scribes is not without interest, for
the study of culture in a given period.

In accordance with the principles laid down, I have given
the text of this Rule exactly as it is found in the MS. Only
the following must be observed. The *i,* which is in the
MS. written undotted, has been printed with a dot over
it. Absolutely wrong forms are starred. Elucidations to
forms in any way remarkable, will be found in the foot-notes,
or in those at the end of the volume [1], or, when the matter is
one of phonological or grammatical interest, in the fifth division
of this Introduction. Italics denote the expansions of the
scribal contractions, when no foot-note is appended. Other-

---

[1] In most cases attention has been drawn to these by the words *see note.*
The editor is sorry to own that, owing to a want of foresight, no very definite, at
least no very scholarly, principle can be laid down as to what notes may be
found at the foot of the page, and what at the end of the volume. As a rule,
palæographical notes are at the bottom of the page, and elucidations of
different nature on p. 119, etc. But various causes prevented this rule being
always adhered to.

wise, those letters are italicised to which attention has been
called in the foot-note. Thus *þæt* means that the MS. has
the contraction *þ*, as no foot-note is there. But the letters
nce in *geswin*ce (1. 6) are italicised merely to call the attention
to the note. Whenever I have thought it necessary to
propose an emendation, it has been only when some reason
for the corruption could be adduced, either from a graphical
error, or a psychical process. But where these reasons were
more or less obscure, I have stated them in words.

Our Anglo-Saxon text is a copy, i.e. the glosses have not
been put over the Latin text only in our MS. Both have
been copied from another text or from other texts, most likely
at the same time, and possibly by the same scribe. The
chances are—indeed, there is every reason to believe—that our
MS. was copied often. That the last copyist had an interlinear
translation before him, is evident from the frequent occurrence
of wrong forms that can only be explained by influence of the
lemma on the gloss, or vice versa (see foot-notes, passim).
When an original Latin text was first glossed, we may
a priori assume two possibilities. Either the glosses were
copied into our original Latin from a ready-made Anglo-
Saxon translation, or the glossators worked without a model
of any kind.

Let us consider the first assumption. If this were true, the
Anglo-Saxon text must have been supplied either from the
text commonly attributed to Aethelwold[1], or from some other
hitherto unknown text. We need, of course, not speak of the
latter possibility, as the establishment of this point, as well as
its rejection, are utterly beyond determination. As to the
text edited by Schröer, it is not likely to have been the
original, for, as we have already seen, the vocabulary of the
two is somewhat different.

We are therefore led to the theory of the gloss-origin.
And, indeed, even if we could have for a moment thought of
the other theory, the evidence in favour of the former is
so overwhelming that there can be no doubt about it; and I

---

[1] Thus Schröer, ib., p. xvii. I am not sure that he has established his point.

have but to refer to the appearance of the text, passim, without entering into particulars in any way.

We find then that our version developed,—just like the glossaries that Henry Sweet has so ably treated of in his Oldest English Texts, p. 7—out of a few interlinear glosses, that have multiplied gradually until, in our MS., the Latin is very nearly fully-glossed, every copyist having contributed some more glosses to those which he found in his original. The scribe of our MS. has also acted as a glossator. His work can be traced, e.g. in the words *gesawen* and *visum* (as its lemma, 13. 3), that he himself put instead of the *ealra, omnium*, which is a misreading that does not belong to the text.

That we can still be positive about the fact that more than one scribe has been at work is rather curious, considering that through the last copy all external traces of former glossators are lost. Yet a place like (13. 1)

leorn forebeon i. cnihtum
preesse   discipulis

can hardly be otherwise explained than as the work of two glossators.

THE 'PAVING' LETTERS.

Those who happen to have looked into the text of our Rule before reading this part of the Introduction will have been struck at seeing numerous letters enclosed—in our print[1]—in square brackets spread all over the volume. In the notes they will be found referred to as 'paving letters' or 'glossletters.' The word, as well as the matter, I now proceed to explain.

As to the letters themselves, they are found in our MS. Tib. A. 3, over most of the Latin words, both in our Benedictine Rule, and in those tracts that Wanley styled the Regulae S. Fulgentii (supra, p. xxiv), but, so far as I have been able to find out, they do not occur anywhere else. No one I could consult—I may thankfully and especially mention Dr. E. Maunde Thompson, now Chief Librarian of the British

---

[1] Not so in the MS. See next paragraph.

C 2

3 ★

Museum—knew of their existence in any other manuscript. The only man who mentions them is that accurate worthy, Wanley, who, at p. 199 of his Catalogue, speaking of these letters, says: 'N.B. Super voces Latinas, exaratas esse Literas Saxonicas, quae, quo ordine construendae sunt, ostendunt.' Had Wanley written in English, his would have been the task, which now devolves upon a foreigner, of bestowing an English name on these 'Literae.'

He would, no doubt, have followed the ordinary school-crib *ordo*, which gives the English construing order of a Latin author, and would have called these unfortunate waifs '*order-* or *sequence*-letters.' But when I talked to Dr. Thompson on the subject, he said that the Rugby boys' slang term for this process was *paving*—paving smooth (I suppose) the rough road of learning Latin. The term struck me as a happy one, suiting Wanley's *construendae*, and so I adopted it, though perhaps without due consideration of how it would puzzle readers to whom 'paving' suggests only laying stones on a carriage-road or a footpath.

That Wanley is right in saying that these 'paving' or sequence letters show the order of construing Latin into Anglo-Saxon, is not so apparent at first sight as on closer investigation. The idea must have been, of course, to put the letters over these words that wanted construing, in such a way that they had but to be arranged in the alphabetical order thus indicated, in order to yield an intelligible meaning[1]. Now it is, e. g. not clear why the scribe at one time begins with *a* and goes on to the end of the alphabet, whereas at another time he proceeds only as far as *g* or *l*, or almost any letter, and begins again at *a*. The Latin wanted 'paving,' not the gloss-text. A friend suggested to me that it must have been the Anglo-Saxon text whose syntactical word-order was thus pointed out. 'In order to get an Anglo-Saxon translation, not glosses' — thus my friend writes—'some one put in those "paving" letters to indicate the word-order of the vernacular text. A later copyist, not being able to read the text well, copied the paving letters,

---

[1] See below, V, § 6.

but omitted the glosses.' I am inclined to think that this view is not correct. It must be admitted that the several blunders—see the starred forms—for which we must blame one or more of the scribes, point to an imperfectly legible text [1] at one time or another. But is it likely that the gloss should have been unintelligible so wholesale, and the paving letters quite clear? Must we not *a priori* accept the fact that the Latin text stood in need of comment? What could have been the object of him who thus tried to transmute the interlinear translation into a more or less paraphrastical one? I do not wish to lay undue stress on the fact that the gloss-letters are in Latin characters, like the Latin text, whereas the A.-S. text is naturally written in A.-S. characters. I only say that, although it perhaps remains an open question, the likeliest thing seems to be, that we must look upon the gloss-letters as 'paving' the Latin text.

At one time we find two gloss-letters over one Latin word, not only where this is glossed by *two* Anglo-Saxon ones, but also where only one A.-S. rendering is given. At another, a few non-paved words may be seen intervening between two sets of paved ones. Sometimes these non-paved words must be taken into account when construing the sentence, whereas a little further on we may find an instance where they need not be taken into consideration. From this it is clear that, whatever explanation we fall back upon to solve the difficulty—and none other but the one propounded by Wanley seems plausible, or even possible—we must not strain it; we must rather be content to apply the key somewhat loosely; for there can be no doubt that our 'paving' letters have suffered by the frequent transcribing which our text has undergone. In consequence of this we may expect:—

a. Letters to have been put over the wrong words;

β. Letters not to have been transcribed;

γ. Letters to have been misunderstood as part of gloss-words, which in reality are nothing but gloss-letters;

---

[1] To this cause the same gentleman also attributes the phenomena I have discussed below, V, § 4.

δ. Parts of a word—initial letters, mostly—to have been taken as 'paving' letters, and written separately accordingly.

For the case of *a*, I refer the student to the text passim. For *β*, I would remind him of the fact that unless this assumption be right, the frequent occurrence of a single gloss-letter over a Latin word, amidst a number of non-paved Latin words, cannot be explained. Of the cases under *γ* and *δ* some instances should be adduced :—*asutol, esefor, drenc, aða, bæt*, which must be read respectively as [a.] sutol, [e.] se for (ma) [d.] renc (cf. note to 69. 12), [a.] ða, etc., whereas in *h algena* (sanctorum) the case would seem to lie the other way about.

All this tends to make it tolerably certain that Wanley's supposition is correct, however many difficulties we may find in our way. In the MS. the gloss-letters are always found over the Latin words, sometimes by the side of the A.-S. gloss (either before or after it), sometimes under it, or even over it. To print them in exactly the same place was not feasible, as that would have taken up too much space. I have therefore had to make shift, and to print them in the same line with the A.-S. glosses : this was at once practical, and in accordance with the principle followed throughout in this edition, that whatever must be held to belong originally to the Latin text, whether written by the Latin scribe or by the last glossator, is put in the line of the lemmata, whereas all that partakes of the nature of the gloss—whether A.-S., Latin, or 'paving' letters—has been put in the line assigned to the glossarial renderings.

V. THE LANGUAGE OF THE TEXT. CRUDE FORMS. 'MERO-GRAPHY.' EVIDENCE OF THE LATIN TEXT. ENGLISH SOUNDS. ENGLISH INFLECTIONS.

§ 1. THE language of the present text will be considered in this chapter in its most striking peculiarities. In all essentials, I think, we shall find it a document of the later periods of Anglo-Saxon. External criticism cannot be called in to bear out this statement, for, as we have seen, there is no person on whom to father it, nor is there any external reason to attribute it to an inmate or to inmates of any particular convent. Considering that the only evidence we have—the palæography of the MS.—gives us the limit of about 1020–1030, and further remembering that we have some reason to believe that the MS. was copied more than once, we may perhaps roughly assign it to the first years of the eleventh century.

§ 2. The text will not be treated exhaustively. Such treatment had better be reserved for the works of a standard author of the period. Now that we have a statistical grammar of two representative works of King Alfred's, in Prof. Cosijn's Altwestsächsische Grammatik, it is highly desirable that some one should take up this labour and commence a similar work for, say, Aelfric. A work which is fit for such treatment should yield material not only for phonetic studies, but also for the study of inflections, and also of syntax. Our text lacks the former to a certain extent, and the latter altogether.

§ 3. For the want of inflections, to a certain extent, I refer to what in a letter to the *Academy* (for July 21, 1888), and borrowing a term from Sanskrit philology, I have called 'crude forms.' A glossator wishes to write down the sense of the Latin word merely as an aid to his memory; and without regard to either number or case, he just jots down the word—no more. It is not so much the nominative which he selects, as 'the word' in the abstract, which of course in Teutonic philology always coincides in form with the nominative. I shall here enumerate some cases of crude forms :—

siðfæt (itinera, 3. 12), *twyfeald* (dupplici, 12. 17), *hyrde* (pastoris, 12. 8 ; 17. 5), *leas* (gewitnesse ; falsum testimonium, 19. 13), *lænctenfæsten* (quadragesime, 45. 13, etc.), *vers* (versuum, 50. 2), *mid gewunelic þeaw* (68. 5, 6 ; probably mid was added afterwards to indicate the case; more solido), *gewordenum forecnyll* (facto primo signo, 82. 11), *wrað* (iratum, 116. 13).

Here the crude form is always singular, as also where we find *hæc*, neuter plural, glossed by the neuter singular *þis* (5. 3). But once I found 'utentibus' glossed by *brucendas* (92. 6), which looks very much like a plural crude form. This may be also the case with *bebodu* (preceptis, 21. 17 ; 55. 13 ; and also 54. 2).

Conversely we find a singular glossed by a plural in *gymeleastum* (42. 7), and a nominative by a genitive in *ealra heardnessa* (96. 7), but these must surely be due to a mistake. A similar occurrence is when verbal forms are glossed by infinitives. We cannot be astonished at this, if we think of what a school-boy in the present time, who had to prepare a piece of Latin for translation, would do. Suppose he found the form *taxavimus* in his text; the ending would naturally be clear to him, and he might ask, What is *taxare*, and having remembered it, or having been told, he would *perhaps* write down *we write*, if he took the ending into consideration, but it is quite possible that he would jot down *to write* only. In the same way we must bear in mind that it was quite as often the aim of the glossators to aid their own memory, as to further the use of the text by *others*. This is lost sight of, I think, by those scholars, who look upon any gloss as a *mistake* which does not in all particulars of tense, person, or number, case, etc., correspond with the lemma. For instances, see *beon* (fueris, 75. 4), *underfon* (subjaceat, 91. 8), and *infaran* (96. 13 ; ingredere, which, however, may not be in point, as the glossator was liable to the mistake of looking upon *ingredere* as an infinitive). See note to (97. 2).

§ 4. A phenomenon akin in character to the above, is one which, for want of a better name, I was forced to call ' merography,' because only part of the gloss was in these instances written. It would seem as if the glossator, when writing down only a few letters, thought: 'If I see but this part, I shall remember the whole easily enough ;' or, in cases where the ending is given only : ' I know the word well, it is only the case which I am in doubt of.' Hence, we find forms like the following [1]:—

*becum*an (5. 17), æm *tigað* (5. 17), lea *des* (10. 8), *for* ma (23. 5), eal *dre* (26. 11), *h*læd *dre* [2] (28. 1), hlæd *dran* (28. 9), *monðæs*,

---

[1] The parts which I supply are printed in Roman characters.

[2] The *h* is here, possibly, a corruption of a ' paving ' letter *b*.

monð *es* (39. 10), *on ænde* byrdnesse (41. 15), *ead* modnesse
(53. 8), *under* fo (56. 13), *ge* mæn *sumunge* (? 70. 5 ; cf. 69. 6,
or must we read *gesomnunge?*), *becumen* dum (? 75. 2),
sin gendra (77. 5), ræd *an* (83. 17), anfeald *lice* (101. 16),
genan (probably a mistake for *genam* ian ; 105. 17),
wege dihtað (110. 16, 17), *pra* vost (111. 9), *to wurpon* nesse
(113. 15).

Perhaps also in *rihtwisnesse* (injustitias 33. 11, but it may
more likely have been understood by the glossator as : *in
justitias*), and in *geunrotsaded* (62. 18) which must be supposed
to stand for *geunrotsad* or geunrotseð.

See, for another view of the origin of these glosses, **IV**,
p. xxxvii, note.

§ 5. As regards the lack of syntax, it is but natural that
syntax could not be expected in a collection of glossarial
renderings, constituting a text, like the present. Slight traces
of it may however be found, as when a gloss follows the
government of a preceding English word, instead of the
lemma, e.g. *heardlices*, as gloss to *asperum* (6. 4), being
a genitive dependent on the words *ænig þinc*, going before.
Cf. also the following :—*on ðam*, referring to *hiwe* (masculine, 14. 13), but gloss to in qua ; *lareowlicum hi fylian
regole* (magistram sequantur regulam, 18. 9) ; which may be
also owing to the tendency in Latin, of mixing up dative and
accusative forms.

In *þam geræddum* (qua perlecta, 41. 13), the gloss is wrongly
put in the masculine ; the glossator evidently thinking of the
godspelle which goes before ; whereas in reality the *qua* refers to
lectio.

. § 6. I must remind the reader, at this point, of how
narrowly we have missed possessing a valuable contribution
to the study of English syntax in our document. If we had
but the original, instead of a much defiled third or fourth-hand
copy, how the 'paving' letters would repay the trouble of an
investigation ! For there can be little doubt that if we could
re-arrange the Latin words in the alphabetical order of
the original position of these paving-letters, we should
find that the words were then put in the Anglo-Saxon word-

order, or nearly so. Why this is not now the case, may be
seen above, p. xxxvii.

§ 7. In making my choice as to what I should take up
and what reject, I have been guided by the principle of
noting only that which may be thought in any way to supple-
ment Sievers's Standard Grammar. It is to his second edition
that my quotations of his sections refer, which, however, I
do not always cite. I also give what is characteristic of the
period to which the present text belongs.

In what follows, the evidence will be found to be based,
with one or two exceptions, on material drawn from our Old
English text. But, when lately investigating this matter,
I came to the conclusion that a careful analysis of a Latin
text may sometimes yield valuable matter for phonetic investigation too. In a letter to the *Academy* [1] for Sept. 22, 1888,
I tried to lay down the general principles by which we
should be guided when working at a Latin text for this
purpose. What will be found there, may be summarised as
follows :—Where we know a Latin text to be written in the
country whose language we are investigating—in our case,
English,—and where we know that the spelling-differences
presented by the text under consideration are deviations from
the ordinary Latin taught in the Middle Ages; that is, where
we have reason to suppose that the peculiar spellings in this
text are due to an *English* scribe, we may take those Latin
spellings into account to corroborate the evidence of the
spelling in our English text.

Now although our MS. dates from the eleventh century,
i. e. about four centuries after the reported introduction of
Benedictinism into England, yet the ultimate source is a
Latin original. The fact, however, that the other MSS.
appear *not* to present the peculiarities of this manuscript,
enables us to rely more on the following evidence, especially
in conjunction with that of the Anglo-Saxon. I have here
brought together the little evidence that our text yields.
But my knowledge of Middle Latin is so slight that I am by

---

[1] See also the subsequent numbers of that periodical.

no means confident of having been at all consistent in distinguishing between what is general, and what is peculiar to the
English scribe. (See above, p. xxix.)

§ 8. That *ae* becomes *e* (passim) is, of course, quite general,
but perhaps the reverse process may be thought to illustrate
what will be found stated below in § 15. Cf. *desiderænt* (24. 13),
itæm (31. 13), *occupæntur* (82. 4.) The general levelling of
unstressed vowels may be perhaps exemplified by *corda* (19.
10), *murmurantis* (25. 10, 11), *opore* (35. 16), *leganter* (38. 15),
memoriter (39. 16), etc. As to what has been said of the
possible existence of nasal vowels, if any importance is to be
attached to the examples in §§ 41, 70, we may here instance
atiphona (43. 7), *emendaverit* (= -*int*, 59. 4), *injugat* (80. 16,
etc.). Do, perhaps, spellings such as *completori*, *subsellis*,
versum (40. 11, 46. 6, 50. 2, for *completoriis*, etc.) prove that
our scribe was accustomed to indicate vowel-length by
doubling the letter ?

As to § 42, cp. *sompno* (2. 9, 28. 2), *comtempnentes* (28. 16,
where *p* is added below the line), *amplicet* = *applicet* (21. 1), etc.

For the pronunciation of *b* = *v*, cf. in our text *habitavit*
(3. 16, etc.), which, however, is of very frequent occurrence
(as in the O.S. *Heliand*, e.g. *bar* = *far*). See Sweet, O.E.T.,
p. 185. If, as I have reason to suppose, this change obtains
only in this ending, -*abit*, -*avit*, I doubt whether it is anything but a graphical, or a continually occurring, blunder.

As to § 50, see *debead* (63. 12), *prospiciad* (68. 14), *capud*
(73. 15), *hospidum* (75. 8), *deliquid* (79. 15), and compare *jube
addare*, which is, of course, *jubeat dare* (91. 5). Hence in
(64. 14) I put *agad* in the text, not *agat*, on account of the
deo following.

Medicetur (96. 2, þæt he smæge, MS.) = *meditetur*, is equally
interesting, as the word *secende* = *setende* (below, § 63). Ad
§ 66, cf. *siens* = sciens (97. 5).

As to § 72 compare *habbatis* (79. 8), *coherceat* (15. 12), *in has
signato* (75. 3 = in (h)*assignato*), as well as *omnibus* (MS., evidently a corruption of *ominibus* = hominibus, 30. 6), *ospitum*
(61. 15), *ospite* (88. 12), *abitant* (91. 11), *ortu*(s) (112. 15), etc. ;
nichilum (4. 8) is, I believe, quite common elsewhere.

We shall now have to examine the Anglo-Saxon text.

§ 9. SOUNDS.—A. Stressed short *a* before nasals has passed through the second *o*-stage (Sievers, § 65), and has again become *a*. passim, e.g. *underfangen* (97. 4), *langsumum* (97. 7). Stressed short *a* otherwise placed is stable ; the only cases where it is found as *o* are *ut to foranne* (65. 16 ; cf. § 20), and *upahofennesse* (22. 7).

Half-stressed and unstressed *a* passes into *e* and *o*. Cf. *andsweras* (3. 1), andswore (112. 6, 112. 9), and for the latter case *eadmodren* (14. 9), *forhicgenden* (15. 4), *witen* (72. 13), and befrinonne (26. 12).

§ 10. O. Stressed short *o* is sometimes found as *eo* before *r*, *f*, and *h* : *feorwyrðe* (interitum, 57. 5), *godes leof* (ambrosianus, 38. 7, but *lof* and *lofsang*, passim), to geleohgenne (92. 8). I also find *ŏ* represented by *u*, *stuwe* (36. 10) and *lucað* (110. 12), which latter is possibly a mistake for *lociað*.

§ 11. Stressed long *o* is represented by, possibly its umlaut, *e* in *werigende* (*vagari*, 112. 17), but *u* in *du*=do (103. 7).

§ 12. Unstressed *o* becomes *a* in *abbade* (116. 2 ; Latin influence?). It is rendered by *u*, e. g. in *furður* (26. 13), and often by *e* in the case of the ending *-æst* of the superlatives (e. g. *leofestan*, 3. 9, etc.). Cf. also *nygeða* (37. 4), *nigeða* (37. 11).

§ 13. U. There is little to be said of the *u*'s in stressed syllables : on a possible nasal *ŭ*, see below, § 41.

u, in unstressed syllables, is represented by *o* in *hohfolnesse* (54. 1 and 57. 18), and by *a* in *oðram* (14. 9).

§ 14. Ĕ, Ǽ. Genetically speaking, *e* is either palatal or guttural. Traces of this may be seen in the fact that *g* is retained longer before guttural *e*'s than before palatal ones, where it soon runs into the palatal spirant (j). Thus we find the prefix ge- (=ga) unswervingly represented in this way. It is not until the end of the eleventh century that we find it represented by *i* (Vices and Vertues, ab 1200, passim, icleped, idon, etc.).

§ 15. Short *ĕ*, stressed, half-stressed, and unstressed, very frequently becomes *æ* ; conversely *æ*, in all three positions is often written *e*. The natural inference is, that the two sounds have run together, and are assimilated. In fact, three originally different vowel values may be said to have dwindled down into one. $e =$ West Teutonic i; $e = a + i$, and $e = æ =$ W. S. a before non-nasals + palatal vowels (Sievers, § 49; Sweet, History of Engl. Sounds, second ed., § 413).

Cp. *ændebyrdnesse* (14. 3), *ælfræmedne* (20. 5), *ælles* (28. 4), *bigænge* (86. 3), *þænce* (104. 16).

wæfæls (32. 14), *monðæs* (39. 10), *lufiænde* (68. 1), *hei aspendæ* (98. 9), etc. In *ælmæssan* (99. 16), and in *hæftemæst* (76. 5), the non-italicised symbol may owe its sound to a confusion with *mæsse, -mæst*, due to and explained by popular etymology.

§ 16. Æ.—Both short and long *æ* are often found in our text represented by *a*. *þarrihte* (23. 16), *stape* (28. 13), *hwar* (36. 1), *radan* (72. 10), *mage* (72. 15). They are also written *e*: *seigð* (2. 18), *stepe* (31. 9), *gemenlica* (communis, 34. 12), *geedleht* (51. 17), *efterfilige* (54. 10), *afered* (prostratus, 78. 11), and lastly, both short and long *æ* is expressed by the symbol *ee*: *geedleehte* (51. 3), *geþeef* (101. 16).

§ 17. *æ* is *ea* possibly in *eallþeodscipa* (89. 5), if it is not a mistake, influenced by *eall*; *gehealdenne* (61. 2), which must then be supposed to be wrong for *getealde* (but cf. note, infra, on p. 123), and perhaps in *teallic, = tællic* (54. 7).

§ 18. *æ* is *y* in *gystes* (94. 5).

An *i* has developed after a long *e* in the case of *hei aspendæ* (98. 9). It may be due to the analogy of the *e* in some cases, e.g. aweig (1. 7), etc., where a *g* followed.

§ 19. *ĕ* has developed into *ea* in *fealaspreocala* (35. 5; cf. infra § 30); into *eo* in the same word *fealaspreocala*, as well as in *beotwux* (51. 8), and in *neodbeheofe* (69. 14, but regularly *behefe*, 81. 14, etc.).

§ 20. *e* becomes *o*, *swoðunga* (fomenta, 59. 11), and possibly in *ut to foranne* (65. 16), where, however, the *o* may equally well be the representative of *a*; cf. § 9).

§ 21. *ĕ* has become *y* in *bið beiyten* (adquiritur, 65. 9), and *i* in *æthwigan* (92. 16).

§ 22. *ĕ* in unstressed syllables is very frequently represented by *a*; thus in *forasþræc* (1. 2), *foraglæwlice* (18. 7), *forabeon* (11. 9, 24. 13), *forahradian* (55. 4, 5), *forascawunga* (73. 11);

in the following two verbal forms: *he gemuna* (meminerit,
16. 14), *of acerfa* (amputet, 108. 11); then in the gen. sing.
m. g. *lareowas* (10. 8, etc.), *bebodas* (22. 2).

Conversely, the ending -*as* of the plural being written -*es*
occasioned the corruption *asyndrodest* (56. 9).

§ 23. This *a* for *e* is most probably phonetically correct in
the above-mentioned cases. In *to smeagenda* (26. 11), *hlæddra*
(28. 7), it may be from the influence of the respective lemmata.
The lemma has probably also influenced the gloss in the case of
gewrita (32. 5, scriptura).

§ 24. Syncope of *e̯* follows the rule as laid down by Sievers
(§§ 144, 293). Hence we find forms like *regolicere* (63. 10),
regollicere (103. 15), by the side of *regolicre* (113. 16, 115.
16), etc.

§ 25. I, Ẏ. Although of different origin, these two vowels
may, in the stage to which the language of the present Text
belongs, be safely considered together, as they are both levelled
under one sound, probably the *i*. That this should be under
the former sound, is first of all made likely by such spellings
as *forþig* (17. 16), *ingehide* = *ingehygde* (94. 12), in both of
which cases the *ig*, *i* represents the long *ī*, and is secondly
borne out by the subsequent history of the letters, both of which
are diphthongised into the present *ī*. Hence we find such
spellings as *kin* (genus, 10. 6), *cinehelm* (31. 14), *mycel* having
again (cf. Sievers, § 31 note) become *micel* (72. 15, etc.).

§ 26. I, *y* are rendered by *u*, in *wursan* (11. 4), and in *cwude*
(24. 14), *oferfull* (71. 9), *gefullan* (81. 4).

§ 27. *e* for *i* resp. *y̆* is found in the following instances:—
gef (3. 1), *smeðe* (officium, 23. 1), *þen*(g) (71. 7), *tender* (75. 17),
gement (decreverit, 78. 17), *begeme* (intendat, 96. 5), etc.

§ 28. For an apparently long *ī* in *lilic*, see § 42.

§ 29. EA, EO. That these were stressed on the second ele-
ment, in the period to which this text belongs, and that, consequently, the first *e* had become a half-vowel is, to my thinking, beyond doubt. I adduce in support of it the following
forms:—*iornfullestan* (1. 12), *iarcie* (16. 17), which may easily
be multiplied from the present and other texts. *eode* is spelt
(58. 17) *gode*, and in conjunction with forms like *gereordgenne*

(74. 2), *hadgenne* (107. 4), but especially *gebisgode* (82. 4, which cannot be anything but *gebisiode*, cf. also below, § 68 *f*). I have no hesitation in looking upon this *gode* as a case in point. See Sievers, § 212; anm. 2, and § 214, sub 7.

§ 30. *ea* and *eo* interchange. See *neorwan* (24. 8), and for *feola*, *feala*, supra, § 19, Paul Beiträge 4. 345, 6. 55. The former is found monophthongised in a great many cases in full syllables, as well as in half, and unstressed ones. The monophthong *e* thus born, is sometimes found interchanged with *æ*.

nextan (4. 6), *ege* (13. 13 bis), *geþehte* .(19. 7), *hlehtregamene* (21. 11).

þeh (21. 17), *scel* (58. 8, 102. 8, etc.).

þrege (15. 9) and *þræiungan*, (59. 7) *foreglæwlice* (18. 7), *glæwnesse* (58. 9, 59. 14).

gimlæslice (63. 9) and *gimlæslic* (MS. *gunlæslic*, 62. 2), as against *gemeleasan* (15. 3) and passim.

§ 31. The spelling *scamen* (76. 11) and *gescad* (109. 2), etc., is no monophthonging at all, because the vowels never were diphthongs, see § 66. *Salmos* (51. 9) is Latin influence.

§ 32. In *andwyrde* (presentem, 30. 11) and *beþyrfendra* (93. 15), *ea*, probably through *e*, is represented by *y*.

§ 33. *eo* is *e* in *ceriende* (20. 15), and possibly in *ateriað* (89. 10), but see note. Hence in *cyrigende* (55. 12), *eo* becomes *y*.

In *forrane* (29. 13) and *forsig* (64. 13) *eo* has become *o*.

§ 34. U, in consonantal value, presents the usual contractions: *noldon* (2. 7), *sutol* (9. 7), *gesutulað* (29. 10 ; cf. *geswutulað*, 29. 11), for which see Sievers, § 172 note, who does not mention *ucan* (52. 7), *ucuþena* (66. 12), and see note to *uwucan* (52. 4).

It is superfluous in *hwiwrædenne* (107. 11), whilst *ðryrnyssum* (32. 12), *anfealde* (91. 4, etc.), *þeahfæstnÿsse* (100. 13), are mistakes due to the misreading of *r*(ɼ), *f*(ꝼ) and *h* respectively for *w* (ƿ).

Is *awÿrtlian*= *avÿrtwalian* (108. 7) a mistake, or the outcome of a phonetic process ?

§ 35. I, in consonantal value, need not be treated separately,

4

as it has become identical in sound, as well as mostly in symbol, with the spirant palatal *g*, for which see below, § 68. Thus we find *geornlice* (23. 2), as well as *geond* (11. 4); *iornfullestan* (1. 12), as well as *iond* (50. 1).

§ 36. R is omitted, whether phonetically or graphically it is difficult to say, in *foahrædigende* (106. 11), *tobedde* (109. 15, *inflati*), *hicce* (32. 9), *bæd* (54. 7). *R* is inserted in *mæssepreostrum* (100. 10, see note, but preosta 101. 6), *ætbredendrum* (32. 13), *hefigran* (65. 7, cf. 66. 9), and of course by mistake in *frynd* (20. 11, inimicos).

§ 37. We may further note a case of svarabhakti in *merigenlicum* (66. 13), and *merrigenlice* (37. 14), as also two instances of metathesis, *hærdlicor* (24. 6), and *wryhta* (33. 16, etc.). In the case of *merrigenlice* it is also possible that the *ig*, resp. *rig*, represents only the vocalisation of the *g*. Cp. the spelling *meriendlice* (44. 7, 45. 16, 46. 4).

§ 38. L has disappeared in *æfwyrðe* (16. 6), and has been doubled in *welleorniaþ* (100. 4).

§ 39. M. Apart from the ending of the dative plural, where an older *-um* is usually supposed to have dwindled down into *-an*, *m* is often found represented by *n*. Graphically speaking, the difference is so slight that e. g. in a word like *wylne* (fervore, 9. 19) we must perhaps assume a scribal error; on the other hand, forms such as *þan* (40. 4, 99. 2) and *medenlicum* may be phonetic.

A case of assimilation may occur in *belippendan=belimpendan* (73. 11, but see note). For *lilic=lim(p)lic* (21. 11), see § 42.

§ 40. N. Not written in *fadung* (9. 19), *windrucen* (20. 13), *drihtelican* (50. 1), *gedihtere* (51. 4; cf. *gedihtenre* 50. 17), *ære* (semel, 54. 7), *þearflices* (82. 3), *si geþeoda* (injungatur, 84. 3), *wacmodes* (84. 5), etc.

Added in *geþeondan* (57. 14), and assimilated to *d* in *eddebyrdnesse* (78. 17), doubled in *inn eode*, which was misunderstood or mistranscribed and written *in neode* (103. 18).

§ 41. Misreading a word so as to put an *n* where it was not, or *vice versa*, is admittedly of very frequent occurrence, owing to the fact that *n* is often denoted by a stroke over the preceding letter. All our instances may be due to this. But if Sievers is right in assuming the existence in early Teutonic of nasalised vowels (ib. 45. 5), and if Zupitza's account of Kent. Glosses 795 *strenð = strengð*, etc., is correct[1]— that is, if we may lay down the principle that certain sound values are thus symbolised in a preceding letter, it is just possible that some of the cases above indicated owe their origin to this principle, and that this aided the spreading of the then only apparent loss of *n*. Cf. § 70.

§ 42. P. Omitted in *cam dom* (abbreviated in the MS. as cā dō, 14. 6); *iýl* (jactantiam, 22. 7), *gelimlic* (96. 3) This last word occurs also (21. 11) under the form *lílic*, where the sign of length ⁻ must be taken as indicating *m*.

§ 43. An epenthetical *p* obtains in *luftempre* (dulcius, 3. 8). No doubt under the influence of the lemma a *p* is retained in *psealmas* (38. 7). The word *reps* = Latin *responsorium* is perhaps another instance of metathesis, as to which see Sievers, § 204. 3; otherwise the form may be explained as representing *re*(s)*p*(on)*s*(orium) and not *resp*(onsorium).

§ 44. B. The close relationship that exists between *m* and its corresponding stop *b* explains at once forms like *emfaran* (83. 6), and perhaps also *gemysgunge* (occupationem, 89. 16), and *si forhæmed* (abstineatur, 71. 12), although in the latter word a mixing up with *hæmed* is the more probable origin of the extant form.

§ 45. *b* is misread as *h* in *heode* (56. 8), and *hetelicum* (=betehtum, 31. 1).

§ 46. F, V. In the instances to be mentioned lower down, both F and V express the voiced labial spirant, and hence they are here mentioned together—*vers*, *verse* (41. 7, 47. 13, 50. 2, etc.), in each case as gloss to a Latin *versus* (or oblique cases), the writing of *v* may be due to Latin influence. Not so in *pravoste* (54. 10), *pravostum* (104. 4), *pravostscire* (111. 15); see also *se sylva* (12. 16), and *weouedes* (62. 1), and compare Sievers's remark that this representation by *v* is characteristic of the oldest English (§ 192. 2).

---

[1] 'Das *n* behielt natürlich in allen diesen fällen seine gutturale natur, Z. f. D. A. 21. 11.

§ 47. An original voiced *f* (= Gothic *b*, or Latin *f*) before
n admittedly often becomes *m*, 'especially in the later period'
(Siev., § 193. 2, and see note). Bearing this in mind, we must
be struck to find *stefne* and *efnum* constantly, which forms
are indicative of an older period; and on the contrary, the
following English adaptations of the Latin word *antiphona*:
antiphonas (81. 1), *antiphonam* (41. 1); *antemn* (79. 1), *antemne*
(38. 5); *antemp* (56. 10, 79. 12), and *antempne* (42. 12; 43. 4).

§ 48. Are any traces found of an interchange between
f and *w*; and is this phonetic, or, as is certainly very possible,
merely graphical? The constancy of the occurrence of the
gloss *anfealde* to *potestate* in our text (which I have starred;
91. 4, and passim) would almost make me inclined to think
that the change was phonetic. If so, we may look upon *liw*
(61. 13) as an analogue. Here, however, the *w* has been
changed into *f* (contemporarily).

f is dropped in *frore* (solacio, 10. 1), and has been added, no
doubt erroneously, in *ȝfefle* (31. 5).

§ 49. T. The resemblance in shape of this symbol to
c may often account for forms like the following: *orseclena*
(9. 18), *uncruman* (109. 6). Whether *wice* (poena, 25. 12),
secende (ponens, 28. 14) must not be viewed in a different
light, is a matter which will be found treated of below,
§ 63).

§ 50. Traces of the voicing of final *t* to *d* are numerous:—
gemed (modus 45. 8, 72. 14), *gild* (33. 10), *tramod* (118. 2).
Of this last word, Schröer's texts have on p. 133 of his edition,
tramet, which is also in the Durham MS. in the corresponding
passage on fo. 123 b. Schröer asks (glossary, in voce) if the
word is masc. or neuter. The following references may give
an answer to this question. Gospel of S. Matthew, ed. Skeat,
p. 2, l. 10: *trametas ł wægas ł stige*: tramites; and Prudentius
glosses, Germania 23, p. 398 b. *trametas*: paginas.

t, the outcome of the combination -teþ, becomes voiced in
the following cases: *si gebed* (emendaverit, 25. 13), *anded*
(confitebitur, 29. 14), *agild* (deliquerit, 80. 4), *hæd* (91. 3)
and as the result of -deþ being contracted in: *asend* (mittit,
36. 13), *læd* (ducit, 117. 3).

Observe the spelling *geledt* (impediatur, 87. 4).

§ 51. *t* is dropped very frequently. Finally in *geþeah*
(17. 14), *higeleas* (75. 17). Cp. also *sceornesse* (39. 13),
cræfican (=cræftican, 94. 10), swa *of* swa (94. 5), etc.

Inwardly in *drihne* (1. 8), *tihende* (suadentem, 4. 7), *tearum*
(61. 1, probably a mistake for *teartum*) influenced by the
thought of *tearum*=lacrimis ; *wæsmas* (82. 3).

Initially it is, with a following *e*, misread for *æ* in **ælendne*
(=*telendne*, detractorem, 20. 15), and **arlicor* (=teartlicor,
115. 5).

§ 52. *t* is found added after *s* in *gewist* (38. 6), in *cost*
[certainly in (88. 3), and probably also (20. 7), if *pacem* may
be taken to mean *pacis osculum*], and through a mixing up
of forms in *asyndrodest* (=asyndrodas, privati, 56. 9). Owing
to influence of the lemma, it is added in *þeniant* (serviant,
65. 15). See a very interesting article, Mod. Language
Notes I, 3, and ib. I, 97.

§ 53. *t* becomes *ð* in *si gescȳrð* (53. 13), *wurð menð* (87. 15),
and also in *swa hwæð swa* (1. 11). This latter instance,
unlike the former which is *isolative* (Sweet, H. E. S., § 47),
is *combinative*, influenced by the following *s*. Other combinative changes of *t*, but through a preceding *s*, are found
in these words: *aþreht* (78. 10, 98. 7), and *þrengestan* (1. 9).
Instead of becoming *þ*, the *t* of *st* is dropped in *æt nyxan*
(2. 7).

§ 54. D. This sound is very frequently unvoiced. *Myrrent*
(stirpator, 62. 3), *mænifealt* (113. 15). It is retained etymologically in *gemildsa* (39. 7). The frequently occurring forms
abbot in the nominative as well as in the oblique cases (e. g.
79. 8, 80. 15, etc.) are not likely to be all due to the form
of the lemma ; they may on the contrary present examples in
point here.

Hlutclipol (35. 11) and *stuntmælum* (38. 10) may be
instanced as exemplifying the unvoicing of a *d* at the end
of a syllable, and the following words as a specimen of the
same process inwardly, so far as they may be thought to
indicate phonetic and not merely graphical changes.

fotum (alimentis, 68. 15), wið *meten* (mercedi, 85. 13,

d 2

4 ★

probably a blunder), *atreogenlic* (agenda, 37. 12), *to motgenne* (superbiendi, 110. 4, cp. § 69), *stete* (111. 15). For the apparent change of *d* into *g*, see below, note to 5. 9 (p. 119).

§ 55. *d* is represented by *ð* in the following cases: *æfwyrðe* (16. 7), *beon gesæið* (22. 3), *belaðod* (65. 6, 65. 13). See for *wiðscripel* (10. 16, 17), where *d* is influenced by the following *s*, § 53 above. Owing to the want of length-designation in our MS. it is difficult to decide whether *wið-* here represents *wið* or *wĭð*. In the former case the change would be combinative and internal; in the latter isolative and external (Sweet, H. E. S., § 46.*f*).

§ 56. The close relationship existing between the *d* and *n*, *n* being formed exactly in the place of the *d* but with free breath-passage, throws more or less light on the following instances, most of which, if not all, may represent truly phonetic changes. See also below, § 92.

*ablicen*dum earum (2. 10), *tundgan* (3. 3), *angitfullum* (13. 3), *gewiten*d*licum* (16. 11), *merien*d*lice* (44. 7, etc.), *ion* (per, 49. 2), etc. etc. See Sievers, § 198.

d is represented by *n* in *gegearcon* (exibetur, 25. 3), is doubled in *gepreadd* (104. 6), and assimilated to *n* in *cumenne*, etc. (95. 11).

§ 57. Þ, Ð. The sound symbolised by these letters is in our text often found represented by *d*. Cp. *nytwyrdnyssum* (19. 6, 65. 14), *sodes* (89. 7), *læigd* (98. 2), *sede* (115. 15). This *d* by unvoicing becomes *t* in *underfeht* (16. 1), *det* (108. 6, where the possibility of Latin influence is not excluded). It is assimilated to *t* in *attan* (77. 16).

þ, *ð*, as sign of the 3 p. s. are often omitted; cp. *sæig* (24. 9), etc.

Inwardly, *þ* has disappeared in *swyrian* (59. 14), and possibly in *lareow*. So says Sweet, as regards this last word, in the Anglia, III, p. 152. But is this derivation correct? Speaking *a priori*, a *þ* is more likely to be added by analogy than to disappear phonetically between *r* and a *vowel*; *lateow* from *ladþeow* is no fit analogue. Or must we presuppose, for a transitional stage, **laþreow*? Even then our *swyðrian* is but a meagre analogue, occurring as it does only once or so, as against the constancy with which *lareow* obtains. On the whole, Reimann (Die Sprache, etc., cp. § 64, p. 36),—who assumes *larþeow* to be a twelfth century neologism,—seems to me most likely to have hit the mark.

Original *dh* is represented by *dd* in *anddettan* (21. 15), *þ* is written *f* in *stæfnysse* (55. 5), a very probable phonetic interchange.

§ 58. s. *S* is assimilated to *t* in *blettian* (33. 3), and is prothetic—if phonetic in this place, which is at least doubtful —in *stalu* (= *talu*, detractionis, 110. 7).

§ 59. C, K. Both these symbols express either a guttural or a palatal voiceless stop. In our text the following words occur with *k* by the side of forms with initial *c*. *ofkyrfes* (abscisionis, 60. 2), *gekynd* (5. 14), *kyð* (69. 10), *beon gekydde* (29. 9), *kyre* (18. 4), *kyn* (9. 17), *kin* (10. 16), *kapitol* (47. 9), etc.

c is sometimes voiced: *begimð* (76. 4), *drencg* (potus, 78. 1), *godgundre* (81. 10), *geswing* (84. 4), *swingan* (109. 3).

c is represented by *t* in *fæte* (37. 13) and *geferlætenn* (102. 13). For the reverse process, see § 49 above, and for the explanation, § 63 below.

§ 60. As regards the pronunciation of this *c*, I have already stated that it is either palatal or guttural. The guttural pronunciation occurs of course before guttural vowels, and possibly also in a few cases before purely palatal vowels, but only when the *c* is there owing to a secondary development. Thus, when we find *re* glossed by *þince* (33. 9), it is difficult to believe that the *c*, which has grown out of *g*, and is thus a purely guttural stop, can be palatal in the oblique cases. Before guttural vowels a palatal pronunciation is not likely to have obtained.

§ 61. What is the nature of this palatalisation? Sievers expressly and distinctly states, in various sections of his grammar, that the palatal *c* = *tsch* (§ 196. 3), i.e. a ' pronunciation resembling the present English *ch*[1] ' (§ 206, anm. 3).

---

[1] Sievers does not restrict his statement to any later period. The following may therefore be of interest. That this assibilation of the *c* cannot be established for the older periods—I here refer to the Corpus Glossary—may be seen from Dieter, § 43, who gives *mertze* (Wr. W., 32. 25) as representing

However strange it may be that the author of the ' Grundzüge der Phonetik' must have here made the slip of con-
founding palatalisation with its consequence, assibilation,
the fact is proved by referring to p. 62 of the third edition
of the Grundzüge, where a correct statement is given. But
the words quoted above still stand in the A.-S. grammar, and
the wrong notion there expressed, pervades the whole treatment of the c.

§ 62. Let us examine the facts on which Sievers's theory
is based. They are :—

(1) The transition of *ort-geard* into *orceard*, afterwards
orcerd, *ordceard*.

(2) The transition of *fetian* into *fecc(e)an*.

Now the interchange of guttural c and t, i.e. of the voiceless guttural and dental stops, is no matter of wonder; and
as such, the matter might be explained without more ado [1];
but there is more which tends to explain the change. A
palatal c, as in A.-S. *rice*, before having attained the present
stage of pronunciation—assibilation to *tsch* in *rich*—must
have passed through the *tj* stage—i.e. exactly through the
place where the *tg* (i. e. *tj*) of *ortgeard* must have been formed.
No wonder then, that t + palatal vowels, or rather t + palatal
semi-vowels, should be confused *in writing* with c + palatal
vowels, i.e. semi-vowels. Hence the transition of *ortgeard*
into *orceard*. Hence possibly also the form *feccean* by the
side of *fetian*, although the possibility of two distinct verbs
being apparently merged into one is not excluded [2]. Thus
then I believe with Sievers, that *orceard* proves a pronunciation *ortjard*, but no more. I shall now examine the re-
maining grounds against this supposition. The c originally
sufficed because, as is very likely (Siev., § 206), palatalisation is an Anglo-Saxon phenomenon. But when the palatals
began to develope, k was sometimes used to denote the
guttural sound. This at least is very probably the meaning
the middle Latin *mercem*. If c had then been *tsch*, the scribe would not have
had recourse to the unusual *tz* to express this sound, then so akin to that
of c.

[1] See Mod. Language Notes II. 222, III, 126, 192.

[2] Whence does Bosworth-Toller get his preterite, *fœhte*?

of *k* (Sievers, § 207); but that the distinction was not always
kept up, that is, that the distinction was evidently too
delicate to be palpable to the untrained ear, is clear from the
list of words above, § 59, where the *k* occurs before vowels
originally palatal as well as those originally guttural. But
however rough and obtuse an ear may be, the distinction between *k* and *tsj* must be sure to be heard and to find expression
consistently. How then was it afterwards expressed? By
the adding of *h* to the palatal *c*; but this did not happen
until the beginning of the Middle English period (Koch,
§ 172 ff.). I do not believe that the *ch* of the Northumbrian
documents represents *tsj*, but I wish to reserve my judgment
until the grammar of these texts, which may be expected from
the hands of Professor Cook, has placed before us the necessary
material on this subject.

§ 63. We may now safely conclude that the evidence in
Anglo-Saxon does not do more than prove that palatal $c = tj$
at the utmost, not yet *tsj*. See also on this subject the
remarks of Professor March, Englische Studien, I. 315.

Hence it is that I have left the above-mentioned forms
fæte, geferlætenne, etc., unstarred, since they are just as likely
to represent the palatal *c*, as would be done by this symbol
itself, and it is probably owing to this confusion of *c* and *t*
that we find such forms as *wice, secende*, cp. supra, § 49.

§ 64. A word must be said about the *c*-epenthesis, although,
of this phenomenon proper, I have not found an instance in
our text. Traces of it may, however, be perhaps discovered.
For instances of it, see Sievers, § 210; Cosijn, Altwests.
gramm. I, § 131, i.e. Sweet, Pastoral Care, p. 482 f.;
Zeuner, Die Sprache des Kentischen Psalters, § 39; Dieter,
Sprache und Mundart der ältesten Englischen Denkmäler,
§ 45, p. 63; Reimann, Die Sprache der Mittelkentischen
Evangelien, § 28, sub 3; Schröer, Die Winteney-Version der
R. S. B., p. xxvii, etc.

§ 65. What is the nature of this epenthesis, i.e. what is
here the sound of *sc*? I think that *c* must be supposed to
indicate the change of *s* (not only of *sc* as Zeuner has it,
note 2 on p. 80) into the *palatal* sibilant, and I am happy

to find that the only writer who does speak of the nature of the sound—Reimann, l. l.—is of the same opinion. It is curious that so far as my instances go, the older periods present this insertion only between s and l, m or n, not before p and t[1], as in modern South German. Here *stein* and *spalte* become[2] *ŝtein* and *ŝpalte*; there it is only such words as *snīden* which would become *scnīden*. Now in German this *ŝ* from *s* has run into the sound *sc*, (etymologically) *sch* $= sk$. In modern English an original *sk* has often also become ' *sc* ' (i.e the palatal sibilant), as in *shadow* from *scadu*. In § 31, I have stated that the spelling *scamen*, etc., does not present a case of monophthonging. This must be now further explained.

§ 66. If the above view of the *c*-epenthesis be accepted, we need not be surprised to find this *c* written so comparatively rarely. Even in Anglo-Saxon times we may safely assume pronunciation to have been in advance of spelling, so that when the former began to change, the latter followed only tentatively, and not always consistently. Suppose therefore, that the sound-change, under certain conditions, of *s* to *sc* $= ŝ$ were pretty general, it is quite possible that in the majority of cases it should yet be written *s*, especially since the difference between the two is not so very great. Now the *sk* before palatal vowels would easily become *stj* (cf. §§ 60–63); and owing to the presence of the *s*, it would further dwindle down to *sj* $(= ŝ)$.

If it be objected that I here give a pronunciation to the *c*, which was denied it in the §§ cited, I must emphatically state that this is owing to the influence of the *s*[3]. That a stop should be slurred over sooner *between two continuants* than that at the beginning of a syllable (ri-ce) a *tj* should develop a sibilant, no one will care to deny, I think. Another possibility must here be disposed of. Could *sk* have developed into *ŝ* through the intermediate stage of *sχ* ? $(= s +$ the un-

---

[1] I now find *cæsctra* (castellum) in the Northumbrian Gospel of S. Matthew, 21. 2.

[2] By *k* in the rest of this section I denote the guttural voiceless stop, and by *ŝ* the palatal sibilant.

[3] See Mod. Language Notes, as quoted in § 52.

voiced palatal spirant). It is possible, but not likely. Spellings
like *schyldo* (Mt. prologue 17. 12) and *bischead* (corr. from
bigschad. Praef. Eusebii, 9. 13), as well as *sgiire -monn* (dis-
pensator, Luke 12. 42) in the Northumbrian Gospels, would
indeed seem to favour this view, but for a reason pointed
out above, I do not wish to lay too much stress on these
forms.   For my own self, I am inclined to look on the above
forms as all indicating the pronunciation *śyldo* (= sgyldo),
biśead, *śiiremonn*, etc.   But there is more.   Do spellings like
schamian occur?   i. e. *sch* before guttural vowels?

As to *sk* before the guttural vowels, whatever may have
originally been the impetus that set *sk* changing into what
is now spelt *sce* (Sievers, § 76), it did change in this direction,
and as soon as forms like *sceamu*, *sceadu*, had developed themselves, the way was open to change in the same manner as the
sk before palatal vowels.   Sievers, in reply to Kluge (Anglia,
V, anz. 83) has treated of these *ea*'s, etc. in the Beiträge,
(Paul and Braune) 9. 205 f.   His reasonings have not con-
vinced me, and I continue to hold with Kluge that the *ea*
in *sceamu* is no real diphthong.   Thus we find that *ce* in
sceop is the symbol for one sound (just as *sh* in *shall* is
the expression for only *one* sound), and the *o* has not become
diphthongized by the palatal *c*, i. e. the stress is on the *o*.
Now when the palatal *ś*, as developed out of *s* in the case
of *scniden*, had come to be expressed by *sc*, and when the
sound thus symbolised was also expressed by *sce*[1], we need
not be surprised to find that the *j*-sound originally expressed
by the *e* now got sufficiently known to be inherent in the
symbol *sc* (=*ś*) and that consequently a return to the spelling
scame may gradually be observed.   This is what I meant
above when saying that slight traces of the *c*-epenthesis
might perhaps be found in our text.

§ 67.   I have said that we must expect to find *sc* written
for *s* only rarely, whereas it may have been pronounced
so much oftener.   We may now go further, and say that

---

[1] This nearly always in conjunction with *a* and *o*, so that they can be
looked upon as the diphthongs *ea* and *eo*, which by this time had also the
stress on the *á* and *ó*.

a spelling *mænnisnesse* (68. 11) need not be a mistake for *mænniscnesse*, as *s* probably had here the value of *š*. See also *flæslican*[1], Cura Past. 234. 14. (Cosijn, I, § 131.)

Cosijn (I, p. 123) instances *menniscu, -escu* from the Pastoral Care (71. 12), without *sc* making the preceding vowel long through position. Was *sc* already palatal *š*?

§ 68. G. The following selection of forms, which might easily be multiplied, bears out the various statements of Sievers in his Grammar on the pronunciation of this letter:—*beiym* (47. 7), *aiyldenne* (19. 4), **asmaidan* (29. 11, read asmaiand = asmeagend*), *adli* (morbida, 60. 4), *scyldine* (36. 3), *sæde* (36. 6), *gesæið* (22. 3), *secce* (38. 12), *cræftican* (94. 10), *forhicgende* (12. 14), *underfænc* (16. 12), *þince* (33. 7), etc. etc. The combination *hg* occurs twice: *geleohgenne* (92. 8), gelohgenlican (63. 5). See also above, § 29. As regards the transition of *g* to *w*, it is exemplified in our MS. e.g. in *suwian* (11. 5, cf. Siev., §§ 214. 8, 416. 8), but the form *forgæwað* (107. 14) by the side of *forgæian* (75. 8) is rather curious. (Cf. note to 86. 17.)

§ 69. To one statement of Sievers's (§ 216, 3) I must take exception. He says: '*dg* has caused *cg* in *micgern*, fat (for **midgern*, O. H. G. *mittigarni*), which is extant in comparatively late texts only. This transition presupposes for its time (tenth century) a pronunciation of *cg* as *dz*.' I must claim for this *cg* the pronunciation *tj*, and refer my readers to § 63. O. H. G. *mittigarni* presupposes A.-S. **midgern*. This would readily become **mitgern*[2], i. e. *mitjern*; see above, § 62, where I have shown how this combination could be written *micgern*.

The pronunciation of *cg* as *dz* is therefore not proven.

---

[1] This word has lately been treated of by *Osthoff* (Beiträge, 13. 401 ff.; see especially p. 407). I suppose that the Kentish word *flæc*, which Kluge cites in his new ed. of his Etymol. Wörterbuch, is part of *flæchaman* in the Kentish Psalm 143. Zupitza, Z.f.D.A. 21. 12, thinks that this is a mistake. The suggestion may be hazarded that *c* (= *š*) should stand for *sc*, but I cannot support this spelling at present, except by the selfsame words *percce ðerccedum*, which Zupitza instances from the Kentish Glosses, and by the Northumbrian *oncæccen bið* (denegabitur, Luke 12. 9). Cp. perhaps the spelling *fiðer fete flæsð*, =*fiðerfete flæsa* (71. 11), for the *d* presupposes an *a*, rather than *ca*.

[2] Cf. *motgenne = modgenne* (110. 4), and *gemodigenne* (114. 10).

§ 70. ŋ, i.e. guttural *n*. This is usually, and in our MS. also continually, expressed by the letters *ng*, *nc*. While referring the student to § 41, I may here comment on the possibility that there may be something more than mere accident in the occurrence of the following forms:—

forspennigum (11. 3), *geondsprecend* (= geondsprengend, 12. 1), **gespinð* (i. e. geswinð, 82. 5; cp. 80. 2), *ginran* (106. 11), etc. etc. In the first two instances *g* and *c*, in the last two *n*, may denote what I have written *ñ*.—See *Zeuner*, Die Sprache des Kent. Psalters, § 32.

§ 71. If *midlum* (59. 1) is not an adverbial dative, then *ñ* is here denoted by *m*.

Note also *aflingede* (84. 5)=*afligede, alinge* (78. 10), *alenge* (79. 4), and *cantincas* (41. 5) by the side of the more usual *canticas*.

§ 72. H. We find an *h* added in some words, e.g. in *hæfte-mæst* (76. 5), *upahræred* (94. 14).

On the other hand we find: *efenlyttan* (consortes, 6. 14), *nexode* (molliti, 10. 9), *ofreow* (19. 8), *wilce* (26. 11), *wanon* (30. 13), *wælreow* (58. 12), *rægelhuse* (98. 15), *reod* (108. 8), *rædlice* (109. 13), *lyst* (auditus, 113. 12), etc. This dropping of the *h* most likely denotes a voicing of the *hw*; this is also expressed by the following spellings, *æiwhepera* (81. 11) and *whænne* (103. 2).

h is misread as *b* in **bræd* (promptus, 35. 6) and ** bada* (14. 7).

§ 73. Doubling of consonants, and conversely haplography [1], is exceedingly frequent in our text. I am not sure that in each case a phonetic corresponding process is thereby intimated. I select the following instances:—

goddra (53. 17), *fett* (pedes, 66. 2), *estmettas* (20. 1), *be-healdenne* (29. 6), *aworpones* (34. 8), *hederne* (80. 2).

§ 74. INFLECTIONS. I begin my notes on the inflections by giving a couple of instances of the absolute cases. They are of course imitations from the Latin, and although not restricted to interlinear translations, they are very frequent there, owing to influence of the lemmata.

---

[1] The writing of one symbol instead of two.

aw(ec)cenduthe gewrite (2. 8), *rihtwisnesse dihtendre* (14. 2), *gedihtenre endebyrdnysse* (50. 17), etc. etc.

§ 75. SUBSTANTIVES. Nominative. *intingu* (occasio, 91. 6, misreading?). Twice I have noticed the use of an accusative instead of a nominative case, *neode* (57. 19) and *forgimeleaste* (68. 8). See, however, (69. 16), where *neod* under the same circumstances is used in the nominative case.

Genitive. *cræftis* (22. 11), *biscopis* (107. 8). This ending -*is* may be owing either to influence of the respective lemmata, or it may be the natural reflex of -*ys*, which is very common in some texts. See Sievers, § 44, anm. 2. Is *breðer* (13. 12) perhaps wrongly influenced by the preposition *on*?

Dative and Instrumental. *gebeda* (orationi, 21. 13), *gebeda* (oratione, 21. 14), *eallra sawla* (anima, 19. 11), *dara* (noxa, 56. 17), are instances of a dative form, which (only in the two last words) may be due to Latin influence.

Accusative.—*repse* (Si quis dum pronunciat responsorium, 79. 11). Whence this dative form? Is this (as well as the accusatives instead of nominatives recorded above) to be looked upon as a trace of the mixing up of forms, to which Sievers, § 1, anm. 2, has drawn attention?

§ 76. Nom. Acc. Plural.—*broðra* (fratres, 57. 19), *gebroðra* (73. 13), *gebroðran* (3. 9, 105. 3), *beboda* (13. 4, 13. 6, etc.), *andsweras* (3. 1), *kynna* (9. 15), and other instances probably exemplify this same principle.

§ 77. If we did not find the words *geongra cildra* (pueri parvi, 106. 11), I should be inclined to look on *cildra* (pueris, 105. 14) as a misreading for *cildrū = cildrum*.

§ 78. The dative plural ends in -*on*, -*an*, -*um*, passim. There is no need to give instances. *Heofonum* (28. 8, 36. 9) may be a dual (Kluge, Beitr. 8).

§ 79. Of dative forms of the ADJECTIVES we notice the following, which are worth mentioning:—*orsorgi* (securi, 10. 3), which *i* may be due to the Latin ending[1], and forms like *ungehȳrsumude* (12. 8), *gecwemlice* (78. 5) as exemplifying the form-mixing spoken of above.

§ 80. Of plural forms compare the following :—*godu* (13. 2),

---

[1] Another possibility is, that, with the *ge* following, the word may be *orsorgige*.

feawa (35. 10), *þurhtogenes* (74. 11), *sinderlices* (85. 1), in most
of which cases the presence of the lemmata makes us doubt
whether the changes are not merely graphical blunders.

§ 81. The dat. plur. ends in *-on, -an, -um.*

§ 82. As regards the NUMERALS, a form *sex*, which, if it is
not caused by Latin influence, resembles the Northumbrian, is
found (reference missing).

§ 83. Of the Ordinals, I note the following forms which
are not found in Sievers, or of which he doubts the cor-
rectness :—

 9. *nȳgeþan, nigeþan* (37. 4, 11).
 30. *þritteoga* (43. 9):
 40. *feowerteogaða* (43. 10).
 50. *fifteogaða* (42. 13, 43. 10), *fyfteoða* (45. 19), *fiftugeðan*
  (43. 6).
 60. *syxteogaða* (42. 11, etc.).
 70. *seofonteoða* (42. 14).
 80. *hundeahteoða* (43. 13), *hundeahtoða* (43. 13).
 90. *hundnigenteoða* (43. 14, 51. 3), *hundnigenteoðan* (76.
  2, 3).
 100. *hundteontiga 7 eahtateoðan* (48. 16), *hundteonteoðan*
  (49. 16, 17).

§ 84. PRONOUNS. In *c, us, y,* as possible pronominal gloss
to *nobis*, see below, notes to (27. 2). *Inc* may be a pronoun
(19. 5), but there is no corresponding lemma. A peculiar
case of a declined ' genitive ' (see Sweet, A.-S. Reader[2], p. lix)
is found (54. 3), *abbodes heores* (abbatis sui).

þis (a neutral singular) is gloss (5. 3) to the neuter *þis.*

Seo, as a masculine pronoun, occurs (43. 11) and (70. 4), and
possibly also (36. 13). It thus bears out the statement of
Sievers, § 337, anm. 2. Conversely *se* would seem to be a
feminine pronoun in *se romanisca laðung* (aecclesia, romana,
44. 3).

§ 85. VERBS. Only a few verbal forms are interesting
enough to be noted. Of these we find the following third
persons : *beheald* (respicit, 30. 16), *stynt* (97. 1), and some
others where there is no suffix (see Cosijn, Altwestsächsische
Grammatik, I, § 148, p. 200). *sweg* (118. 5), *sæig* (30. 6), etc.

§ 86. Of plural forms, the corrupt *sed gat (22. 2) points to secgat, which antiquated form (Sievers, § 360) may itself have been the cause of the corruption ; cf. secgat (17. 17).

§ 87. Of infinitival forms, we may notice hatian (jubere, 11. 17), which, however, is probably a mistake for hatan ; gecian (vocari, 17. 17), which, according to Sievers, § 408. 3, is mostly found as cigan. The rarer forms in -on occur pretty frequently. See, for instance, ahyrdon (2. 12), and unwrigon (33. 7), as infinitival gloss to the imperative revela (supra, § 9). Of infinitives in -a, I found lysta aððe gehyra (audire, 21. 12).

§ 88. Of the verb sculan, the text has the following notable forms :—scel (debet, 26. 3, 102. 8), scell (69. 2), scyll (112. 7), scealan (debent, 81. 9), and scealan as infinitive (32. 10).

§ 89. The 'participium necessitatis,' which Sievers mentions in § 350 as found in later texts, and as formed after the Latin, occurs pretty frequently in our text. For the form given by him we may instance to campiende (5. 14), to specende (26. 7), to smeagenda (a is owing to the lemma, requirenda, 26. 11), to andedende (46. 10).

By the side of this we find even more frequently, however, forms in -enne, e. g. to campienne (1. 9), etc.

§ 90. That this future participle should also be found declined might be expected. Accordingly we have eardigendes (5. 11), and be gegearnendum to ræde gebroðra (de adhibendis ad consilium fratribus, 17. 10). In this case to is, as a matter of course, suppressed (31. 5, I find *aræriende, for ariende or æriende,—as gloss to parcendo : here to would also seem to be omitted).

§ 91. The same notion is sometimes expressed by adjectives in -lic, e. g. þa sendlican (dirigendi, 113. 4), on donlicum þingum (in faciendo, 23. 12), which same ending I have once found glossing a present participle, becumendlicum (87. 12). Here supervenientes was possibly mistaken for superveniendi.

§ 92. 'Formed on the pattern of the Latin :' these words of Sievers's convey the impression that Latin only is answerable for the development of this d. I think that, viewed in the light of § 56, d will probably prove to be of a purely phonetic origin. . When once the *d* began to develop phonetically, its growth and spreading may have been aided by a more or less conscious association with the Latin participle; but I hold that analogy and phonetics both share the paternity of the new form.

§ 93. I may here mention *beon gelogodre* (reponantur, 98. 15). How the passive voice of a verb can be glossed by what is apparently the dative feminine of a past participle, I am unable to understand. With partial dittography the same ending is probably found in *behyd(dad)edre* (100. 1, 2). See however note on p. 124, Compare (26. 16) where the infinitive *aperire*, which may be construed in a passive sense, is glossed by an apparently masculine dative (*geopenodum*). Equally strange datives occur (66. 15) *þa utgangendum*, (74. 12) *þa gehyrendum*, and (87. 12) *ofer becumendlicum*. But they may perhaps exemplify the mixing up of datives and accusatives, which is characteristic of the later Anglo-Saxon.

§ 94. To any one who has looked into the text, or into the foregoing §§, many Kenticisms must be apparent at a glance. Thus we have the *e=æ* (*supra*, § 15, etc.; Sievers, § 151, 1); the *e=y* (§ 27, Siev. § 154); absence of diphthongisation of *e* into *ea* (§ 30, Siev. § 157. 2), to mention only the most striking peculiarities. But it will also have been seen that these do not appear throughout, and that West-Saxon influence is traceable. Now has a Kentish text been copied by a West-Saxon scribe or *vice versa*? I think a case like *betehtum* (31. 1), which was misread as *hetelicum*, is singularly instructive. *Telendne*, (=tælendne) which was misread as *ælendne* (20. 15), tells the same tale. An interchange—graphical—of *h* and *b*, *te* and *æ*, and of *h*, and *li* is quite common. Was it not the *strange* forms *betehtum*, *telendne*, instead of *betæhtum*, *tælendne*, which led to the confusion? If so, the Kentish text must have been the original, and the West-Saxon the copy.

THE RULE OF S. BENET.

—••—

IN NOMINE D*OMI*NI N*OSTRI* IESU CHR*IST*I INCIPIT RE(GULE) |
foraspræc   fæderes   þæs   haligan   þæs   eadigostan   benedictes
PROLOG*US*   PATRIS   EXIMII   BEATISSIMI   BE*N*EDICTI)

hlẏst   eala bearn   beboda   lareowes   7   ahẏld   eare
AUSCULTA   FILI   PRECEPTA   MAGISTRI ET INCLI*N*A)   *aurem*

heortan   þinre   7   mẏneguncge   arfæstes   fæderes   lustlice
cordis   *tui*   *et*   *ammoniti(onem)*   *pii*   *patris*   *libenter*

underfoh 7 fremfi   ge'ẏll   þœt þu to him þurh gehẏrsum-
excipe et *effica(citer)*   *comple ut ad eum*   *per*   *oboedi-*   5

nesse geswince gehwẏrfe forþam þurh ungehẏrsumnesse asolcenesse
entie laborem   redeas   a quo per   *inoboedientie   desidiam*

þe þu aweiggewite   eornostlice nu   min spræc is asend
recesseras ;   Ad t'e)   ergo   nunc meus sermo dirigitur

swa   wið cweþende *aþenum   lustum   drihne   criste
quisquis   abren(un)tians   propriis   voluptatibus   domino christo

þamsoðan   cinge   to campienne gehẏrsumnesse   þa   þrengestan
vero   regi   militaturus   oboedientie   fortissima

7 þa þurh beorh*tan* wæpna swa underfehst ealra ærest þœt
atque   precla(ra)   arma   assumis.   In   primis ut 10

þu swa hwæð swa to donne   þu on   god   fram him beon
quicquid   agendum in(choas) bonum ;   ab eo per-

gefremmed þam iornfullestan gebede bid   se þe us iallinga
fici instantissima oratione   dep(oscas). ut qui nos iam

bearna   gemedemode on getele getellan   *ut* þœt he na sceole
in filiorum dignatus est nume(ro) computare ;   non   debeat

---

5. *fremfi*, see note.   6. *geswince, nce* not clear. First *s* of *asolcenesse* not
at all clear.   8. *aþenum*, read *awenum*.   9. *þam-*, *a* may be *æ*. ð of
soðan may be *d*.   10. *beorhtan, tan* is by no means clear.   11. After
on part of the MS. is torn away.   12. After *bid*, part of the MS. torn away.
13. *ut*, Latin in glossator's hand.   It is in none of the other texts.

1. RE not very clear.   3. AU-SCULTA in two lines by way of illumination
by the side of *In nomine—foraspræc—prologus—fili.*   5, 6. *oboedientie,*
MS. *oedientie; inoboedientie,* MS. *inoedientie.*   7. *t* of *t(e)* not clear.

æhwænne be uru*m* ẏfelum da   beon geunrotsode swa soðlice
aliquando de malis act(ibus) nostris   contristari ; Ita enim

him on ælcere tide be   his   on us is to earcienne ł
ei omni tempore de bon(is) suis in nobis   parendum

hẏrsumienne þ*æt* he ne na þ*æt* an swa swa ẏrre fæder his
est ; ut non solum ut irat(us) pater suos non

oðer hwile bearn beerfwerdige ah swa swa egeful hlaford
aliquando filios exheredet, sed nec(ut) metuendus dominus

swa geẏrsod fram ẏfelu*m* urum þ*æt* he swa swa þa wyr
5· *irritatus a malis nostris   ut   nequissimos*

þeowan to þam ecan na betæce to wite we þe him fẏlian
servos perpetuam tradat ad poenam qui eum sequi

noldan to wuldre uton arisan   æt nẏxan æt sumon cẏrre
noluerint ad gloriam; Exsurgamus ergo tandem aliquando

aw . . cendum us gewrite 7 secgendum   hit is us
excitante nos scriptura Ac dicente ho(ra) est jam nos

of slæpe uparisan   geopenedum eagum urı . . | god-
de sompno surgere. Et apertis oculis nostr(is) | (ad d)eifi- (118 b.)

cundan leohte mid ablicendum earum 7 utan gehẏran þagod
10 *cum lumen; attonitis auribus audiamus   divina (co)-*

amlice clipiende hwæt us mẏngie stefn   to dæg
tidie clamans quid nos ammoneat vox dicens. hodi(e si v)ocem

gegehyraðð nelle ge ahẏrdon eowre heortan   eft
ejus audieritis nolite obdurare corda vestra. (et) iterum ;

se ðe hæfð earan to gehẏranne gehẏre hwæt
Qui habet aures audiendi ; audiat quid spiritus (dic)at

gelaðungum 7 la hwæt sæigð cumað la gebearn gehẏrað
aecclesiis ; Et quid dicit ; Venite filii audite me

. . . htnes ege 7 ic lære eow ẏrnað lifes leoht þa hwile ðe
15 *(timorem domini docebo vos ; Currite dum lumen vite*

ge habbað þẏstru deaðes eow þæt ne gegripan 7 secende
habetis (ne) tenebre mortis vos comprehendant ; Et querens

meniu folce þam he þas ðinc clẏpað his wrẏhtan
dominus (in) multitudine populi cui haec clamat operarium

ł seigð la hwylc is man se ðe wẏle lif 7
suum (ite)rum dicit. Quis est homo qui vult vitam et

---

1. After *dadum* part of the MS. torn away.   4. One letter erased between
oðer and *hwile*.   5. After *wyr* part of the MS. torn away.   6. *to?*, very
indistinct.   8. In *aw . . . cendum* two letters indistinct, probably *aweccendum*.
9. *u* of *geopenedum* reads like an *i*. Read *urum*.   11. Read *dæghwamlice*.
15. Read *drihtnes*.   18. *ł*, last letter of *eft*.

---

7. *s* of *exsurgamus* add. afterwards.   8. *dicente*, see note.

gewilnað . . . on dagan gode þæt gef þa gehýrende andsweras
cupit (vi)dere dies bonos; quod si tu audiens respondeas.

. . . gð þe gode gif þu wilt habban þæt soðe lif 7 þæt
Ego (di)cit tibi deus; Si vis habere veram et per-

ece lif . . . eond tundgan þine fram ýfele 7 þine
petuam vitam (proh)ibe linguam tuam a malo et labia

weleras 7 þæt hi na sprecan . . . n gecýr fram yfele 7 do
*tua ne loquant*ur *(dol)um; Deverte a malo et fac*

god smea oððe sec sibbe . . . ýlig hýre 7 þonne þas
bonum. inquire pacem (et) sequere eam; Et cum haec 5

þincg gedoð eagan mine ofor 7 mine earan to eowrum
feceritis. oculi mei super (vo)s et aures mee ad preces

benum 7 ær þonne geclýpian me ic secge eow æfre ic her eom
vestras. Et antequam me in(vo)cetis dicam vobis. Ecce adsum;

est luftempre . . . ere stefne gelaðgendre la ge
Quid dulcius nobis (ab h)ac voce domini invitantis nos

þa leofestan gebroðran efne mid his arfæstnesse geswutulað
fratres karissimi; Ecce pietate (sṳa demonstrat

us lifes weg begýrdum mid geleafan oððe mid
nobis dominus viam vite; Succinctis (e)rgo fide vel obser- 10

gehealdsumnesse goddra dæda lendenum . . . . u gebroht
vantia bonorum actuum lumbis (n)ostris perducatum

bodung utan gan his sióffæt þæt we gearnian hine se ðe
evangelii pergamus itinera ejus ut (ṃereamur eum qui nos

geclipode on his rice geseon . . n ðæs rices healle on inne gýf
vocavit. In regno suo videre; (In) cujus regni tabernaculo si

we wýllað buton | mid godum dædum ýrnende nateshwon
volumus habitare. nisi | illuc bonis actibus currendo minime

ne bið becumen* abutan axan mid þam witigan drihten
pervenitur; Sed interrogemus cum propheta dominum. 15

secgende him la hwa wunað on ðinan inne oððe
dicentes ei Domine quis habitavit in tabernaculo tuo aut

la hwa gereð on ðinre haligan dune æfter þýssere ax-
quis requiescet in monte sancto suo? Post hanc interro-

a.)

---

1. Read *geseon.* 2. Read *sæigð* or *sægð.* 3. *eond,* see note. 4. Read
facn. 5. *ýlig,* read *fylig.* 8. *est,* ē in MS.; Latin in glossator's hand.
In no other text. . . . *ere,* read *þissere.* 9. *n* of *gebroðran* erased. 11. . . *u,*
read *urum. gebroht,* see note. 13. . . *n,* read *on.* 15. *abutan,* read
ah utan.

1. *audieris* would seem to have been corrected into *audiens.* b. *et* (after
pacem) pasted over. 11. a of *observantia* corr. from *e.* 12. Erasure of one
letter after *pergamus.* 17. *e* add. above line (*requiescet*).

5 ★

unge   uton   gehýran   andswariende 7 gesutuliende
gationem fratres audiamus dominum respondentem et ostendentem
              his   healle oððe innes 7 seccende se ðe ingæþ
nobis viam ipsius   tabernaculi   ac dicentem ; Qui ingreditur
butan smittan   swýlce wýrcð rihtwisnesse 7 se ðe sprýcð soð-
sine maculu et   operatur justitiam :   Qui loquitur veri-
fæstnesse   heortan on his 7 se ðe na deþ facn on his tungan
tatem in corde suo   qui non egit dolum in lingua sua
se ðe na dýde nextan his   yfel   se ðe hosp   na underfencg
5 *Qui non fecit proximo suo malum. qui obprobrium non   accepit*
agen   his nextan   se ðe þone awýridan deofol sum ðinc
adversus proximum suum. Qui malignum   diabolum aliqua
tihende him sýlfan mid his sýlfan tihtinge fram gesihðum
suadentem sibi   cum ipsa   suasione   a conspectibus cordis
     forseonde se gewrohte   his lýtlan hwædan geþohtas
sui respuens   deduxit   ad nichilum. et parvulos cogitatus ejus
7 heald   betæhte   non
tenuit et allisit ad christum ; Qui timentes dominum de bona
        hi sýlfe þane deð upahafene þa sýlfan on
10 *observantia sua non se   reddunt   elatos   sed ipsa   in*
him sýlfan goda na fram him sýlfan magon   beon
se bona non a se   posse   sed a domino fieri
ahwenende   7 hi mærsiað
existimantes. et operantem in se dominum magnificant. illud cum
      na us
propheta dicentes. non nobis domine non nobis. sed nomini tuo
     ah forðan paulus se apostol be   his bodunge
da gloriam. Sed nec   paulus apostolus de predicatione sua
him sýlfan ah forðam ne tealde
15   *sibi aliquid   inputavit dicens; Gratia dei sum. id quod*
              se ðe wuldrað   wuldrie he
sum; Et iterum ipse dicit. Qui gloriatur in domino glorietur ;
þanon   sæigð   sæde
Unde et dominus in evangelio ait ; Qui audit verba mea
þas þinc | ic *onlocie hine wisum were
hæc et facit ea | similabo eum viro sapienti. qui edificavit (119 b.

---

9. *betæhte*, first *t* not clear.   18. Above *ea* the gloss is partly cut away;
an *h* is recognisable, and part of a letter which looks like *g*, so *hig*? Read
onlicie.

---

8. *parrulos*, MS. *pa.rulus.*   13. *sed*, MS. *se.*   18. *a* of *ea* partly cut away.

            comon   flodas   bleowan
domum suam supra petram. Venerunt flumina. flaverunt venti

7 hi ætspurnon on   ðam huse   7 hit ne feoll forþam þe
et impegerunt in domum illam et non cecidit; quia fun-

hit wæs gestaðelod ofor þam stane þis gefyllende
  data   erat   super petram ; Hæc complens dom:nus ;

anbidiað   mid dædum
expectat nos cotidie. his suis sanctis monitis   factis   nos

        we sculan forþi   for   bote
respondere debere. Ideo nobis propter emendationem ma'orum 5

þises lifes dagas to fyrstum sind to alætenne
hujus vite dies ad   inducias relaxantur ; dicente apostolo ;

nyte ge la þæt ge godes geþyld   eow
An nescis quia   patientia   dei   vcs ad penitentiam te

læt   þa synfullan
adducit ; Nam pius dominvs dicit; Nolo mortem peccatoris.

     þæt he gecyrre   þonne   we axiað
sed ut   convertatur et vivat : Cum ergo interrogassemus

            be wunungum
dominum fratres de habitatore tabernaculi ejus. audivimus 10

eardigendes   bebod   ah gyf we gefyllað wunigendes þenunge
habitandi preceptum. Sed si compleamus habitatoris officium.

we beoð   sin to gereccanne
erimus heredes regni celorum; Ergo   preparanda   sunt

     7 lichaman   haligre   beboda   gehirsumnesse
corda et corpora nostra sancte precep'orum   obedientie

to campiende 7 þæt hwonlic þæt þe on us gekynd acumenlic
militanda et quod minus habet in nobis natura possibile.

ac uton biddan   his gife þæt he iarcie   fultum
* rogemus dominum ut gratie sue   jubeat nobis adjutorium* 15

þenian 7 gif fleonde helle   wite   life we wyllað
ministrare ; Et si fugientes gehenne poenas ad vitam volumus

becum to ðam ecan   tigað 7 þa hwile æt þisum
pervenire perpetuam. dum adhuc vacat. et in hoc corpo-

lichaman þe we sin   ealle þas þinc þurh þisne leohtes weg
* re sumus :   et hæc omnia per hanc lucis viam*

---

7. Second *e* of *nytegela*, being written too close upon the *l*, is not quite clear.
8. *þa*, read *þæs*. 17. Read *becuman. tigað*, end of *æmtigað*.

---

7. *vos*, not in other texts ; *te* is crossed out. 10. *habitatore*, MS. *habitatorum* ; see note. 15. *jubeat*, MS. *habeat*, a wrong transcription for *jubeat*,
which all other texts have? The gloss *þæt he iarcie* would lend support to
this view.

gefẏllan ẏs to ẏrnanne 7 is to donne nu |
v(acat) implere currendum et agendum . est modo. | (120 a

þæt hit on ecnesse framme is ,to settanne fram
quod in perpetuum nobis expediat; Constituenda est ergo a

us drihtenlices scole þeowdomes on ðære we hihtað ænig þinc
nobis dominici scola servitii. in qua institutione, nihil

heardlices ænig us to gesettanne we hopiað gif
asperum nihilque grave nos constituturos speramus; Sed et si

hwæt litles forðstepð stiðlicor dihtende rihtwisnesse gescad for
5 *quid paululum restrictius dictante aequitatis ratione propter*

bote oððe drohtnunge soðre lufe forðstypð
emendationem vitiorum. vel conversationem caritatis prccesserit

þærrihte ac þu na forfleo hæle se ðe
non ilico pavore peiterritus refugias viam salutis que

nis buton mid stige to onginnenne mid forðsteppinge
non est nisi angusto initio incipienda ; Processu vero

drohtnunga heortan onunasecgendlicere lufe
conversationis et fidei dilatato corde inenarrabili dilectionis ·

werednesse urnen beboda godes fram his
10 *dulcedine curritur via mandatorum dei. ut ab ipsius*

æfre lareowdome oð
nunquam magisterio discedentes. in ejus doctrina usque ad

deaþ on minstre se þurhwunigende þrowungum
mortem in monasterio perseverantes. passionibus christi

þurh geþẏld þæt we beon dælnimende rices his
per patientiam participemur. ut et regni ejus mereamur

efenlyttan
esse consortes. AMEN. EXPLICIT PROLOGUS REGULE BEATI BENE-
15 DICTI ABBATIS. PATRIS MONACHORUM.

I. De generibus monachorum vel vita.

II. Qualis debeat esse abba.

III. De adhibendis ad consilium fratribus.

IIII. Que sint instrumenta bonorum operum.

20 *V. De oboedientia discipulorum qualis sit.*

---

5. *forðstepð*, probably copied here by mistake by scribe, who must have seen
it a line lower down. Cf. infra, note to l. 3 (*hihtað*). 7. *þærrihte*, *æ* or *a*
not clear; first *r*, but for context, might have been put down as *f*, the *l* of *ilico*
being blended with it.

---

6. *conversationem*, MS. *conservationem*. 7. *pavore*, MS. *pavorem*. 9. *o*
of *dilatato* corr. from *a*. 19. Q of *Que* wrongly rubricated in the MS. as *D*.

19. *XXV.* This is a mistake for *XXIV*, and the mistake is continued throughout in this list, so that ch. *XLIIII* as given lower down (*De his qui* etc.), ought to be ch. *XLIII*. *esse* not in the MS.   21. *XXVII.* A word erased after *abbatis*, probably *junguntur*, which is therefore added in brackets. 22. *XXVIII. communicatos*, *o* of *os* corr. in MS. from *i* by writing *o* over *i*. 24. Second *e* of *debeant* above line.

---

8. *occurrunt* supplied here as the reading of all the MSS. used by Schröer.
Cf. A. Schröer, Die Winteney-Version der Regula S. Benedicti, p. 10. The
text of the Winteney Version (S = Schröer's C) has *occurrerint*, and our text
(fo. 146 b) has *veniunt*. From *XLIII* down to the closing of the bracket the
omission in the MS. has been supplied from our text (corrected).   12.
XLVII. The heading for this chapter not being in our MS., it is supplied
from the readings of the other MS.; cf. Schröer, W. V., p. 96.

(121 b.)   EXPLICIUNT CAPITULA.   INCIPIT LIBER BEATI BENEDICTI |

ABBATIS.   PATRIS EXIMI MONACHORUM MILITUM CHRISTI.

DE GENERIBUS.   EORUM VEL VITA.

            feower   kynna [b.] [c.] beon   [a.]sutol   is
Monachorum *quattuor*   *genera*   *esse*   *manifestum*   *est.* 15

þæt forme   mynstermanna þæt is   mynsterlic campiende [h.]
 Primum   *coenobitarum* *hoc est* *monasteriale* *militans*

under regule. oððe abbude.   [b.] syððan þæt oðer   kyn is
 sub   *regula* *vel* *abbate* ;   *Deinde*   *secundum genus est*

dan.* orseclena þæt is westþensetlena. [g.] þissera [h.] þaðe na
anachoritarum *id est* *heremitarum*   *horum*   *qui non*

drohtnunge *wylne mid niwum [p.] ac mid mynstres [o.]fadunge
conversationis fervore   *novitio ;*   *eed monasterii*   *probatione*

[u.] *landsumere [h.] leornodon ongean þone deoful mænigra
  diuturna   *didicerunt*   *contra*   *diabolum*   *multorum* 20

---

18. Before *dan.* erasure (see note). *g. þissera* added in margin, possibly by
the original glossator.   19. Read *wylme*.   *ac mid* ? *c* may have been there,
but it has been made into first stroke of *m*, which now, by mistake, of course,
looks like *m* with four strokes.   20. Read *lancsumere*.

---

7. *LXVIIII* and following numbers are not in the MS. ; *ut in monasterio*
etc., the title of ch. *LXVIIII* follows in our MS. directly after the *ad mensam
tarde* of the title of ch. *XLIIII*, without a capital letter or rubric being used
for *ut*, so that it looks like one chapter. A page must have been skipped here.
12. EXPLICIUNT, MS. EXPLICIT.   18. *horum* added in marg., possibly by
glossator.   19. *conversationis*, MS. *conversionis*.

[l.] mid frore, eallunga gelærede [i.] winnan ⌊q.] bene getẏde
    solacio jam docti pugnare;   *et bene instructi*

of broðorlicere færrædene to anfealdan gewinne westenes
    *fraterna ex acie ad singularem pugna*m *heremi*

georsorgi. ge buton frofre oðres mid anre [t.] hand
    securi jam sine consolatione alterius sola   manu

[u.] oððe [u.] earme . agean leahtras flæsces [i.] oððe geþohta
    vel   brachio contra vitia carnis vel   cogitationum,

gode gefultumiandum [v.] winnan [q.] 7 hi nihtsumiað
5 *deo   auxiliante   pugnare   sufficiunt;*

þæt þridde [c.]   [d.]   þæt atelicost [b.] kin [a.] sẏlfde-
Tertium vero monachorum teterrimum . genus est. sarabai-

mera [a.] þa on ænigum regole na afandode uel oððe afundennessa
tarum. qui   nulla' regula   approbati experientia

lareowas [h.] [n.] [m.] ofenes. [n.]   ahge . . des on gekynde
magistri sicut aurum fornacis; sed in plumbi   natura

nexode [i.] þa git. [r.] mid weorcum. healdende [o.] weorulde.
molliti adhuc   operibus servantes seculo

[p.] truwan. leogan. [b.] gode þurh scere [a.] sẏnd acnawene
10 *fidem.   mentiri   deo per   tonsuram noscuntur;*

þa twẏfealde þreofealde oððe soðes anlepie gangende ambulantes
Qui bini aut terni.   aut certe   singuli sine

butan hẏrde hig on drihtenlicum heordum. ac heora agenum
pastore, non   dominicis sed suis

beclẏsde   fore æ heom is gewilnunga. lust
inclusi ovilibus pro lege eis est desideriorum voluptas.

þonne hi hwæt wenað tellað oððe geceosan þæt secgaþ halig
cum quicquid putaverint vel elegerint. hoc dicunt sanctum

7 þæt þæt hi nellað þæt 7 hi wenað | na beon alẏfede. þæt
15 *et quod noluerint. hoc   putant | non licere. Quar-* (122 a.)

feorðe soðlice kin is [a.]   þæt is genemned wið
tum vero genus est monachorum quod nominatur gyro-

scripel þa on eallon heora life geond mislice sciru þrim
vagum. qui tota vita sua per diversas provincias. ternis

---

1. *frore,* i. e. *frofre,* and see note on this word.   *bene,* Latin copied into
gloss.   7. *n* in *ænigum* of irregular shape.   *vel,* Latin; see note.
11. *gangende* in the MS. is gloss to *ambulantes,* which has been put in by
glossator spontaneously. It is not found in the other texts.   17. Uncertain
whether *scira* or *sciru.*

---

2. Erasure after *heremi?*   13. *eis* above the line.   16. *est* above the
line and erasure.

oðer feoweru dagum geond mistlicora þinga hus cumliðiað
aut quaternis diebus per diversorum cellas hospitantur
æfre worigende 7 næfre staðolfæste agenum lustum
semper vagi et numquam stabiles. et propriis volup-
7 gýfernesse 7 forspennigum þeowgende geond ealle þinc
tatibus et gule illecebris servientes et per omnia
wursan þam sýlfdemerum þara ealra drohtnunge be ðære
deteriores sarabaitis ; De quorum omnium miserrima conver-
earmæstan betere hit is suwian þonne sprecan. þisum forlætenum
satione melius est silere quam loqui ; His ergo ommissis ; 5
[c.] to [e.] mýnstermanna [d.] þæt strengoste [d.] kýn
ad cenobitarum fortissimum genus
[c.] gedihten [b.] fultumiendum [h.] [a.] uton cuman.
disponendum. adjuvante domino veniamus ; QVALIS
DEBEAT ESSE ABBAS. (CAP. II.)
se abbud seðe forabeon [d.] wýrðe is [c.] [f.] on mýnstre [h.]
ABBA QVI PREESSE DIGNVS EST *monasterio. semper*
gemunon [a.] sceal þæt he is gesæd 7 naman oððe [m.]
meminisse debet quod dicitur et nomen majoris 10
middædum [m.] 7 gefýllan [k.] [e.] [b.] [h.] don
factis implere ; Christi enim agere
[c.] spelunga [f.] [a.] he is *gelýst ðænne his [i.]
vices in monasterio creditur. quando ipsius
he is geciged to forenaman secgendum [a.] [k.] [e.] ge under-
vocatur pronomine. dicente apostolo ; Acce-
fengon gast gewýscednýsse on ðam we cleopiað
pistis spiritum adoptionis filiorum ; in quo clamamus
arwurða fæder [a.] [a.] 7 forð [c.] naht [h.] butan [g.] bebode [g.]
abba pater ; Ideoque abbas nihil extra preceptum 15
[g.] þæt feorsi [h.] na sceall [h.] oððe læran. [d.] [a.] oððe
domini quod absit debet aut docere. aut
gesettan [e.] oððe [f.] hatian [f.] ahsi hæs [b.] his [b.] oððe [c.]
constituere vel jubere. sed jussio ejus. vel
lar [c.] * býsn [o.] godcundre [e.] rihtwisnesse [e.] leornincg
doctrina. fermentum divine justitiae in disci-

---

1. oðer, read oððe ; feoweru, read feowerum.   12. Read gelyft.   18. bysn,
read byrma (=beorma)?

---

5. Er. of one letter (e?) after ergo.   7. dum crossed out before -te of
adjuvante.   13. pro added afterwards.

cuihtas [g.] [dm.] [p.] geþancum geondsprecend mýndig tig [a.]
pulorum   mentibus   conspergatur ;   Memor   sit

æfre [b.] þæt [n.] [e.] his lare [g.] [g.] oððe [h.] leorninc cnihta
semper.   abbas   quia   doctrine   sue   vel   discipulorum

gehýrsumnesse [h.] æghwæðera [k.] [k.] on ðam egesfullan [l.]
oboedientiae.   utrarumque   rerum   in   tremendo

dome [l.] gode to donne he[e.] is he[e.] is[e.] oððe [f.] 7 wite [a.]
judicio   dei. facienda   erit | erit   discusio.   Sciatque (122 b.)

se abbod [b.] gýltes [d.] hýrdes onsigan [c.] [f.] swa hwæt on
5 *alba   culpe   pastoris   incumbere   quicquid   in*

sceapum [g.] se hiredes ealdor [g.] nýtwýr ðr.esse hwonlicor swa
ovibus   paterfamilias   utilitatis minus potuerit

mæg gemetan swa micel [d.] eft [d.] * srig [c.] he bið gif unstilre
invenire;   Tantum   iterum   liber   erit.   si   inquieto

oððe ungehýrsumude [g.] hýrde [e.] ælc. [f.] geornfulnýssa
vel   inoboedienti   greji pastoris fuerit   omnis   diligentia

bið forgifen 7 gif adligum [c.] heora [c.] dædum [c.] eall [b.]
attributa.   et   morbidis   earum   actilus   universa

býð [a.] [b.] gýman gegearcod hýrde [e.] heora [e.] on dome [g.]
10 *fuerit   cura   exhibita.   pastor   eorum   in   judicio*

drihtnes tolýsed [f.] ut * þæt * ece mid þam witigan
dom:ni   absolutus   dicat   cum   propheta   domino ;

[b.] þine rihtwisnýsse [b.] ic ne be hýdde on minre hecrtan
Justitiam tuam   non abscondidi   in   corde   meo.

þine [e.] soðfæstnesse [e.] 7 halwendan [f.] [f.] þinre ic sæde
veritatem tuam   et   salutare   tuum   dixi.

hig [g.] forhicgende [h.] forsawon [g.]   7 [a.] þonne [b.]
ipsi autem contempnentes   spreverunt   me.   Et   tunc

æt lýxtan [e.] ungehýrsuman gýmene [f.] his [f.] sceapum to wite
15 *demum   inoboedient:ibus   cure   suae   ovibus: pena*

[a.] bið heom swýðrenda sesylva [c.] [c.] deað [b.] þonne
sit   eis   prevalens   ipsa   mors;   Ergo   cum

ænig [g.] underfehð [f.] naman [i.] [h.] þæs abhodes. on twýfeald
aliquis   suscipit   nomen   abbatis.   dupplici

---

1. *dm* stands above *g*, *p* under *g*, both to the right. See note on *geond-sprecend.*   7. *srig*, read *frig.*   11. *ut* in line of gloss by hand of glossator. *þæt ece*, i. e. *þ̄ ece*, read *secce* ?

---

10. MS. *earum*, an *o* above the *a*, which does not seem to me to be one of the 'paving' letters, but a correction by glossator of *earum* into *eorum.*

he sceal [a.] lare [e.] his [d.] leorn [c.] [c.] forebeon i. cnihtum
debet　　doctrina　　suis　　　　　　　preesse　　discipulis.

þæt is ealle [b.] godu. [b.] 7 halige middædum [e.] swyðor
id est omnia　　bona　　et sancta　　factis　　amplius

þænne [f.] [f.] mid wordum he atiwige angitfullum leornicenihtum
quam　　　verbis ostendat ; ut capacibus　discipulis

beboda [i.]　　　　　mid wordum [k.] his foresette [g.] þam heard
mandata domini　　verbis　　　prcponat.　　duris vero

heortan [d.]　　bilehwitum mid his [c.] dædum [c.] þa godcundan
corde　et simplicioribus　factis　　suis　　divina　5

beboda [b.]　he geswuteliað ealle þino. [b.]　þe leornincenihtum.
precepta　demonstret ;　Omnia　vero que　discipulis

he læræð beon [h.] wiðræde on his dædum he gebicnige na
docuerit　esse　contraria in suis factis　indicet　non

to donne þæt oðrum bodiende [m.] he sylf [k.] wiðercora
agenda　ne　aliis　predicans　　ipse　　reprobus

ne si gemett þæt ahwenne him na secge [c.] syngendum
inveniatur　nequando　illi　dicat　deus　peccanti.

to hwi na ðu cyðst rihtwisnyssa mine 7 þu underfæhst
Quare　tu enarras　justitias　meas. et　assumis　10

gewitnysse mine þurh þinne muð þu　hatodest steore
testamentum meum per　os tuum　Tu vero odisti disciplinam

7 ðu awurpe spræca | mine *bestande 7 þa ge on breðer þines
(123 a.) *et projecisti sermones | meos post te et　qui　in fratris tui*

ege　mot　gesawe on ðinon ege beam ne gesawe þu la
oculo festucam videbas. in　tuo　trabem non　vidisti ;

[a.] Na si [c.] fram him [b.] had on mynstre [d.] [a.] asyndrod
Non　ab · eo persona in monasterio　discernatur.

na si an swiðor gelufod mid godum dædum oððe gehyrsum-
non unus plus ametur　bonis　actibus aut　oboedi- 15

nesse *ænne oðer butan þaneþe he met beteran ne si
entia quam alius nisi　quem invenerit meliorem; Non

forasett se æðelborenne þeowdome ge [c.] cyrrendum [e.] buton
preponatur　ingenuus　ex servitio　convertenti.　nisi

---

1. *leorn*, which belongs to *cnihtum*, has been put before *forebeon*. For *leornincenihit*? 12. *ðu* not quite clear, a stroke running through *ð* and along the top of the *u*, making it look like *a*. *bestande*, read *beftan ðe*. 16. *ænne*, read *þænne*.

---

12. *meos*, MS. *meo. post te*, MS. *poste*. 15. *bonis*, MS. *actionis*; clearly the scribe's eye was caught by the next word.

wenunga sum gesceadwislic [f.] intinga [e.] wunige þæt [a.]
forte aliqua rationabilis causa existat ; Quod

gif bi**ð** rihtwisnesse dihtendre [c.] þam [b.] abbude sewen ge. [a.]
si ita justitia dictante abbati visum fuerit.

[g.] be sumere be ændebȳrdnesse þæt [h.] hedo elles
et de cujus libet ordine id faciat; Sin alias ;

agenre [a.] higehealdan [b.] stowa for**ð**am swa þeowa [g.] [h.] swa
propria . teneant loca. quia sive servus sive

fræc [h.] ealle [d.] on chri**s**te an. [e.] þe we sin [a.] 7 under ane
5 *liber ; omnes in chri**s**to unum sumus. et sub uno*

drihtene gelicne [b.] þeowdomes ca**m** dom [b.] 7 we abera**ð** for**ð**am
domino æqualem servitutis militiam bajulamus. quia

þe *þe is mid gode *bada *anstangynnes [b.] þæt an [b.]
non est apud deum personarum acceptio ; Solum modo

[a.] **ð**isum dæle [c.] mid him [d.] he tosyndraþ gif beteran
in hac parte apud ipsum · discernimur. Si meliores

o**ð**ram [h.] [h.] on godu**m** weorcu**m** [h.] 7 eadmodren we beo**ð**
aliis in operibus bonis et humiliores inveni-

gemette gelic [b.] [a.] si fram him [g.] eallum [d.] [k.] so**ð**lufu
10 *amur; Ergo equalis sit ab eo omnibus karitas ;*

an sigegearcod on eallum æfter [b.] gearnunge steor [f.]
Una prebeatur in omnibus secundum merita disciplina; In

lare [h.] witodlice on his se abbod [e.] apostolice [a.] sceall
doctrina namque sua abbas apostolicam debet

þæt he æfre [f.] hiwe healdan on **ð**am he sæig**ð**. [g.] þrea
illam semper formam servare in qua dicit ; Arguae.

halsa cid þæt [a.] is [a.] mængcende tidum tida [c.]
obsecra. increpa. id est miscens temporibus tempora

ogum. egesum. geswæsnyssa 7 re**ð**e [e.] lareowas [b.] arfæst
15 *terroribus blandimenta; Dirum magistri. pium*

fæderes [c.] heatiwe [a.] lufe [b.] þæt is [f.] þæt ungeþeawfæstan [i.]
patris ostendat affectum. idem indisciplinatos

---

6. *cam dom, cā dō* in MS. Meant for *campdom.* 7. *þe,* read *ne.* Read *hada.*
anstangynnes, e cor. from other letter ; read *andfangynnes.* 14. First
[*a.*] on erasure.

---

6. The glossator has once more written *servitutis* over the same word in
the text, and over that the gloss *þeowdomes.* 8. *ipsūm,* sic in MS.
9. *operibus, p* has a line through the downstroke as a sign of contraction for *er,*
and yet *er* has been written. *humiliores,* MS. *humilio.* Of the other texts AC
have *humiliores,* the others *humiles.* 13. *servare, rv* on erasure. It is
possibly to be regarded as an unsuccessful attempt to correct the *servire* of the
MS. into *servare.*

7 þa ungedefan he sceall stiðlicor þrean [h.] þa gehýrsuman
et   inquietos   debet   durius   arguere.   obedientes

soðlice | 7 þa [d.] liðan [e.] 7 þaðildigan [e.] [r.] þæt hi [g.] beteron
123 b.) autem | et   mites   et   patientes.   ut   in   melius

geðeon debere âhalsian [b.] þa gemeleasan [d.]   7 ða for-
proficiant   obsecrare.   Neglegentes   autem et con-

hicgenden [d.] þæt he ðræge 7 þæt he gestande [c.] [c.]
tempnentes.   ut   increpet et   corripiat

* þe myngiað ne he * bennðe hiwige sýnna agyldendra ahhe
ammonemus ;   Neque dissimulet peccata delinquentium. sed 5

sona * þonne hi onginnað upasprungan grundlunga hig beðam þe he
mox   ut ceperint   oriri   radicitus ea   ut pre-

mæg ofadoceorfe .sit. frecednýssa   sacerdes of silan 7 þa
valet amputet. memor periculi heli sacerdotis de silo; Et

arwurðan witodlice 7 þa andgýtfulran mod mid þære forman
honestiores quidem atque intellegibiles animos;   prima

oððe oþrasýðan mýnegunge mid wordum [a.] 7 hegeþrege
vel   secunda ammonitione   verbis   corripiat

þa ðwýran   7 þa heardan 7 þa modigan oððe þa *ungehýr-
inprobos autem et duros ac superbos vel inobedi-   10

sumantes mid swinglan oððe lichaman oððe oððe þreagunge
entes   verberum   vel   corporis   castigatione ;

on ðam sýlfan angýnne sýnne he þreage witende awriten
in ipso initio peccati coherceat sciens   scriptum ;

se dýsiga mid wordum na bið geðread 7 eft sleg. sleh.
Stultus   verbis   non corrigitur ; Et iterum ; Percute

þa bearn þine midgyrde 7 *þa alyst sawle his of deaðe
filium tuum   virga et liberabis animam eius a morte ;

gemunan [a.] sceal æfre [a.] seabbod þæt þe he is cweden 7
Meminisse debet semper abba   quod   dicitur ; et 15

witan þæt bið þam ðe mara bið befæst mare fram him
scire quia cui plus committitur; plus ab eo exigitur ;

---

2. þæt, þ torn in two.   3. MS. deð, which Latin addendum is in
hand of glossator.   5. þe, read we.   bennðe, read bemiðe, and see note.   d of
-dra above the line.   6. þonne, sic in MS.   Read ponne.   7. sit, Latin in
hand of glossator.   silan or silon.   10. ungehýrsumantes, probably after
having written ungehyrsuman, which read, the scribe's eye was caught by
the -tes which must have been in the Latin original.   13. geðread, wrongly
glossed by original glossator, who must have read corripitur in his text.
14. þa, read þu.

---

10. inprobos, MS. inprobus.   inobedientes, MS. inobediendos.   16. cui, in
accordance with other texts and with the gloss, MS. cujus.

6

[a.] 7 he wite [b.] hu [b.] be earfoðe [b.] he underfeht 7 sticol
*Sciat*que   *quam   difficilem   rem   et   arduam*

[b.] gewissian sawla 7 mænigra þeowan þeawum 7 sumne
suscepit   regere   animas. et *multorum   servire   moribus* et *alium*

witodlice mid geswæsnyssum oðerne   mid þræigum
quidem   blandimentis   alium   vero   increpationibus; alium

mid larum 7   æfter   ge æghwylces   hwylcnysse   oððe
suasionibus; Et   secundum   unius cujusque   qualitat.m   vel

andgit   hinc sy'fne on eallon þingan 7 he gehiwige 7
5 *intelligentiam.   ita se omnibus conformet   et*

he geþæslæce þæt he na þæt an nyðerunga. æfwyrðe heorde
aptet   ut   non solum   detrimenta   gregis

hims ylfan befæstre │   þolige   cac swylce on [g.]geeacnunge
sibi   commissi │ non pat.atur.   verum   in   augmentatione (124 a.)

godre heorde he geblissige toforan eallanþingan   behiwiende
boni gregis   gaudeat; Ante   omnia   non dissimulans

oððe for * forht taliendre   hæle   saule   him sylfan. bi. fæstra
aut   parvi   pendens   salutem animarum   sibi commissarum.

swiðor he ne do hohfulnesse   be þingum gewitendlicum 7
10 *plus   gerat   sollicitudinem de   rebus   transitoriis.   et*

iordlicum 7   gewitendlicum ah   he þence þæt he
terrenis atque   caducis; sed semper cogitet   quia

saula   underfænc togewissianne be ðam 7 gescead þe he his
animas   suscepit   regendas. de quibus et *rationem reddi-*

to gyldenne [a.] 7 þæt he na cide be læssan færunga   landare
turus est; Et   ne   causetur   de minori   forte   substantia

he gemuna   gewrit   æræst   [q.] secað   godes   rice
meminerit   scriptum ; Primum   querite   regnum dei et

rihtwisnesse 7 his 7 ealle þas þinc beoð hihte   7   eft
15 *justitiam   ejus* et *haec   omnia   adicientur vobis; Et iterum;*

naht wana nis ondrædendum hine [a.] 7 he wite [b.] þæt he
*Nihil   deest   timentibus   eum; Sciat*que   *quia*

se ðe underfehð sawla to gewissianne iarcie hine to gescead
qui   suscipit animas   regendas   preparet se ad rationem

6. *æfwyrðe*, read *æfwyrdle*? 7. *g* before *geeacnunge*: as there are no
'paving' letters in this passage, *g*. may be an anticipation of *geeacnunge*.
9. *forht*, *o* and *h* cor. from two other letters ; see note.   10. *ne*; but for
context, *n* might be read as *m*.   13. *na cide*, *a* and *cide* possibly on erasure.
14. [q.] Is this one of the ' paving' letters ?

7. *augmentatione*, MS. *aumentatione*.

ageldenne [a.] 7 swa micel undergýmenne   gebroðia hine
reddendam; Et   quantum   sub cura   sua fratrum   se

habban [a.] swa he wite [a.] getel he oncnawe to soðan þæt he
habere   scierit   numerum; agnoscat   pro certo. quia

                    sýlfra   ealra   þara sawla   sceall agýldan
in die judicii ipsarum omnium animarum est   rediturus

                    buton twýn to gehiht   his agenne sawle
domino rationem. sine   dubio   addita   et sue   animae;

[a.] [d.] [e.]   [f.] [g.] þa toweardan smeagunge [h.] hýrde
Et   ita semper timens   futuram   discusionem pastoris 5

[i.] of befæstum sceapum mid   ælfremedum sceadwisnyssum
de creditis   ovibus; cum de   alienis   ratiociniis

wærnað he si gewordan [c.]   [b.] hohful [a.] þonne
cavet   reddatur   de suis sollicitus;   Et   cum

he mýnegungum be his   bote   oðrum [a.] þenað he si
ammonitionibus suis emendationem aliis subministrat, ipse

geworden fram leahtrum   rihtlæcð
efficiatur a   vitiis   emendatus.

be gegearnendum to   ræde   gebroðra.
DE ADHIBENDIS AD CONSILIUM FRATRIBUS. (CAP. III.) 10

swa oft swa sind [ƀ.] ænige healice þinc [a.] to donne
QUOTIENS ALIQUA   PRECIPUA   AGENDA

(124 b.) [a.]   on mýnstre mýnstre [d.] gelangige [e.] se abbod
SUNT   IN   Mo | *nasterio;   convocet   abbas*

[f.] ealle [f.] gegæderunge 7 he sýlf secge [h.] hwanon
omnem congregationem.   et   dicat   ipse unde

[h.] he beo astired [i.] [l.] gehýrende [m.] geþeah gebroðra
agitur;   et   audiens   consilium   fratrum.

7 he smæge [k.] mid him sylfan [n.] þæt [o.] is nytwyrð-
tractet apud se;   et   quod (est) uti- 15

licor. [n.] 7 he deme   forþig   ealle to geþeahte
lius judicaverit [faciat] Ideo autem omnes ad consilium

gecian we secgat forþam oft þam gingran drihten þe unwryhð
vocari diximus; quia sepe juniori   dominus   revelat

---

10. *gebroðra*, both context and lemma make one expect *gebroðrum*.
14. *astired, i* of peculiar form below the line.

---

6. *ratiociniis*, MS. *rationem.*   7. *sollicitus*, MS. *sollicitur.*   15. *est* a
little erased.   See note.

C

þæt betere is swa   syllan   geþeaht mid ealre
quod melius est; Sic autem dent fratres consilium cum omni
eadmodnesse. underþeodnesse þæt na gędýrstlæcan gemahlice.
humilitatis   subjectione   ut non presumant procaciter
bewerian. þæt hieom heom gesawen biÞ ah furþor
tendere quod`   eis   visum fuerit. sed magis
on þæs abbodes hit stande kýre be þam *hwonlicor oÞÞe
in   abbatis   pendeat arbitrio eo quod salubrius
gesælicor þe he demÞ ealle gehýrsumian [a.]ah [e.]swa swa
5 *judicaverit   cuncti obediant.   Sed   sicut*
leorniccnihtum gedafenaÞ [f.] þæt gehyrsumian [g.] lareowe
discipulis   convenit   obedire   magistro.

[b.]7 him foraglæwlice 7 rihtlice gedafenaÞ [d.]ealle þinc
ita et ipsum   provide et juste condecet cuncta
[c.] gedihtan [d.]on eallum þingum [b.]iornostlice ealle [c.]
disponere;   In   omnibus   igitur   omnes
[c.] lareowlicum [a.]hi fýlian [e.]regole [f.] [h.]fram him
magistram   sequantur regulam ; ne ab ea
[i.]þristelice [f.]na na si gebogen fram ænigum [a.] na [b.]ænig
10 *temere   declinetur a quoquam;   Nullus*
on minstre [a.]na fylige [c.]agenra heortan willan
in monasterio . sequatur proprii cordis voluntatem.
[f.] ne ne gedýrstlæce [f.] [g.]ænig [n.]midhis abbude [n.]
neque presumat   quisquam pro abbate suo
[l.] wurÞlice [h.]wiÞ innan [h.]oÞÞe wiÞutan [m.]on mýnstre
proterve   intus   aut   foris   monasterium
[k.] flitan [a.]þæt gif gedýrstlæcÞ [b.]ænig [e.]regolicore
contendere;   Quod si presumpserit quisquam disciplinae

---

3. *ealra* along with its lemma *omnium* is found in the text, after *heom*,
see Latin note to l. 4.   4. *hwonlicor*, see note.   Sign for *oÞÞe* above
line.   6. *leorniccnihtum*, read *leornic*, i.e. *leorninc*.   7. *him*, last stroke
of *m* erased, by mistake, when the *g* of *sigut* was erased. *gedafenaÞ*, *d*
corrected from some other letter.

---

1. Before *melius* the word *faciat* is erased ; it is found after *judicaverit* in
the other Latin texts. *dent*, *e* corrected from *i*.   3. *omnium* erased
before *visum*. *visum* in margin in glossator's hand, by way of correction
for the misreading *omnium*.   4. *pendeat*, written by glossator over
gaudeat, which is erased.   5. *siqut*, corrected into *sicut*.   6. MS. *discipulus*. Some one, seeing that this word ought to be *discipulis*, began wrongly
to erase *s*, then stopped this, and indicated correction from *u* into *i* by putting
a dot over second stroke of *u*.   10. *quam* (other texts *que*) erased after *ne*.
12. *pro*, other texts have *cum*. That this has been in original of our text
is probable, as the gloss has *mid*.

[e.] styre [c.] he underhnige [b.] sẏlf swa ðeah. [b.] se abbod
regulari   subjaceat ;   Ipse   tamen   abbas

[e.] mid godes ege   [f.] 7 gehealdsumnesse regules [t.] ealle þinc
cum   timore   dei   et   observatione   regule.   omnia

[a.] do. witende hine buton twẏn be eallum his domum þa riht-
faciat.   sciens   se procul dubio de omnibus   judiciis   suis

wisestan deman gode gescead to aiẏldenne gyf [e.] hwẏlce
equissimo judici deo rationem rediturum ;   Si   qua

[b.] [f.] læssan þe inc syndon to done   [g.] on
vero minora   agenda   sunt   in 5

(125 a.) [h.] mẏnstres [g.] on nẏtwẏrdnẏssum ealdra [i.] þæt an
monasterii   utilita | tibus   seniorum   tantum

[a.] he bruce [o.] geþehte swa swa hit awriten is ealle [l.]
utatur   consilio   sicut   scriptum   est ; Omnia

[k.] do mid ræde [m.] 7 [n.] [o.] * æter dædum 7 hit þe ne ofreow
fac   cum   consilio.   et   post   factum   non   penitebis ;

hwẏlce beon   tol   godera   weorca.
QUE SINT INSTRUMENTA BONORUM OPERUM. (CAP. IIII.)

ealra æræst drihten   god   lufian   ealre   heortan mid
In   primis dominum   deum diligere ex toto   corde   tota 10

eallra sawla mid ealre mihte sẏððan nextan ealswa þe sẏlfne
anima   tota   virtute ; Deinde proximum. tamquam se ipsum ;

debemus ofslean   unrihthæman na   don   þeofæ
Deinde   non occidere   Non   adulterare.   non facere furtum.

ne   gewilnian   na   leas   gewitnesse   secgan arwurðian
non concupiscere. non falsum   testimonium dicere ; Honorare

debemus ealle   men   him sẏlfan æni beon þæt ðæt nele
omnes   homines et quod   sibi   quis fieri   non vult.

oðrum 7 þæt ne do wiðsacan. sic hine sylfne   himsylfum þæt
Alii   ne   faciat ; Abnegare semet   ipsum   sibi ;   ut 15

---

3. *þa*, read *þam*.   7. [o.] perhaps *ō=on*.   8. *æter*, read *æfter*.
12. *debem'*, in glossator's hand, not in other Latin texts; cf. l. 15; p. 20,
l. 15, and passim. *þeofæ, þ* corr. from some other letter.   14. *debem'*,
cf. l. 13.   15. First *þæt* added later on by glossator. *sylfne, f* added
later on by glossator. *sic*, stands by the side of *wiðsacan*, not over *se*.

---

2. *timore*, MS. *timorem*.   5. The words *aut major* (read *majora?*) are
found after *agenda*; they are probably originally a marginal note copied
into our text, and not in the other texts.   6. *seniorum* to *sicut* inclusive,
together with gloss, left out by copyist, and put in top margin.   10. *corde*,
MS. *corda*.

C 2

he fẏlige   crist   licḥaman   þrean   estmettas   befon
sequatur christum.   Corpus   castigare; Delicias   non   amplecti
fæsten debemus lufian þearfan   fedan   nacodne et scredan
Jejunium amare; Pauperes   recreare; Nudum   vestire.
untrume 7 geneosian deadne bebyrgian on   gedrefednesse
Infirmum   visitare. Mortuum   sepelire.   In   tribulatione
gehelpan sargenne   gefrefrian fram weorulde [a.] dædum
subvenire. Dolentem   consolari.   A   seculi   actibus
don   ælfræmedne æniþincg cristes lufan na foresettan ẏrre
5 *se facere   alienum;   Nihil   amori christi   preponere. Iram*
non debemus gefremman ẏrsunge timan na   healdan   facn
non   perficere.   Iracundie tempus non reservare; Dolum
on heortan na healdan lease sibbe   cost   na syllan þa soðe
in   corde   non tenere.   Pacem   falsum non dare.   Kari-
lufan na na forlætan   na   swerian þe he hine forswerige
tatem non   derelinquere. Non   jurare   ne forte   perjuret.
* soðfæsten debet of heortan 7 of muðe forðbringan. ẏfel for
Veritatem   ex   corde   et   ore   proferre. Malum pro
ẏfele debemus agildan   tregan debemus   gedonne dæde
10 *malo   non reddere. Injuriam non facere. sed et factam*
geþẏldelice ah forþyldian * frynd   lufian   þa awẏrigendan
patienter   sufferre; Inimicos diligere;   Maledicentes
[c.] non debemus agen wẏrian ah swiðor bletsian   [d.] ehnesse
se non   remaledicere   sed magis benedicere. Persecutionem
for rihtwisnesse þolian. beon   ðe modig   na windrucen
pro   justitia   sustinere. Non esse superbum. non vinolentum;
na mycelæte | na*sia   na *sceac   mur- (125 b.)
non multum | ædacem; non somnolentum; non pigrum; non
nigende naceriende   na * ælendne   hiht his gode
15 *murmuriosum;   non detractorem; debet spem suam deo*
betæcan   god   æni þinc on him sylfan þonne he gesẏhþ
committere; Bonum aliquid in se   cum viderit:

---

2. *debemus*, in glossator's hand, not in other Latin texts. *et scredan*,
MS. *& scredan*; did the scribe find *ed-*, *æt scredan* or 7 *scredan* in his
original? 6. *non debemus* over *gefremman*. 9. *soðfæstne*, read
soðfæstnesse. 11. *frynd*, read *fynd*. 12. *non debemus* in margin.
13. *ðe*, see note. 14. *nasia*, read *slapol*? *sceac*, read *sleac*. *ælendne*,
read *telendne*.

---

1. *Delicias*, MS. *dulcias*; it would seem that an attempt was made to
correct it. 3. *visitare*, underlined in MS. repeated by mistake after
Mortuum. 10. *factam*, see note. 13. *superbum*, MS. *desuperbum*,
see note. 15. *detractorem*, o corr. from a.

gcde ne betæce na him sylfan yfel him. sylfan æfre fram
deo applicet non sibi; Malum vero semper a se
gedon he wite him sylfan 7 getelle domes dæig
factum sciat; et sibi reputet; Diem debemus judicii
ondrædan helle aforhtian þæt ece lif mid ealre gast-
timere; gehennam expavescere; vitam æternam omni concu-
licere gewilnunge gewilnian [b.] deaÞ [c.] dæghwamlice
piscentia spiritali desiderare; Mortem cotidie
[e.]ætforan eagan [d.]gewenedne [a.]habban dæda lifes his
ante oculos suspectam habere; actus vitæ sue 5
on ælcere tide gehealdan on ælcere stowa gode hine besceawian
omni hora custodire; In omni loco deum se respicere
[a.] tosoÞan [b.]witan geþohtas þa yfelan heortan his to becu-
pro certo scire: Cogitationes malas cordi suo adveni-
menne sona to christe *aslidan þam gastlican ealdre
entes; mox ad christum allidere; et seniori spiritali
7 gesutulian he his muÞ fram yfele fram yfele oÞÞe þwyrlice
patefacere. Debet os suum a malo vel pravo elo-
spræce gehealdan mycel swyÞe [b.]spræcan na. [a.]lufian
quio custodire; Multum loqui non amare. 10
idele word hlehtregamene. oÞÞe lilic micelne leahtor oÞÞe
Verba vana aut risui apta non loqui; Risum multum aut
to sceacenne lufian halige rædinge lustlice lysta. oÞÞe
excussum non amare; Lectiones sanctas libenter audire;
gehyra gebeda [o.]*frædlice 7 onsigan his forÞgewitena yfela
orationi frequenter incumbere; Mala sua preterita
mid tearum oÞÞe geomorunge dæghwamlice on gebeda gode
cum lacrimis vel gemitu cotidie in oratione deo
anddettan of Þam sylfan yfelum þærto eacan betan.
confiteri; de ipsis malis de cetero emendare; 15
gewilnunga lichaman [d.] gefremman willan agenne
Desideria carnis non perficere. voluntatem propriam
[d.]hatian bebodu on eallum þeh þe sylf do
odire; preceptis abbatis in omnibus obedire; Etiam si

---

1. *ne*, wrong gloss. 8. *aslidan?* Perhaps the scribe found *aslean* in his
text, and his eye was caught by the *allidere* of the Latin. 13. *frædlice*,
see note; *yfela*, top part of *l* erased by erasure in *audire* (Latin notes on l. 12).
15. *anddettan*, first *d* above line, and at the end of line, but probably belongs
to the word.

---

1. *applicet*, MS. *amplicet*. 2. for *debemus*, see note to p. 20, l. 15.
See *infra*, l. 9. 9. *Debet*, see note to l. 2. 12. *audire*, erasure of about
two letters between *i* and *r*. 16. *propriam*, *i* above line.

he　elles　þæt　feor　sig　sýlf　do　gemýndige　þæs　drihtenlican
ipse aliter quod. absit　agat;　memor　illius. dominici

bebodas　þa * sed　gat　doð　þa ðinc　　　þe hi doþ　don
precepti.　Que　dicunt facite;　que　autem　faciunt　facere

nelle　na　nellan beon gesæið　halig　ærðamþe　hesig
nolite;　Non　velle　dici　s nctum　antequam　sit;　sed

ær　ah　beon　þæt　soðlicor　þæt　þæt　he　is　gesæd godes beboda
prius　esse.　quod　verius | 　dicatur;　　Precepta　(126 a.)

　　mid　dædum　dæihwamlice　gefýllan　clænnesse　lufian
5*dei　factis　cotidie　adimplere;　Castitatem amare;*

nehne　non　æfest 7　andan　　habban geflit. oððe ceaste
nullum　odire;　zelum　et　invidiam non habere;　Contentionem non

　　　upahofennesse　idelne * iyl forfleon　7　þa yldran
amare;　elationem　vel　jactantiam fugere;　Et　seniores

arwurðian　þa iýnran　　on christes * lufian for feondum
venerari;　juniores　diligere.　in　christi amore pro inimicis

gebiddan　mid　þam　ungeþwærum　ær　nýðersige. oððe gange
orare;　Cum discordantibus　ante　solis　occasum

on sibbe gehwýrfan non be godes mildheortnesse debemus næfre
10*in pace　redire;　et de dei　misericordia　numquam*

geortruwian efne þas sind　tol　cræftis gastlices þæt þonne
desperare;　Ecce . hec sunt instrumenta artis spiritalis que cum

beoð gefýlde fram　us　unablinnendlice dægges 7 nihtes
fuerint　a　nobis　die noctuque incessa-

unateoriendlice to gefýllanne　on domes dæge 7 betæhte
biliter adimpleta;　et in　die judicii reconsignata.

seo med　us fram drihtne bið agolden þe he sylf　behet
illa merces nobis　a domino reconpensabitur quam ipse promisit;

　　eage þæt ðe ne geseah　eare ne ne gehýrde ne ne on
15*Quod oculus　non　vidit. nec auris　audivit;　nec in*

heortan mannes astah þa ðinc þe gearcode　þisum. þa ða
cor　hominis ascendit;　que preparavit deus his qui

---

2. *sed gat*, *d* of unclear shape in MS., but no *c*: read *secgat*.　6. *non*
Latin, over *odire*? cf. infra, l..10, perhaps to be taken to *neh ne*, and to be
read *mon*.　7. *iyl*, read *iylþ*.　8. *lufian*, read *lufun*.　12. *unablin-*
nendlice, the fourth *n* corr. from some other letter, probably *a*.　Read *d. 7 n.*
unabl. unateor. adimpleta, glossed as if *ad implenda*.

---

1. *memor*, MS. *memoris*.　3. *dici*, MS. *dice*.　10. *dei*, MS. *dim*, *m*
misread from sign of contr. above *i*, for *e* of *dei*.　11. *u* in *cum* corr. from
some other letter.

lufia𐌳   hine   [c.] sme𐌳e [b.] * iþærwe   [i.]   ealle þas   𐌳inc
diligunt deum ;   Officina   vero ubi   hæc   omnia

[k.] geornlice   [i.] wỹrcean [d.] clỹsunga   [a.]   [e.] mynstres   7
diligenter   operemur.   claustra   sunt   monasterii ;   et

sta𐌳olfæstnys   [g.]
stabilitas   in   congrejatione ;

DE OBEDIENTIA DISCIPULORUM QUALIS SIT. (CAP. V.)

[e.]se for witodlice [f.] eadmodnes [e.] se forma stæpe ans [c.] gehỹr-
PRIMUS ITAQUE HUMILITATIS GRADUS EST :   obe- 5
sumnes [d.] butonỹldincge [b.] þas𐌳inc [a.] gerist [c.] þisom [d.]
dientia   sine mora ;   Haec   convenit   his   qui

naht [g.] himsỹlfum [h.] criste [f.] leofre [e.] ænigþincg [d.] þadene-
nihil   sibi   christo   carius   aliquid   exis-

wena𐌳   [i.] for𐌳am þeowdome haligan [k.] þe hi [k.] beheton
timant :   propter   servitium sanctum   quod   professi

[k.]   [l.] o𐌳𐌳e [l.] for [l.] hogan helle [m.] [o.] o𐌳𐌳e [o.] forwuldre
sunt :   seu   propter   metum   gehenne :   vel   gloriam

(126 b.) [p.] lifes [p.] þæs ecan is sona   [s.] ænig þinc [r.] þonne bi𐌳be-
vite   aeterne ;   Mox   ut | aliquid   impera- 10

boden [d.] fram ealdre [r.] [a.] acswilce [x.] godcundlice [a.] hitsibe
tum   a maiore   fuerit :   ac si divinitus   im-

boden [c.] ỹldincge et þrowian hỹ niton on donlicum þincgum
peretur.   moram   pati   nesciunt   in faciendo ;

[a.] be 𐌳am   [b.]   [a.] sæig𐌳 for   [c.] hlỹste   [d.] earan
De quibus   dominus   dicit :   ob auditu   auris.

[a.] he gehỹrsumede [b.]   7   [a.] eft he seig𐌳 [a.]   [b.] lareowum
oboedivit mihi ;   Et   iterum   dicit   doctoribus ;

[e.] se 𐌳e [f.]   eow [e.] gehỹr𐌳 me [c.] gehỹr𐌳 þas o𐌳𐌳e þillice 15
Qui   vos   audit :   me audit ;   Ergo hi tales

[f.] forlætende [g.] þarrihte [h.] þe heora [h.]   7   [k.] willan
relinquentes   statim   que   sua sunt ; et voluntatem

[k.]agenne [i.] forlætende [m.] sona [n.] gebỹsgodum [n.] handum
propriam   deserentes ;   mox   ex occupatis   manibus

---

1. *iþærwe,* sic in MS. : probably *i* as 'paving' letter. *þær* as gloss to *ubi,* and *we* belonging to *wyrcean.*   5. *for,* read *forma.* The MS. has *csefor.-ans* over *est,* I cannot explain.   7. *þadenewenað,* i. e. *þa ðe ne wenað.*   10. *is.* Latin ? the gloss above *ut* is illegible.

---

8. *sanctum* (scm), MS. *secundum* (scdm).   12. Above the *o* of *moram* there is written a *z.*

7 þæt hi didon [p.] unfulfremed [i.] forlætende [e.] mid [h.]
et quod agebant   inperfectum   relinquentes :   vici-

gehendum [g.] gehýrsumnesse [e.] fet bebeodendes [c.] stefne
no   oboedientiæ   pede   jubentis   vocem

[d.] middædum [a.] hi fýllian [a.] 7 swýlce [d.] onanre [d.] hand-
factis   sequuntur ;   Et   velut   uno   mo-

hwile [b.] seoforesæda lareowas [b.] hæs [e.] 7 fulfremed
mento   predicta   magistri   jussio   et   perfecta

[f.] leorninccnihtas weorc [g.] onhrædnesse [h.] godes eges [h.]
5   discipuli   opera   in velocitate   timoris dei

[k.] bute þa [k.] ðinc [l.] gemænlice [m.] hærdlicor 7 be ongefýl-
ambe res   communiter   citius   explican-

ledc þam [n.] to þam [a.] ecan life [q.] [p.] to gangenne
tur.   Quibus   ad   vitam   æternam   gradiendi

[o.] lufu [u.] onsigð for þone neorwan weig hi gelettað þanon
amor   incumbit.   Ideo   angustam   viam arripiunt : unde

sæig se nearwa weig is se læd to life þæt heora
dominus dicit   angusta   via   est que ducit ad vitam : ut non

agenre kýre na libbende   heora gewilnungum 7   lustum
10 suo arbitrio viventes :   vel   desideriis suis   et   voluptatibus

gehýrsumiende   ac gangende on ælfræmedum dome 7   on
obedientes   sed   ambulantes   alieno judicio   et im-

anwealde   on mýnstrum drohgende abbod heom sýlfum fora
perio   et in coenobiis   degentes : abbatem sibi   pre

beon hine gewilnian buton twýn þas. swilce þone   [a.] ge-
esse   desiderant ;   Sine dubio   hi tales   illam domini imi-

efenlæcean   cwude   [c.] þam ic na com don minne willan
tantur   sententiam; qua dicit ; Non veni facere voluntatem

ac þæs se ðe asende me [a.] ah [b.] þeos sýlfe [b.]
15 meam ;   sed ejus qui   misit me :   Sed   hec   ipsa

[b.] gehýrsumnesse [c.] þonne [d.] anfenge [b.] bið gode 7 wýnsum
oboedientia   tunc | acceptabilis erit   deo et dulcis (127 a.)

mannum gif hwæt bið beboden   forhtlice ne lætlice ne
hominibus ;   si quod   jubetur ;   non trepide ; non tarde ; non

---

2. *bebeodendes,* second *e* above line.   3. *handhwile,* the two *h's* above the
line.   5. *hrædnesse, h* above line.

---

3. *momento,* MS. *monumento, nu* crossed out.   7. *gradiendi,* MS. *gra-*
dienti.   13. *desiderant,* MS. *desiderent.*   16. *acceptabilis,* MS.
acceptabis.

erhlice oððe mid ceorunge oððe oððe mid andswere [e.]
tepide ; aut cum murmurio. vel cum responso

nellendes biðgeworden. [a.] forðam þe [b.] bið gehýrsumnes
nolentis efficiatur : Quia oboedientia

    ealdran [d.] se ðe bið iarcod [c.] gode [a.] gegearcon hesýlf
que majoribus prebetur : deo exibetur. Ipse

       sæde se ðe eow þegehýrð [b.] * m. [a]gehýrð [a.] 7 [d.] mid
enim dixit ; Qui vos audit me audit : Et cum

godum mode [c.] fram * leornincchintum [b.] beon gegearcod
bono animo a discipulis preberi 5

[a.] hit gedafenað [e.] forðam þoneglædan sýllan [e.] þelufað
oportet. quia hilarem datorem diligit

gode [a.] soðes na bið [g.] mid ýfelum [g.] mode gif gehýrsumað
deus. Nam cum malo animo si obedit

leorninccniht 7 na þæt an on muðe ac eac swýlce on
discipulus : et non solum ore. verum etiam in

heortan gif he ceorað 7 gif he gefýlle hæse [c.]
corde si murmuraverit. et si impleat jussionem ; tamen

[b.] anfenge [a.] [a.] [d.] se ðe heortan his besceawað ceori-
acceptum jam non erit deo ; qui cor ejus respicit mur- 10

endes 7 he for swýlcere dæde ænigne ne begitt þanc
murantis ; Et pro tali facto nullam consequitur gratiam.

[b.] gif git swiðor [c.] wice [d.] ceorigendra [a.] onbecýmð gif
Immo penam murmurantium incurrit si

[e.] he hit mid fulre dædbote [e.] na gebed
non cum satisfactione emendaverit.

De Taciturnitate. (Cap. VI.)

utondon þæt ðe sæde se witega ic sæde ic gehealde wegas mine
Faciamus quod ait Propheta. dixi custodiam. *vias meas :* 15
þæt ic na gýlte on minre tungan icsette muðe minon heord-
ut non delinquam in lingua mea ; Posui ori meo cus-
rædne ic adumbede 7 ic eom geeadmed 7 ic suwode
todiam : obmutui et humiliatus s m et silui

---

3. A letter (s?) erased before *gode.*   4. *m*, probably no 'paving' letter,
but for *me* (m̅).   5. *leorninchintum,* read *leorninccnihtum.*   10. *his, i*
above line.

---

           i
4. *Qui vos,* MS. *Quos.*   10. *murmurantis,* MS. *murmorantis.*   *nullam,*
MS. *millam.*

fram godum [a.] her geswutulaðð [a.] [b.] gif [e.] fram godum
a bonis : Hic ostendit propheta ; si a bonis

[e.] spræcum oðerhwile interdum for [g.] * salnesse beon gesuwod
eloquiis propter taciturnitatem

[c.] scel beon gesuwod lahu micele swiðor fram ýfelum
debet interdum tacere : quantomagis a malis

wordum for wite sýnne þeah sig be godum 7
verbis propter penam peccati ; Ergo quamvis de bonis | et (127 b.)

haligum et timbrunga [d.] spræcum 7 fulfremedæ [b.]
5 *sanctis et aedificationum eloquiis et perfectis*

leorningccnihtum. fore. [f.] stilnesse stæððinesse * sýlfsýne
discipulis propter taciturnitatis gravitatem rara

to specende [a.] geunnen [e.] leaf forðam þe hit is awriten on
loquendi concedatur licentia ; quia scriptum est ; In

manifealdre þu ne forflihst sýnne on oðerstowe deað 7
multiloquio non effugies peccatum. Et alibi : Mors et

lif on handum tungan soðes sprecan 7 læran lareowum
vita in manibus lingue ; Nam loqui et docere magistrum

gedafenað suwian 7 heorcnian leorniccnihtum gedafenað
10 *condecet ; Tacere et audire discipulo convenit ; Et*

gif wilce þincg sind to smeagenda fram dre mid ealre
ideo si qua requirenda sunt a priore cum omni

eadmodnesse 7 underþeodnesse 7 beon gesmeade befrinonne þæt
humilitate et subjectione reverentie requirantur ;

ne si gesewen furður spræcan þonne hit gefremige higlista
non videatur plus loqui quam expedit Scurilitates

oððe idelword stirienda ecei clýsunga
vero vel verba otiosa et risum moventia ; aeterna clausura

on ealle stowum we ne fordemað to hwýlcere spræce
15 *in omnibus locis dampnamus ; Et ad talia eloquia*

leorninccniht geopenodum muð 7 we ne ðafiað
discipulum aperire os non permittimus.

---

2. *interdum* in glossator's hand. *oðerhwile*, as gloss to *interdum*,
stands above it. *salnesse*, read *stilnesse*. *et*, MS. &. 6. *sýlfsýne*, see
note.

---

2. *eloquiis*, MS. *eloquris*. 3. *quantomagis*, *n* above line. *malis*,
l partially erased ? 5. Second *et* above line. *perfectis*, MS. *perfectus*,
but *i* written above *u*. 7. MS. *liquendi*, but changed into *loquendi*.
12. *reverentie* in margin. 13. *Scurilitates*, *li* above line in later
hand.

DE HUMILITATE. (CAP. VII.)

[b.] clẏpað c. vs. ẏ. gewritt [d.] þæt [d.] godcunda eala [a.]
CLAMAT NOBIS SCRIPTURA DIVINA FRATꞋES

[e.] seccende [b.] ælc. [d.] se ðe [c.] hine [c.] upahefð [a.] bið ge-
DICENS. omnis qui se exaltat humilia-

eadmet [e.] 7 bið [f.] se ðe [f.] geeadmeð upahafen þonne
bitur et qui se humiliat exaltabitur : Cum

þas þinc [o.] sæigð geswutulað [a.] us 7 ælce upahafennesse
haec ergo dicit ; ostendit nobis omnem exaltationem 5

cẏn beon modinesse hine warnian se witiga þæt gebẏcniaþ
genus esse superbie quod se cavere propheta indicat

la drihten nis upahafen heorte mine nana upahafen
dicens ; Domine non est exaltatum cor meum neque elati

sind eagan mine ne ic na ferde on mærlicum þingum na
sunt oculi mei ; Neque ambulavi in magnis ; neque in .

on wundorlicum ofor me ah la hwæt sæig he gif ic ne ge-
(128 a.) mirabilibus super me. Sed quid sinon humiliter

eadmodlice þwærlæhte ac ic upahof mine sawle swa swa is
sentiebam sed exaltavi animam meam sicut 10

þæt * openodum cild puer [a.] ofor his meder þu forgẏldst
ablactatus est super matrem suam ita retribues

on minre sawle [a.] wanon. [k.] gif healicere eadmod-
in animam meam ; Unde fratres si summe humili-

nesse we wẏllað geþincðe [m.] hreppan [o.] ad illam
tatis volumus culmen adtingere et ad

[o.] [o.] [o.] [p.] to þære þurh andweardes lifes
exaltationem illam celestem ad quam per presentis vite

eadmodnesse [p.] bið astigen hrædlice becuman dædum
humilitatem ascenditur volumus velociter pervenire. actibus 15

---

2. c. vs. ẏ, sic in MS.; see note. 3. seccende, second c changed into e.
9. geeadmodlice, a letter between g and e? 11. openodum, read awenode.
puer not in other texts, added by glossator, as the word to which ablactatus
refers. 13. ad illam in glossator's hand-writing.

---

3. qui, dot under u, as if it were meant to be expunged. 5. ergo, MS. ĝ.
11. ablactatus, MS. ablactatum. retribues ; of the other Latin texts (cf.
Schröer, W. V., p. 30, and see Schmidt, p. 17), S has retributio, T and U
have retribues, and G has bues erased. Our MS. had first retributio, then o
was erased, i lengthened into s, and t changed into e. With this newly-
fabricated retribues the gloss corresponds. 15. ascenditur, some other
ending changed into itur.

urum   upastigendum   h dre   [b.] seo hlæðð. is up to aræranne
nostris   ascendentibus   scala   illa erigenda   est

[c.] seo [e.] on swefne   [d.] þeatiwde [c.] [f.] þurhðage [g.] him
que   in sompnio   iacob   apparuit ;   per quam   ei

7 niðer astigende [h.] 7 upastigende   [f.] sutulodan
descendentes   et   ascendentes   angeli monstrabantur ;

na bið ælles buton twýn se nyðerstige se 7 upstige fram us
Non aliud sine dubio   descensus ille et ascensus a nobis

understandan   buton   mid   upahafennesse   nyðerastigan   mid
5 intellegitur   nisi   cum   exaltatione   descendere ;   et

eadmodnesse   upastigan   [c.] seo sýlfe   [b.] uparærede
humilitate   ascendere ;   Scala   vero   ipsa

hlæddra ure [d.] is [a.] lif [d.] on [e.] worulde   [f.] seo bið
erecta   nostra   est   vita   in   seculo ;   Que

geeadmedre heortan [k.] [g.] uparærede to heofonum [c.] sidan
humiliato   corde   a domino ; erigitur ad celum ;   Latera

[b.] sint þære [e.] dran [a.] we secgað urne [g.]   [f.] beon
enim   ejus   scale ;   dicimus   nostrum   esse

[g.] lichaman 7 sawle. [g.] on ðære sidan [a.] gesætt [d.] mistlice
10 corpus   et animam ;   in que latera   diversos

[d.] stapas   eadmodnesse   oððe [f.]   lare   gecigednýss [b.]
gradus   humilitatis   vel   discipline :   evocatio

[b.] seo godcund [c.] þa upastigændan   a an
divina   ascendendos   inseruit ;

[b.] se forma   [c.]   [d.] eadmodnesse [b.] stape is [a.] [e.] godes
Primus   itaque   hvmilitatis   gradus est :   siti-

ege him sýlfum [k.] aetforan [k.] eagan [i.] æfre [h.] secende
morem dei sibi   ante   oculos   semper   ponens

[g.] foregýtelnýsse [f.] eallunga [e.] gif he flihð   he sig
15 oblivionem   omnino   fugiat ;   et semper   sit

gemýndig ealraþinga þæt bebead god   [a.]   [d.] þa forhic-
memor   omnium   que precepit deus ; Qualiter   contemp-

genden [d.]   gode   [h.] on   helle   forsýnnum   [a.] hi on
nentes   deum ; | in   gehennam   pro peccatis   inci-   (128 b.)

---

1. hdre ; hlæðð, probably both words are meant for hlæddre.   12. a an
over inseruit, see note.   14. secende, sic in MS.

---

2. sompnio, p corr. from n.   5. cum added in the margin ; exaltatione,
MS. exaltationem.   11. MS. gradis, marked in MS. to be changed into
gradus.   16. contempnentes, p below line.

---

befeollan [f.] 7 þæt ece lif þæt [k.] adrædendum god [k.] is
dunt ; et vitam aeternam que timentibus deum pre-
gegearcod is [h]on his mode æfre [g.] [f.] 7 he wealce 7
parata est animo suo semper revolvat. Et

gehealdende hine fram synnum 7 leahtrum þæt is
custodiens se omni hora a peccatis et vitiis id est

geþohta tungan eagana handa fota oððe agenes
cogitationum lingue ; oculorum manuum pedum, vel volun-

willan ah gewilnunga lichaman ofadon he ofeste wene
tatis proprie ; sed et desideria carnis amputare festinet ; Estimet 5

man of heofonum fram gode æfre beon behealdenne
se homo de celis a deo semper respici

on ælcere tida 7 his dæda on ælcere stowe fram gesyhðe
omni hora ; et facta sua omni loco ab aspectu

godcundnysse 7 beon gesawen fram englum on ælcere
divinitatis videri ; et ab angelis deo omni

tide 7 beon gekydde gesutulað us þæt witega on urum
hora renuntiari ; Demonstrat nobis hoc propheta cum in

geþancum esse esse andweardne þonne he geswu-
cogitationibus nostris deum semper presentem ostendit 10

tulað asmaidan heortan 7 lendenu god
dicens ; Scrutans corda et renes deus ; et item

can geþohtas manna idel 7
Dominus novit cogitationes hominum quoniam vane sunt ; Et

eft he sæigð þu understode mine geþohtas forrane 7 þæt
item dicit Intellexisti cogitationes meas a longe; Et quia

geþanc mannés anded þe soðes þæt hohful sig
cogitatio hominis confitebitur tibi ; Nam ut sollicitus sit circa

soðes oððe secge se nydwyrða
cogitationes suas perversas ; dicat semper utilis 15

broðor on his heortan þonne ic beo *ungewennned toforan heom
frater in corde suo ; Tunc ero inmaculatus coram eo ;

gif ic gehealde me fram minre unrihtwisnesse willan
si observavero me ab iniquitate mea ; Voluntatem vero

---

11. *asmaidan,* see note. 15. *soðcs oððe secge,* see note. 16. *unge-*
wennned, read *ungewemmed. foran, o* crossed, as if corrected from *e.*

---

1. *aeternnam. a* MS., *e* added later. 3. *omni hora* added by glossator.
17. *observavero,* second *o* in MS. *ð. mea,* MS. *me.*

ageure   don   we forbeodaÞ þonne sæigÞ gewrit   us
propriam ita facere prohibemur   cum   dicit scriptura nobis
fram þinum willan 7 si Þu awend 7 eft 7 uton biddan god
*Et a voluntatibus tuis   avertere ;   Et ite*m *roge | mus deum* (129 a.)

on gebede 7 þæt gewýrÞe his   willa   on us we beon
in oratione ut   fiat   illius voluntas in nobis; Docemur

gelærede rihtlice   urne na don   willan þonne we gewarniaÞ
ergo   merito nostram non facere voluntatem cum   cavemus

þæt   þæt   sæig þæt halige gewrit sýnt wegas þa beoÞ
5 *illud quod dicit sancta scriptura ; Sunt vie   que*

gesawene fram mannum rihtlice þara enda   oÞ dýpan * helde
videntur ab ominibus recte quarum finis usque ad profundum

besent   7   eft þonne we gewerniaÞ þæt be þam
inferni demergit ; Et cum   item   cavemus   illud quod

gýmeleasum þæt Þe is gesæd   gewemmede sýnt 7 laÞe
*de neglegentibus   dictu*m   *est ; corrupti sunt et abo-*
oÞÞe andsæte 7 insint geworderie willum   on heora on
minabiles facti sunt   in   voluntatibus suis ; In

gewilnungum soÞlice lichaman swa us   god semper we lýfaÞ
10 *desideriis vero carnis. ita nobis deum   credamus*

æfre beon andwýrde þonne sæiÞ se witega ætforan þe is
semper esse presentem; cum dicit propheta ; Ante te est

eal gewilnunc min is to wearnienne   ýfel gewilnunc
*omne desideriu*m *meu*m *; Cavendum est ergo ideo malum desiderium ;*

deaÞ wiÞ infereld gelustfullunc forÞam þe is gesæd wanon
quia mors secus introitum delectationis   posita est ;   Unde

gewrit   * behýt secgende æfter þinum gewilnungum
scriptura precipit dicens ;   Post concupiscentias   tuas

ne farÞu   gif besceawiaÞ
15 *non eas ; Ergo si oculi domini speculantur bonos et malos*

7 he beheal
*et dominus de caelo sempe*r *respicit supe*r *filios hominum.*

þæt he * oseo gif he is to understandenne oÞÞe secende god
ut videat si   est   intellegens   aut requirens deum ;

---

5. *sæig*, for *sæigÞ.*   6. *helde*, read *helle.*   7. *besent*, read *besenct.*
9. *insint*, see note.   10. *semper* added by glossator.   14. *behýt*, read
bcbyt.   17. *he oseo*, read *he seo.*   See note.

---

1. *prohibemur*, MS. *prohibetur*, marked by glossator to be changed into
prohibemur.   4. *cavemus*, MS. *cancmus.*   6. *ominibus* (for *hominibus*),
MS. *omnibus.*   11. *est*, MS. *eos.*

7 gif fram englum * hetelicum dæghwamlice dæges 7 nihtes
et *si ab angelis nobis deputatis cotidie die noctuque

drihtne urum scÿppende ure weorc gif beoð gecyððe is to
domino factori nostro opera nostra enuntiantur: caven-

warnienne on ælcere tide swa swa sæigð on * ða * sealmo
dum est ergo omni hora fratres. sicut dicit in psalmo

þæt us bugande to * ÿfefle 7 unnÿtwÿrðe 7 ge-
propheta ne nos declinantes in malum. et inutiles factos

(129 b.) wordene on ænigera tida þæt * ne * besceal 7 * aræriende us on
aliqua hora aspiciat deus et parcendo | nobis in 5

ðissere tide forðam þe is 7 he anbidað us gecÿrran to
hoc tempore quia pius est; et expectat nos converti in

beteran us on toweardum þas þinc ðu dÿdest
melius cotidie ne dicat nobis in futuro. Haec fecisti

7 ic suwude.
et tacui. II.

se oðer eadmodnesse stepe is gif ænig na
Secundus humilitatis gradus est: si propriam quis non

lufiende willan his gewilnunga ne gif gelustfulað gefÿllan
amans voluntatem. desideria sua non delectetur implere 10

þas stefne drihtnes mid dædum ac he geefenlæce. secgendes.
sed vocem illam domini factis imitetur dicentis;

ic na com æfter
Non veni facere voluntatem meam sed ejus qui me misit. Itæm

lufe hæfð wite 7 neodþearfnes 7 akenð
dicit scriptura. Voluptas habet penam et necessitas paruit

cinehelm se ðridde stæpe is þæt under æni for
coronam. Tertius humilitatis gradus est: ut quis pro dei

godes lufan mid ealre gehÿrsumnessa hine sÿlfne þeowde ealdre
amore omni obedientia se subdat majori; 15

geefen læcende drihtnes be ðam þe he seið se apostolo wæs
immitans dominum de quo dicit apostolus;

he wæs geworden gehÿrsum oð deað
Factus obediens usque ad mortem; IIII.

---

1. *hetelicum*, read *betehtum*. 3. *ða*, read *ðam*. *sealmo*, with Latin ending, the scribe's eye being caught by the *almo* in *psalmo* under it. 4. *ÿfefle*, read *ÿfele*. 5. *ne besceal*, read *he be sceawie*. *aræriende*, read *ariende*. 14. *under*, see note. 16. *þe, þ* corr. from *h* ? *apostolo*, read *apostol*.

---

2. *factori*, MS. *facturi*. *cotidie*. Not in any other text. 9. *Secundus*, MS. *secundum*. *propriam*, MS. *propria*. 12. *Itæm*, sic in MS. 16. *apostolus*, MS. *apostolis*.

se feorða eadmodnessa stæpe is on ðære sylfra gehyrsumnessa
Quartus   humilitatis   gradus est; si   in   ipsa   oboedientia

stiðum þingum.   7 wiðerweardum   oððe eac swilce sumum
duris et   *contrariis rebus;   vel* etiam *quibuslibet*

on gebrohtum teonum mid stillum ingehyde   gif he
inrogatis   injuriis;   tacita conscientia   patientiam am-

befehð   7 for þyldigende oððe aweig gewite
plectatur et *sustinens   non   lacescat   vel   discedat :*

secgendum gewrita seðe þurhwunað   oð ænde   þæs
5 *Dicente   scriptura :   qui   perseveraverit   usque in finem ;   hic*

hæle bið oft he seið dicit si ge strangod þin heorte 7 forþyldiga
*salvus erit; Item   confortet*ur *cor tuum;* et *sustinet*

drihten   gesutuliende   swa swa
*dominum ; Et ostendens fidel*em *pro *nos deus igne nos*

þu afandodes swa swa bið afandod   seolfor   þu ongelæddest
*examinasti.   sicut   examinat*ur *argentum.   Induxisti*

us on grin þu gesettest gedrefednessa on urum *hicce   7
nos in laqueum.   posuisti   tribulationes   in dorso nostro; Et

þæt getiwe under ealdre | us scealan beon he fylige
10 *ut ostendat   sub   priore* | *debere nos   esse. subsequitur dicens;* (130 a.)

þu ongesettest men ofer urum heafdum ah ge   bebod
Inposuisti   homines super   capita nostra.   Sed et *preceptum*

drihtnes on *ðryrnyssum 7 on teonum þurh geþyld gefyl-
domini in   adversis   et   injuriis   per   patientiam adim-

lende þa þe synd geslegene hleor *hiercian 7 oðer æthredendrum
plentes. qui percussi in maxillam.   prebent et *aliam : Auferenti*

      7 forgifan   7   wæfæls genydde twamilan hi gan
tonicam.   dimittunt et *pallium.   Angarizati miliario.   vadunt*

---

6. *dicit,* in glossator's hand.   9. *hicce,* read *hricce.*   12. *ðryrnyssum,*
read *ðuyrnyssum.*   13. *hiercian,* read *hi iercian.*

---

3. *patientiam,* MS. *patientia.*   4. *lacescat,* MS. *lasescat.*   6. *con-
fortetur,* MS. *confitetur.*   7. *pro nos,* a whole passage has been here
left out between *pro* and *nos* by the scribe, the Latin of which in S runs
as follows:—pro (Domino universa etiam contraria sustinere debere dicit ex
persona sufferentium: Propter te morte afficimur tota die, estimati sumus
ut oves occisionis, et securi de spe retributionis divine subsecuntur gaudentes
et dicentes. Sed in his omnibus superamus propter eum qui dilexit nos;
et item alio loco scriptura Probasti) nos.   10. *nos,* MS. *non.*   14. *angarizati.* All other texts have *angariati.* But as our form occurs not only
here, but also twice in 'Wright-Wülker's Anglo-Saxon and Old English
Vocabularies' (353. 30; and 479. 17), I dare not change it, to which Wülker
apparently sees no objection; cp. ib. I, p. 479, note 19.

þa leasa gebroðra
pergere unum et *duo Cum paulo apostolo*   falsos   fratres
hi forðildian
sustinent.   et *persecutionem propter justitiam patiuntur* et
7 þa awýrgedan hig 7 hig blettian.
maledicentes.   *se*   *benedicunt.*   V.

[b.]   [c.]   [b.] [a.] [d.] ealle ýfele geþohtas [g.]
QUINTUS *humilitatis gradus est   si   omnes   cogitationes   malas*
[i.]   [i.] [h.] cumende [k.]   [k.]   [m.] [l.] digellice
cordi   suo   advenientes   vel   mala   a se   absconse   commissa 5
þurh eadmode andetnesse abbote gif ne bediƕ gað his tiht
per   humilem confessionem abbati   non celaverit   suo hor-
[a.] [b.] be ðisum þince gewrit [d.]   [e.] unwrigon drihtne
tatur nos de hac   re   scriptura dicens :   revela   domino
weig þine 7 hiht on higne 7 eft he seið [a.] andetað
viam tuam et spera in eum et item dicit   confitemini
drihtne [b.] forðam [c.] þe is [d.] god forðam þe is   [g.]   his
domino   quoniam   bonus,   quoniam   in seculum mise-
mildheortnesse [f.]   [f.]   [b.] gild mine [b.]
ricordia   ejus Et item propheta delictum   meum 10
cyð [c.] ne ðe [d.] ic [a.] dýde 7 rihtwisnýssa mine
cognitum   tibi   feci.   et   injustitias   meas non operui :

Dixi : pronuntiabo *adversum me injustitias meas* domino. et *tu*
arleasnessa   minre heortan
130 b.) *remisisti im | pietatem cordis   mei*   VI.

mid ealre wacnisse æftergenc-
SEXTUS *humilitatis gradus est.   si   omni   vilitate   vel ex-*
nýsse. oððe endemestnesse hýlde gýf bið   to eallum
tremitate   contentus sit monachus   et ad 15
þingum himsýlfan þa ðe beoð geðeodde swýlce ýfel wrýhta
omnia   que sibi injunguntur   velut   operarium

---

6. *bediƕ gað, ƕ* corrected from other letter ; then erasure. *gað,* lower down,
read *bediƕligiað.*   11. Erasure before *cyð.*

---

1. The words *pergere unum* are not in the other texts. *twamilan* would
seem to be the gloss to *et duo.*   6, 7. *hortatur* ; after this some letter only
faintly discernible.   14. *humilitatis,* MS. *numilitatis.*

D

       7 hedeme unwurðne   to
malum se judicet et indignum dicens sibi cum propheta Ad

  nahte   ic eom agen gehwӯrfæd 7 ic ne cuðe swa swa nӯten
nichilum   redactus sum et nescivi.   *ut jumentum*

ic eom
factus sum apud te. et *ego semper tecum.* VII.

                 he eallum 7 læssan
SEPTIMUS HUMILITATIS GRADUS EST. SI OMNIBUS SE *inferiorem et*

  wacran na   þæt an mid his tungan gif hit ahhe eac swӯlce
5 *viliorem non solum   sua lingua pronuntiet sed   etiam*

mid incundre   gelӯfe lufe geeadmetende hine sӯlfne
  intimo   cordis credat affectum humilians se et dicens

mid þam witegan ic eom   *wursan 7 na man
cum propheta. ego autem sum vermis et non homo.

      manna 7 aworpones folces sum upahafen 7 ic eom
obprobrium hominum et abjectio plebis Exaltatus autem et humi-

geeadmed   gescӯnd   god me þæt þu geead-
liatus sum et confusus. et item. bonum mihi quod humi-

mettest þæt ic leornige þine beboda
10 *liasti me. ut discam mandata tua.* VIII.

              gif nadeð naht se munuc buton
OCTAVUS HUMILITATIS GRADUS est. *si nihil agat monachus nisi*

þæt þe se gemenlica   rego mӯnstres oððe ealdra tihtað
quod communis monasterii regula vel majorum cohor-

oððe lærað bӯsna
  tantur exempla. VIIII.

---

2. *gehwӯrfæd, r* corr. from another letter, probably *f.*   7. *wursan,* see
note.

---

5. *lingua,* MS. *linguet.*   13. After the word *exempla* there follows in our
MS. the following passage in Latin, which has been put in the note, as it is
unglossed, and as it is not contained in any of the other Latin texts used by
Schröer or Schmidt :—Sicut scriptum est. humiliatus sum usquequaque *domine*
vivifica me *secundum* verbum tuum. Et *dominus* dixit : Discite ame quia
mitis sum *et* | humilis corde *et* invenietis requiem animabus *vestris* ; Et (131 a.)
apostolus dixit petrus ; Humiliamini sub potenti manu dei. ut vos exaltat in
tempore visitationis. omne*m* *vestram* sollicitudinem pr*o*icientes in eum :
q*uoniam* ipsi cura est de vobis Sobrii estote *et* vigilate : quia adversarius
vester diabolus tamquam leo rugiens circuit querens quem devoret ; Cui
resistite fortes infide, scientes eande*m* passionem ei. que in m*u*ndo est *vestra*
fraternitati fieri ;

gif tungan to sprecanne gif
NONUS HUMILITATIS GRADUS EST. *si linguam ad loquendum pro-*
forbidde se munuc stilnesse habbende * oðð̄e ax-
hibeat monachus et taciturnitatem habens usque ad interro-
unge 7 he ne spece swýtelunge write þæt na on
gationem et non loquatur monstrante nobis scriptura quia in
mænifealdum spræce býð forflogen sinn 7 þæt na bið se
multiloquio non effugetur peccatum et quia vir
fealaspreocala wer gerihtlæhð
linguosus non dirigetur super terram X. 5

gif na bið eðhýlde 7 *brǣd.
DECIMUS HUMILITATIS GRADUS EST SI NON SIT FACILIS ac *promp-*
caf. on hlehtre forðam þe hit· is awriten se dýsega
tus in risu. quia scriptum est : stultus in risu
upahefð his stefne ·
exaltat vocem suam. XI.

þonne he sprece se munuc
UNDECIMUS HUMILITATIS GRADUS EST. SI. CUM LOQuitur *monachus.*
liðelice 7 butan hleahtre eadmodlice mid gedreoge oðð̄e feawa
leniter et sine risu. humiliter cum gravitate vel pauca 10
word 7 gesceadwislice gif na sprýcð 7 he na beo hlutclipol on
verba et rationabilia loquatur Et non sit clamosus in
stefne swa swa hit awriten is se wisa wordum gesutulað
131 b.) *voce sicut scriptum est | sapiens verbis innotescit*
mid feawum
paucis XII.

gif na þæt an
DUODECIMUS GRADUS HUMILITATIS EST SI NON SOLUM *corpore sed* et
on heortan se munuc * eadmodnýssum geseondum æfre gif ne
corde monachus humilitatem videntibus se semper in- 15
gebicniað þæt is on weorce on gebedhuse on minstre on
dicet. id est: in opere. in oratorio. in monasterio. in

---

2. oðð̄e, read oð. 5. *feala-*, first *a* above line. 6. *brǣd*, *b* above line,
read *hrǣd*. 11. *hlutclipol.* The MS. has *hut-* ; the *l* is written over the *u*.
15. *eadmodnýssum* under the combined influences of (humilitate)*m* and *ge-*
seondum.

---

3. *monstrante*, MS. *monastrante.* 8. *exaltat*, MS. *expectat.* 15. *semper*
in glossator's hand. 16. *opere*, MS. *opore.*

orcerde on wege on æcere oð̃ðe swa hwar swa he bið̃ fuerit
orto. in via in agro vel ubiq̄ue

sittende gangende oð̃ðe standende ahẏldum he sẏg æfre
sedens. ambulans vel stans inclinato sit semper

heafde gefæstnodum on eorð̃an gesẏhð̃um scẏldine hine on ælcere
capite defixis in terram aspectibus. reum se omni

tida be his sẏnnum wenende eallunga hine on ð̃am
hora de peccatis suis existimans jam se tremendo

* gefullan dome beonge andwerded hewene secgende himsẏlfan on
5 *judicio dei representari estimet. dicens sibi in*

heortan æfre þæt þæt he sæde publicanus ge godspellica
corde semper illud. quod publicanus ille

manfulla gefæstnodum on eorð̃an gesẏhð̃um sæde la ð̃u
evangelicus fixis in terram oculis dixit: Do-

drihten ic ne eom wurð̃e ic sẏnfulla upahebban eagan mine to
mine non sum dignus ego peccator levare oculos meos ad

heofonum dicit mid þam witegan ic eom gebẏged 7
celum; Et item cum propheta: Incurvatus sum et

ic eom geeadmet æghware oð̃ðe on ælcere stowe
10 *humiliatus sum usque quaque: Ergo*

þingum eallum ð̃isum eadmodnẏsse se munuc
his omnibus humilitatis gradibus ascensis monachus

sona to ð̃ære soð̃an lufan godes becẏmð̃ to ð̃ære fulfremed
mox ad karitatem dei perveniet illam que perfecta

ut seo asend ege þurh þæt he ealle þinc ær
foras mittit timorem: per quam universa que prius

buton forhte þe he geheold buton ænigum geswince
non sine formidine observabat. absque ullo labore

swilce gekẏndelice of gewunan anginne gehealde na
15 *velut naturaliter ex consuetudine incipiet custodire non jam*

mid ege helle ac mid cristes lufan 7 gewunan þa sẏlfan godu
timore gehenne. sed amore christi et consuetudine ipsa bona

7 gelustfullunge mihta on his wẏrhtan
et delectatione virtutum. que dominus jam | in operario (132 a.)

---

1. *fuerit* in glossator's hand. 5. *gefullan*, read *egefullan*. 6. *pub-licanus*, Latin repeated as gloss, whereas *manfulla* in l. 7 is the English gloss. *ge*, read *se*. 9. *dicit*, glossator's handwriting. 10. *stowe* or *stuwe*?

---

7. *fixis*, MS. *fixus*.

on middan earde fram leahtrum 7 synnum mid þam haligan
suo   mundo a vitiis et   peccatis spiritu sancto
þa gemedemode geswutulian
dignabit   demonstrare.

DE OFFICIIS DIVINIS IN NOCTIBUS. (CAP. VIII.)

Wintres [k.] on tide [i.][i.] fram clypunge [m.] þæs nygeðan mon-
HÝEMIS TEMPORE   ID EST A   KALENDIS   novem-
ðes [m.] [n.] oð eastran [n.] æfter forasceawunga [o.] [p.]   [b.] æt
bris   usque inpasca. juxta considerationem rationis.   oc- 5
ðære ehtera tida [b.] [c.] is to arisan [a.][a.][d.] æt hwe lytle mare [e.]
tava   hora noctis   surgendum est. ut modice amplius
[a.] þære [f.] [f.] [d.] þæt hi gerestan [n.] [b.]   [i.] hi
de media nocte   pausentur   etiam digesti sur-
arisan [g.] [a.] þæt to lafe [b.] is [a.] æfter uhtsange [c.]   [f.]
gant   Quod vero restat   post vigilias a fratribus
þa þa sealmsanges [i.] oððe rædinge [k.] sum ðinc beheofiað [g.]
qui psalterii   vel lectionum   aliquid   indigent.
smeagunge [e.] si geþeowod [d.] fram [e.] eastran   [f.] oðða
meditationi inserviatur.   A   pasca autem usque ad 10
forasædon. clypunga [f.] þæs nigeðan monþæs [f.] swa [b.]
supra dictas kalendas novembris   sic
si gemedemod [a.] [c.] tid uhtsanga [d.] seo atreogenlice [g.]
temperetur   hora vigiliarum   agenda. ut
betwux þam læstan [n.] fæte [n.] [o.] [f.]   to neodbeheofe
parvissimo   intervallo quo   fratres ad necessaria
gecyndes onðam utgan [m.] gehealdenum sona merrigenlice
nature   exeant   custodito.   mox matutini qui
lofsang. þa sint [i.] onginnendum [l.] leohte [k.] todreogenne
incipiente   luce   agendi   sunt 15
þæt æfter fylian
subsequantur.

QUANTI PSALMI DICENDI SUNT NOCTURNIS HORIS. (CAP. IX.)

[c.] tide foresædon ealra ærest mid ferse   fultum [g.]
Hiemis tempore premisso in primis versu deus in adjutorium

---

13. fæte, i. e. fæce.   14. onðam? indistinct.

---

4. Hyemis, MS. hyems. 5. in, MS. an. 6. surgendum, d'corr. from t,
which is in the text, by writing a dot under it, and a d over it. 7. de media,
MS. dimidia. pausentur, MS. pasountur. 13. quo, MS. que. 17. Hiemis,
MS. hiems.

mine [g.]   begẏm   oðer   sidon   þriwa   is to [a.] singanne [a.]
meum   intende.   in   secundo   tǐr   dicendum est.

[k.]   mine [m.] weleras [m.] þu [l.] geopena [n.] 7   [o.]
domine   labia   mea   aperies   et   os

min [o.] muð   kẏð [n.]   þin lof   [p.]   þam   isto under-
meum   adnuntiabit   laudem   tuam   cui   subjun-

þeoddenne   se ðridde sealm   æfter [c.] þison [c.]   [c.]
gendus   est tertius psalmus et gloria.   Post hanc   psalmus

se feower 7 hundnigon teoða sealm   mid   antemne
5   *nonagesimus |*   *quartus cvm cntiphona aut* (132 b.)

[b.] gewist [a.] is to singanne [a.] est þam æfter fẏlige godes
certe   decantandus.   Inde sequatur   am-

leof   sex * psealmas   mid antiphonum   þam
brosianus.   Deinde sex psalmi   cum   antiphonis.   Quibus

gesungenum [c.] gecwedenum [d.] [d.] [e.] [a.] gebletsige.   [b.]
dictis ;   dicto   versu   benedicat   abbas.

[a.]   [h.]   [h.]   [i.]   7 beon [a.] gerædde
Et   sedentibus   omnibus   in   scamnis   legantur

stuntmælum   [d.]   [e.]   ofor ıædinc scamol [f.] [g.]
10 *vicissim   a fratribus in codice super   analogium   tres*

        betwux [b.] þam [l.] [l.]   [l.]   æfter [n.]
lectiones   inter.   quas. tria responsoria canantur. Post

þære [n.] þriddan [c.] rædinge [n.] se ðe singe he recce
tertiam   vero lectionem   qui cantat   dicat   gloriam.

[d.]   [a.] þonne ongẏnð se sangere singan sona [f.] ealle of
Quam dum   incipit   cantor dicere.   mox omnes de

heora setlum   hi arisan for wurðmẏnte 7 arwurðnesse þære
sed libus   suis surgant. ob   honorem   et reverentiam sancte

halgan þrinnẏsse   [c.]   [b.]   [a.] beon geredde æt uhtsangum
15 *trinitatis.   Codices autem   legantur   in   vigiliis*

godcundlices ealderdomes geðære ealdan. gecẏðnẏsse [f.] geþære
divine auctoritatis   tam   veteris testamenti   quam

niwan [g.] ac eac swilce. forgesetnẏssa heora þa fram þam
novi.   sed expositiones earum que   a

---

6. *est.* Latin in glossator's hand.   7. *psealmas,* read *sealmas.*
16. *cẏðnẏsse,* second *s* above the line.

---

namcuðestan lareowum 7 rihtgelýfendum   fæderum
· *nominatissimis*   *et*   *orthodoxis*   *catholicisque*   *patribus*
wæron [k] gewordene [k.] æfter [a.] þisum [k.] ðrim [b.]
facte   *sunt ;*   *Post*   *has*   *vero*
rædingum [c.]   [c.]   [d.] mid heora repsum [d.] fýlian [a.]
tres   *lectiones*   *cum*   *responsoriis*   *suis sequantur*
oðre sex sealmas [e.] mid alle*lui*an [g.] to singanne [f.] æfter [b.]
reliqui sex psalmi   cum   alleluia   canendi ;   Post
þýsum [b.] rædinc [c.] þæs *apostolos [d.] æfter fýlige [a.]
hos   *lectio*   *apostoli*   *sequatur*   5
butan [f.] bec to reccanne. to singanne [g.]   [h.] 7 halsung
          ex corde recitanda et   *versus* et *supplicatio*
gebedu þæt [k.] is drihten gemildsa us [m.] 7 swa beonge endode
letanie.   id est   kyrieleison.   et sic   finiantur
nihtlice [n.] uhtsangas [n.]
vigilie   nocturne ;   (CAP. X.)

QUALITER ESTATIS TEMPORE AGATUR NOCTURNA LAUS.

          [c.]   [b.] oðða [o.] clýpunga þæs nigeþan monðæs [d.] es
A pascha   autem   usque ad calendas   novembris 10
ælc [e.]   swa swa [a.] hit her bufan gesett sealmsangas [f.]
omnis   ut   supra   dictum   est   psalmodie
mýcelnýss [e.] [a.] sigehealden utasýndredum [h.] þæt [k.] rædinga
(133 a.) *quantitas | teneatur   excepto*   quod *lectiones*
[l.] on bec   for sceornesse [m.] nihta {n.} þæt nateshwonne [i.]
in codice   propter   brevitatem   noctium   minime
beonge [i.] [a.] ah si forðam sýlfan ðrim rædingum anre [b.]
legantur.   sed   pro   ipsis   tribus lectionibus   una
lectio [b.] of ðære ealdan gecýðnysse gemýndelice geræd. oððe
de   *veteri testamento memoriter*   *dica-* 15
sungen   scort [g.] [g.] *fers þam [f.] æfterfýlige [a.] 7
*tur   Quam   breve   responsorium   subsequat*ur :   *Et*

---

5. *apostolos*, read *apostoles*.   10. *es*, cf. Introd., Ch. V, § 4.
11. *gesett*, read *gesegd*.   15. *lectio* added in glossator's hand.   16. *fers*,
read *reps*.

---

5. *apostoli*, corr. in the MS. from *apostolos* by putting *i* over *os*.
7. *finiantur*, MS. *firinantur*.   9. *estatis*, MS. *etatis*.   12. *quod, qu*
corr. from two other letters.   14. *una*, MS. *uno*.   15. *memoriter*, MS.
memoritur.   16. *responsortum*, MS. *responsorum*.

oðre [b.]　ealle ða　ealswa hit bufon is geseed beon [a.] gefyllede
reliqua　*omnia*　　*ut dictum est*　　　*impleantur :*
[d.] [d.] [e.] þæt ne sig [e.] læs [g.] [g.] twelf sealma　[h.]
id est ut numquam minus a duodecim psalmorum
[g.] to micelnysse [f.] to nihtlicum uhtsangum gesungenne utasyn
quantitate　　*ad*　*vigilias nocturnas*　　*dicantur ex-*
dredum þam ðriddan [i.] 7 þan feower 7 hund niᵹoteðan
cepto　　*tertio*　　*et*　　*nonagesimo quarto*
sealme.
5 *psalmo ;*

QUALITER DOMINICIS DIEBUS VIGILIAE AGANTUR.　(CAP. XI.)

on ðam drihtenlicum dæge [c.] [b.] gemetlicor [a.] si arisan [a.]
DOMINICO　　DIE　　　TEMPERIUS　　SURGATUR
to nihtsangum [d.] on ðam uhtsangum si gehealden [a.]
AD　　VIGILIAS ;　*In quibus*　*vigiliis*　　*teneatur*
gemet [b.]　þæt [d.] is ge tɪymedum [f.] swa swa we bufan
mensura.　　*id*　*est modulatis.*　　　*ut supra*
gedihton [f.]　[g.] syx sealmas [h.] 7 fers　[k.] sittendum
10 *disposuimus.*　*sex*　*psalmis.*　*et versu.*　*residentibus*
[k.] eallum gedihte 7 [i.] be endebyrdnysse on sceamolum [c.]
cunctis disposite et　*per ordine*m　*in*　*subselliis*
[i.] beon gerædde [m.]　on　bec　swa swa　we bufan [p.]
*legant*ur　　　*in*　*codice.*　*ut*　　*supra*
sædon [p.] feower [q.] rædinga [q.] mid repsum [r.]　þær [s.]
diximus.　*quattuor lectiones*　*cum*　*responsoriis suis.*　*ubi*
þæt [t.] an [a.] on ðam feorðam repse [u.] gesungæn fram ðam
tantum　*in quarto*　*responsorio dicat*ur　*a cantante*
singendum þane [f.] þonne [e.] onginð [e.]　[b.] sona ealle [e.]
15 *Gloria ;*　*Quam*　*dum*　*incipit.*　*mox*　*omnes*
mid arwurðnessa　[a.] arison　[b.] æfter þisum rædingum [b.]
cum reverentia　*surgant :*　*Post quas*　*lectiones*
fylian　[c.] be endebyrdnesse [d.] oðre syx [e.] sealmas mid
sequantur　*exordine*　*alii*　*sex*　*psalmi*　*cum*

---

3. First *to,* dittography in] the wrong place.　　10. *fers, f* corrected
from *r.*

---

3. *quantitate,* MS. *quantitatem.*　　11. *disposite, dis-* corrected in the
MS. from *des-* by writing *i* over the *e.*　*subselliis,* MS. *subsellis.*

antiphonam [f.] swa swa [g.] þa æreran [g.] 7 mid ferse [h.]
antiphonis   *sicut*   *anteriores*   et   *versu.*

æfter [c.] þam [c.] [b.] eft [a.] beon geredde oðre [d.] feower [d.]
Post   *quos*   *iterum*   *legantur*   *alie*   *quattuor*

rædinga [d.] [e.] mid repsum be endebýrdnesse swa swa we her
lectiones. *cum responsoriis :*   *ordine quo*

bufon sædon. æfter [b.] þýsum beon [a.] geþrý [c.] canticas be
(133 b.) *supra ;*   *Post*   *quas* | *dicantur*   *tria*   *cantica. de*

ðam [d.] witegendum þe [e.] ðe ge [e.] gesette [f.] þa * cantincas
prophetis.   *que*   *instituerit* *abbas. que* *cantica* 5

mid [h.]   [h.]   beon [g.] gesungenne gecwedenum [f.]
cum   *alleluja*   *psallant*ur.   *Dicto*   *etiam*

[f.] verse [a.] 7 bletsiendum [g.] abbude [h.] þam beon [a.] ge-
versu   et   *benedicente*   *abbate*   *legan-*

rædde [b.]   [b.]   [b.] of ðære [c.] niwan gecýðnýsse [c.]
tur.   *alie quattuor lectiones de*   *novo testamento.*

be endebýrdnesse. swa swa we bufon sædon [e.]   [e.]
     ordine quo supra ;   *Post*   *quartum autem*

[e.]   onginne [a.]   [b.]   lofsang   [d.]   [d.]
responsorium *incipiat*   *abbas* *ýmnum.* te *deum laudamus;* 10

[a.] þam gesungenum [a.] ræde [b.] [c.]   [d.] of ðam god-
Quo   *dicto ;*   *legat*   *abbas lectionem de*   *evan-*

ʃpelle [f.] mid wurðmýnte [f.] [g.] 7 mid ege   [h.]
gelio ;   *cum*   *honore*   et *timore stantibus omnibus ;*

þam geræddum andswarian ealle [c.]   [d.]   [a.] 7 þam æfter
Qua   *perlecta*   *respondeant omnes Amen.*   *Et* *subse-*

filige [a.] [b.] se abbod [d.]   [e.] [e.] [e.] [f.] 7 for [f.] gifenre
quatur mox abbas ýmnum. Te decet laus. et *data benedic-*

bletsunge [g.] hi anginnan mergenlicelof þæt [a.] [b.] onænde [æ.]
tione.   *incipiant*   *matutinos ;*   *Qui*   *ordo* 15

uhtsanga [c.] [d.] ælceretide   [d.]   [e.] swa sumeres [e.] swa
vigiliarum   *omni*   *tempore tam*   *aestatis*   *quam*

---

3. The top of the two *b*'s partly erased.   4. After *beon* a piece of the MS.
is away.   5. *cantincas*, read *canticas*.   6. The gloss to *Alleluja* is
erased ; the *h* is probably a 'paving' letter.   7. *bletsiendum*, *u* corr.
from *ei*.   15. *þæt onænde*, as gloss to *qui ordo*, I do not know how to explain
the *þæt*, unless here the contraction *þ̄* stands for *þe* ; *onænde*, however, stands
for *on œndebyrdnesse.*

---

2. Erasure after *alie.*   3. *quo*, *o* corr. from *i*?   5. *instituerit*, MS.
instetuerit.   11. *de, e* above line ; *ad*, which was in the MS., has been corrected into *de* by underdotting the *a*, and adding the *e.*

wýntres gelice [g.] [h.] on ðam drihtenlicum dæge sigehealden [a.]
hiemis   aequaliter   in   die dominico teneatur.

[i.] buton si [k.] þæt næfne na genýrðe lætlicor [l.] arisan
nisi forte.   quod absit tardius surgatur.

sum ðinc of rædlingum [p.] is to scýrtanne [n.] oððe of repsum
aliquit   de lectionibus   breviandum est.   aut responsoriis.

þæt [r.] sig þe ah hwæðere [s.] eallunga [t.] gewarnod [r.] þæt
Quod   tamen   omnino   caveatur   ne

hit ne [k.] belimpe [n.] þæt [a.] gif hit [a.] belimpð [a.]
5   *proveniat;   Quodsi   contigerit.*

wýröfullice þanon [b.] he gebete [b.] gode [d.] on cýrcean [e.]
digne   inde   satisfaciat   deo   in oratorio

[f.] þurh þæs gýmeleastum þe hit becýmð.
per cujus evenerit neglectum.

(CAP. XII.)

on mergenlicum
QUALITER MATUTINORUM SOLLEMPNITAS AGATUR. IN MATUTINIS

[d.] lofsangum [c.] on sunnan [c.] dæge ealre æræst si gesungen se sýx
10   DOMINICO DIE   INPRIMIS   DICATUR   SEX-

7 sýxteogaða sealm se sýx 7 syxtigoða sealm [e.] buton
agesimus sextus psalmus   sine

[f.] antempne forð rihte   [b.] þar æfter þam sigesungen
antiphona   in directum.   Post   quem   dicatur

se fifteogaða sealm [e.]   [e.]   [b.] [b.]   [a.] se hun-
quinquagesimus   cum alleluja;   Post quem dicatur cen-

teontigoða sealm. 7 se seofonteoða sealm 7 [d.] se twa 7 syx-
tesimus septimus | decimus   et   sexagesimus (134 a.)

teogaða [d.] sealm [d.] þanon bletsunga [b.] 7 [c.] lofu [c.]
15   *secundus.   inde   benedictiones   et   laudes.*

of unwrigednesse [f.] 7 an [d.] buton bec [e.] 7 reps [g.]
lectio de apocalipsi   una ex corde   et responsorium.

[h.] 7 godes lof [h.] 7 fers [i.] [k.] lofsanc [i.] of þam godspelle
et ambrosianus.   versus.   canticum   de   evangelio.

gebedu 7 hit bið [n.] geendod [n.]
letania. et   completum est;

---

14. The second word *sealm*, last stroke of *m* erased. *bletsunga*, *e* very
indistinct.

---

3. *de lectionibus*, MS. *dilectionibus*.   12. *antiphona*, MS. *antiphonam*.
15. *benedictiones*, the last *e* corr. from *i* in MS.

QUALITER PRIVATIS DIEBUS MATUTINI AGANTUR.

(CAP. XIII.)

[c.] . [b.]   [c.] on *syndorlicum* dagu*m* æftersanga symboh.ys
DIEBUS AUTEM   PRIVATIS   MATUTINORUM   SOL-
[d.]   si gedon [a.] *þæt* [f.] is [g.] *þæt* sig [h.]   [h.]
lempnitas ita   agatur.   id   est   ut sexayesimus sextus

[h.]   [g.] sungen   [i.]   buto*n* antempne   [k.] teonde
psalmus   dicatur   sine   antiphona.   subtrahendo

æt hwega [l.] swa swa [m.] on ðam [m.] sunnan die dæge *þæt* [n.]
modice   sicut   dominica.   ut   5

ealle becuma*n* [n.]   [p.]   toðan fiftugeðan sealme   se sige
*omnes   occurrant   ad psulmum   quinquagesimum.   qui cu*m

[r.]   [q.] sungen æf*ter* [b.]   *þæm* [b.] [c.] [c.]   [c.]
antiphona   dicatur ;   Post   quem   alii duo   psalmi

beon gesungenne [a.]   æfter   [d.] [d.] [e.] on monan [f.] *d*æge
dicantur   secundum consuetudinem id est   secunda feria.

[f.] 7. se. y 7 þiitteoga sealm 7 se fif þæs * tides dagæs [a.]
quintus.   et   trigessimus   quintus.   tertia   feria

se twa 7 feowerteogaða sealm [b.] 7 se *syx 7 fifteogaða   [c.]
quadragesimus secundus.   et quinquayesimus   sextus. 10

þæs [a.] wodnes dæges [a.] seo þieo 7 *syxteogaða sealm [b.]
Quarta   feria.   sexayesimus tertius

7 se feower 7 syxteogaða sealm se fifta dæig se seofon 7
et   sexuyesimus quartus.   Quinta feria   octogesimus

hun*d*enhteoða 7 se nigoða 7 hund eahtoða sealm þæs frian dæges
septimus.   et   octogesimus nonús.   Sexta feria

se fif 7 *syxteogaða   7 sean 7 hund nigenteoða
septuagesimus   quintus. et   nonagesimus primus.

sæternesdæge   7 hund teontigoða. 7 se twa 7 fcower-
Sabbato   autem   centesimus quadrage-   15

tigoða san.   7 cantic   se *deo todæled
simus   secundus. et canticum deuteronomii   quod dividatur

---

5. *die*, Latin in glossator's hand.   9. *y* over first *quintus*; probably
originally=*fifta*, which must also be understood over the second *quintus*.
tides, read *tiwes.*   16. *san*, pro *salm* or *sang*? *deo*, read *beo.*

---

4. *sine* above the line.   7. *antiphona*, MS. *atiphona.*   12, 13. *octogesi-
mum* and *octogesimus*, MS. *octuagesimus, -m.*   14. *primus* is a correction
of the MS. from *quintus*, which was there first, and which is marked for
expunction by a line of dots over and under it; *primus* is then written
over it.

on twam glorian   soðes [a.]   [b.]   [b.]   an *cantinc
in   duas   Glorias ;   Nam   ceteris   diebus   canticum

anum   anum [d.]   gehwylcum   dæge [d.]   he   [e.]   * sw
unumquodque die suo ex   [prophetis. sicut (134 b.)

[f.] singað   se romanisca   laðung   si gesungen [a.]   æfter þisum
psallit   aecclesia   romana   dicatur ;   Post   hec

filian [a.]   lofu [c.]   capitul   gemimorlice
sequantur   laudes :   Deinde   lectio   una   apostoli   memoriter

to secanne

5 recitanda. responsorium. ambrosianus. versus.   canticum de Evan-
                    gewistlice [b.]   is to donne [a.]
gelio. letania et completum est ;   Plane   agenda

meriendlice lofsang [c.]   oððe [d.]   on æfen [d.]   sanc ne wite [e.]
    matutina.   vel   vespertina   non   transeat

æhwænne [f.]   buton on   ðære ytemesta   endebyrdnysse   [k.]
aliquando.   nisi   in   ultimo ordine

[h.]   bed þæt   drihtenlicge [h.]   eallum   gehyrendum   si gesun-
oratio   dominica   omnibus   audientibus   dica-

gen [g.]   fram ealdre [h.]   for [i.]   aswicunga [k.]   þornum [i.]
10 *tur   a priore   propter   scandalorum   spinas*

þam [l.] upasprungen [l.] gewuniæð [n.] gecyrde [r.]   þurh ða sylfan
que   oriri   solent   ut   conversi   per   ipsius

gebedas   behat [q.]   on ðam [t.] sægað [e.]
orationis sponsionem   qua   dicunt.   dimitte nobis sicut et nos

                þæt [n.]   hi gefeormian [a.]   fram þas [p.]   geræ-
dimittimus   purgent se   ab   hujus-

dum [p.]   leahtre [p.]   [d.]   oðrum [d.]   timam [b.]   [d.]   donlicum
    modi   vitio.   Coeteris vero   agendis :

[c.]   se ytemesta [c.]   þæs gebedes [e.]   sigesungen [a.]   [f.]   fram
15 *ultima   pars ejus   orationis   dicatur   ut   ab*

eallum [g.]   þæt si [f.]   geandswarod   ah   alys   us   fram
omnibus   respondeatur.   sed   libera   nos   a

yfele
malo.

---

1. *cantinc*, read *cantic*.   2. Erasure after *sw*, read *swa* ; even *sw* is barely
visible.   8. *ytemesta* ; it is possible that the *n* we expect here should be cut
away ; first *e* is partly cut away.   14. *timam* in the MS. ; *m*, however, is
underdotted, and a *d* written over it, and *a* seems to be changed into *u*,
yielding for the whole, *tidum*.

---

4. *memoriter*, MS. *memoritur*.   5. The MS. reads *evangelico*, but the *c*
is expunged.

QUALITER IN SANCTORUM NATALITIIS VIGILIE
AGANTUR. (CAP. XIV.)

[c.]   [d.]   [b.] [c.] on freolsungum [m.] oððe on eallum [e.]
IN SANCTORUM VERO   FESTIVITATIBUS   VEL   OMNIBUS

sẏmelnẏssum [e.] swa swa [f.] we sædon [f.] on ðam drihten-
sollempnitatibus.   sicut   diximus   dominico

licum [g.] is to donne [a.] [e.] [i.] sigedon [k.] utasẏndrodum
die   agendum.   ita agatur   excepto   5

þæt beon [i.] sealmas [m.] [n.] oððe antempnes [o.] rædinge [o.]
quod   psalmi   aut antiphone   vel lectiones

to þam [q.] sẏlfum [q.] dæge [p.] gebẏriende [l.] sungenne
ad ipsum   diem   pertinentes   dicantur.

gemed [c.] [b.] þæt foresæde sige healden
Modus   autem suprascriptus   teneatur

QUIBUS TEMPORIBUS ALLELUIA DICATUR. (CAP. XV.)

fram þam halgan [f.] eastran [f.] to [g.] pentecosten [g.]
A   SANCTO   PASCHA   USQUE PENTECOSTEN: 10

butan [e.] to forlætennesse si gesungen [a.] [b.] geon [c.]
SINE   INtermissione   dicatur   alleluia.   tam

sealmsange [c.]   ge [d.] on repsum [d.]   [c.]   [b.]
135 a.) in psalmis | quam in responsoriis : A pentecosten autem

oð [d.] angin [d.] lænctenfæsten [d.] eallum [e.] nihtum [e.]
usque in caput   quadragesime   omnibus   noctibus

mid sex [f.] æftrum sealm [g.] þæt an to uhtsangum sigesungen
cum sex posterioribus   tantum ad nocturnales dicatur :

ælcon [b.] sunnandæge [e.] [s.] butan lænctene [d.] canticas
Omni vero   dominico   die extra quadragesimam. cantica. 15

meriendlice lofsangas.   prim undernsanc [g.] middæigsanc [i.]
matutini.   . prima.   tertia.   sexta.

nonsangc mid [l.] beon sungenne [a.] æftersanc [c.] [b.]
nonaque cum Alleluia   dicantur ;   vespera   vero ;

næfre ne sigesungen sang mid alleluia butan fram eastran
numquam   dicantur cum Alleluia. nisi a pasca.

oððone fẏfteoða dæig
usque ad pentecosten.

---

3. [d.] Top part erased.   11. æt in forlætennesse not clear; t may be d,
and æ probably corrected from a.   17. æfter sanc, probably a mistake for
æfen sanc.

---

10. Pascha, h above line. 15. die, later addition, which is in no other text.

QUALITER DIVINA OPERA PER DIEM AGANTUR. (CAP. XVI.)

swa swa se witega sæde seofonsiðon on dæge lof [a.]
UT   AIT   PROPHETA.   SEPTIES   IN DIE   LAUDEM

ic sanc [b.] ðe þæt [a.] seofonfealde [a.] þæt halige [a.]
DIXI TIBI ;   Qui   septenarius   sacratus

getel [a.] fram us [b.] [a.] syge fylled gif meriendlice
numerus   a   nobis   sic impleatur.   si   matu-

lofsanges [i.] primsanges [k.] as [l.] as [m.] as efensang
5 tini.   primae   tertie   sexte   none   vespere

7 [o] nihtsanges [a.] on tide ures þeowdomes [g.] þenunga
completoriique   tempore nostre servitutis   officia

we gelæston forðam [p.] be þisum [p.] tidum þe he sæde [p.]
persolvamus.   quia de   his   oris   dixit :

[t.]   [a.] on dæge [s.] lof dixi sang þe [x̄.] [a.] soðes
septies in die laudem   tibi;   Nam   de

benihtlicum [c.] [c.] uhtsangum se ilca [b.] se sylfe [b.] witega [b.]
nocturnis   vigiliis   idem   ipse   propheta

[a.] sæde [b.] to midderenihte [b.] [a.] ic aras to andedende [c.]
10 ait;   media nocte   surgebam ad confitendum

þe [d.] [b.] on þisum [e.] tidum [e.] [a.] we gereccað lofu [c.]
tibi; Ergo   his temporibus   referamus   laudes

urum [d.] sceppende [d.] [f.] ofor domes [f.] [g.] his riht-
creatori   nostro   super judicia   justi-

wisnesse [g.] [h.] þæt is æfter sangum primsang undernsanc
tiae sue.   id est   matutino.   prima. tertia.

middægsang nonsanc æfensanc nihtsang 7 on nihte 7 utan arisan
sexta.   nona.   vespera. completorio et nocte   surgamus

to andedtenne him
15 ad confitendum ei.

---

2. Erasure after dæge? 4. bi=the glossator's correction of impleatur
into implebitur, which is in the other texts, is found over the a of impleatur.
5. as, three times, merely the termination of words, which are understood
to be known, showing that the Latin words are plural. efensang, or
æfensang. 8. dixi, omitted in Latin text, and supplied by glossator.
10. andedende, i. e. anlettende ; the last d is corrected from n. 15. andedtenne, read andettenne.

---

4. impleatur, see supra, note to l. 4. 6. completoriique, MS. completorique.
9. ipse above line. 13. sue, MS. tue.

QUANTI PSALMI PER EASDEM HORAS DICENDI SUNT.   (CAP. XVII.)

nu soðes be nihtlicum vigiliis uhtsangum oððe meriendlice
JAM   DE NOCTURNIS.   VEL   MATUTINIS

lofsangas æfter sanges endebýrdnesse [b.] [c.] sealmsauges [g.] [c.]
DIGESSIMUS   ordinem   psalmodie.

nu [g.]   be   æfterfýliendum   tidum [h.]   uton [f.]   wearnian
(135 b.)   nunc   de   sequentibus | horis   videamus ;

on þære [c.] formantide * becna þreo sealmas [b.] sindorlipes [d.]
Prima   hora   dicantur   psalmi   tres   singillatim.   5

7 na under anum glorian lofsang þære ýlcan tide [g.] æfter [h.]
et non sub una gloria. ymnus ejusdem hore post

verse [h.] o [i.] mine [l.] fýlst [l.] beiým [k.] ærðam [ɪn.]
versum.   deus in adjutorium meum intende : Antequam

[n.] sealmas [m.]   æfter gefýllednesse þreora sealma [d.]
psalmi   incipiantur : Post expletionem trium psalmorum

[a.] si gereht [a.] kapitol [b.] [b.] an et 7 fers 7 drihten si mid us 7
recitetur   lectio   una   versus. et   Kyrieleison   et

hit bið geendod [g.] undernsanges. soðlice. middægisanges 7 non-
missa   est :   Tertie   vero.   sexte.   et   10

sanges on ðære endebýrdnesse si gebremod [a.] gebed [b.] þæt is
none   eo ordine celebretur   oratio.   id est

[h.] fers lofsanges þæra ilcan [k.] tidana [k.] þreo sealmas capitol [m.]
versus.   ymni earundem horarum terni psalmi.   lectio.

7 vers [n.]   7 hit bið geendod gif [a.] mare [c.] gega-
et versus. KΥΡΙΕΛΕΙϹΟΝ. et missa est ;   Si major   con-

derunc [b.] bið [a.] mid antempnes soðlice læsse forðrihte beon
gregatio   fuerit. cum antiphonis. si vero minor. in directum psal-

gesungene [c.] æfen [b.] [c.] tidsanc mid feower [d.] sealmas [d.]
lantur ; Vespertina autem sinaxis. quattuor psalmis 15

---

2. vigiliis supplied by glossator. It is only in S. (Schröer's Winteney
Version).   3. The es over psalmodie stands much lower than sealmsang,
making it look as if es were written first by one who only wished to indicate
the ending. Then some one else put in sealmsang. All this appears to have
been carefully copied by our scribe..   5. becna, probably read beon a
(sungenne) or read becweden ?   7. o over deus, no 'paving' letter, but
sign of vocative.   9. et after an by glossator.   10. middægisanges,
g inserted by glossator himself, but probably in the wrong place, middæigsanges
being the word which it was intended to produce.   14. antempnes, s corr.
from r or n.

---

2. Jam, wrongly rubricated in the MS. Nam.   3. psalmodie, MS.
psalmodiet.   12. terni, MS. termi ; the first stroke of m perhaps erased.
14. in directum, MS. in directu.   15. autem here and passim indicated in
MS. by hᶜ.

mid [e.] antempne [a.] si geendod æfter [b.] þisum [b.]
cum antiphonis terminetur : Post quos

sealmum [b.] capitul [c.] is to reccanne [a.] is [a.] þanon [d.]
psalmos lectio recitanda est. inde

reps [e.] godes lof [f.] [g.] [h.] lofsang of ðam godspelle
responsorium. ambrosianus. versus canticum de evangelio.

gebedu [k.] [l.] 7 þæt drihtenlic gebed [l.] [m.] heo beon geen-
letania et oratio dominica. et fiant.

dode [m.] [c.] nihtsanc soðlice þreora [e.] sealma [e.] * forð-
5 *misse ; Completorium autem trium psalmorum dic-*

rihtes [b.] si geendod [a.] þa sealmas [a.] [a.] forðrihtes [b.]
tione terminetur ; Qui psalmi directanei

butan antemne [c.] sint [a.] to singanne [a.] æfter [d.] þisum [d.]
sine antiphona dicendi sunt. Post quos

lofsang [e.] þære ylcan tide [f.] capitol [g.] an [g.] 7 vers [h.]
ymnus ejusdem hore. lectio una. versus.

[i.] 7 bletsung [k.] 7 hi gebeon geendode
kirieleison. benedictio et misse fiant ;

10 QUO ORDINE IPSI PSALMI DICENDI SUNT. (CAP. XVIII.) | (136 a.)

ealra ærest [t.] æfre [b.] on dæghwamlicum [d.] tidum
INPRIMIS ,SEMPER DIURNIS HORIS

[a.] sigesungen mine fultum beiym [d.] eala þu
DICATUR VERSUS *deus in adjutorium meum intende. domine*

drihten to gehelpanne me efest 7 gloria þanon lofsang
ad adjuvandum me festina. et gloria : inde ymnus

anrehwylcre æghwilcre tide syððan on ðære forman tida
unius cuiusque hore. deinde prima hora do-

on sunnan dæge die tosecgenne feower cwydas psalmi þæs
15 *minica dicenda quattuor capitula centissimi*

hundteontiga 7 cahtateoðan sealmas on oðrum soðlice tidum
octavi decimi ; Reliquis vero horis

þæt is undernsang þry capitulas þæs foran
id est tertia. sexta nona. terna capitula supra

awritene sealmas beon gesungenne
scripti psalmi centissimi octavi decimi. dicantur ;

---

6. *forðrihtes,* evidently a mistake for a word that can be a gloss to *dictione*;
for *dihte*? 15. *die* inserted by glossator. *psalmi* added by glossator, to
which the *sealmas* in l. 16 is the gloss.

---

11. *diurnis,* MS. *diurnus.*

æt primsange þæs monan dæges beon gesungenne
Ad primam autem secunde ferie dicantur
þreo sealmas þæt is se forma se oðer 7 se sẏxta 7 swa ion
tres psalmi. id est primus. secundus. et sextus. et *ita per*
ænlepige dæges æt primsange oððane drihtenlican dæg diem
singulos dies ad primam usque ad dominicam
beon geseonde be endebẏrdnesse þrẏ sealmas oððone nigon
dicantur per ordinem terni psalmi. usque ad
teoðan sealm swa gewislice þæt se nigoða sealm
nonum decim*um psalmum. ita sane ; ut nonus psalm*us 5
7 se seofonteoða sealm beon todælede on twam glorian 7 swa
et septimus decimus dividantur in binas glorias. et *sic*
hit beo þæt si æt uhtsangum on sunnan dæge die æfre
*fiat. ut ad vigilias dominico semp*er
fram þam twentigoðan sealme ongunnon to undernsange
a vigessimo. incipiatur. Ad tertiam vero ;
þæs monan dæges *niwe gencwidas þa þe
sext*am et *nonam secunde ferie. novem capitula que*
to lafe synt of þan hunteontigoðan 7 eahtateoþan sealme
residua sunt de centessimo octavo decimo 10
þa sẏlfa þrẏ sealmas geond þa ẏlcan tida beon gesun-
psalmo ipsa terna per easdem horas dican-
genne utasẏndrodum [b.]
tur ; Expenso ergo psalmo centessimo octavo decimo
on twam dagum þæt is asunnandæge 7 on monan dæg
duobus diebus. Id est dominico et *secunda feria.*
7 on tiwes dæg eallunga æt undernsange æt middægsange
tertia feria. jam ad tertiam sextam
oððe æt nonsange beon gesungenne þreo sealmas fram þam
(136 b.) *vel nonam | psallantur terni psalmi a cen-* 15
hundteondtigoðan 7 nigonteoðan sealme *oððe þone hundteon-
tessimo nono decimo usque ad centesi-*
teoðan 7 seofon 7 twentigoðan sealme *niwe 7 þa
mum vigessimum septimum. psalmi novem : Quique*

---

2. *ion* for *iond.* 3. *diem* added by glossator. 4. *geseonde*, corrected
in margine into *gesungenn.* 7. *die* added by glossator after *dominico.*
9. *niwe, novem* glossed, as if *novum*, cf. l. 17. 16. *oððe*, read *oð.* 17. *niwe*,
cp. supra, note to l. 9.

---

1. *secunde*, MS. *secundum.* 2. *tres*, MS. *te es.* 5. *decimum*, *X*ᵐᵘᵐ in MS.,
mum in glossator's handwriting?

sealmas   oððone drihtelican   dæig   iond þa ẏlcan tida
psalmi semper   usque ad   dominicam per easdem horas

eftsonas geedlehte lofsanga eac eacswilcę rædincga oððe   vers
itidem repetantur. ẏmnorum nihilo minus. lectionum vel versuum

gesetnẏssa   anrædlice eallum dagum gehealden 7 swa gewislice
dispositione uniformiter cunctis diebus   servata. et ita   scilicet

æfre on ðam drihtelican dæge fram þam hundteontigoðan 7
semper   dominica a centesimo octavo

eahtateoðan sealme hit si agunnen æfensanc   dæghwamlice
5·   *decimo incipiatur.   Vespera autem   cotidie*

mid feower * sealmorum mid dreame si gesungen þa sealmas
quattuor psalmorum modulatione   canatur. Qui psalmi

beon agunnenne fram þam hundteontigoðan 7 nigoðan sealme
incipiantur a   centessimo nono.   usque ad

centessimum quadragesimum septimum. exceptis his qui in diversis

horis ex eis sequestrantur. id est a centessimo septimo decimo.

10 *usque centessimum vigesimum septimum et a centessimo triges-*
                                    ealle þa oðre
simo tertio. et centessimo quadragesimo secundo; Reliqui omnes

on æfen sind to singanne 7 forðam læs þe cumað þreo
in vespera dicendi sunt. Et quia minus veniunt tres

sealmas forði hig sẏnd todælenne þa þa getele on ðam
psalmi.   ideo dividendi sunt   qui in numero supra-

foresædan strengran beoð gemette
scripto fortiores inveniuntur.   id est centesimus trige-

15 *simus tertius et centesimus quadragesimus quartus. Centesimus*
            forðam lẏtel þe he is
vero sextus decimus. quia parvus est cum centesimo

          si geþeod gedihtenre   endebẏrdnẏsse
quinto decimo jungatur. | Digesto ergo ordine (37 a.)

sealmsanga æfensanga oðre þæt is rædinga repsas
psalmorum vespertinorum reliqua. id est lectiones. responsoria.

---

6. *ssalmorum*, read *sealma*.

---

2. *versuum*, MS. *versum*.   13. *dividendi*, MS. *videndi*.

* imnis versus [i.] oððe canticas swa swa we bufan scripsimus
ẏmni ;   vel   cantica.   sicut   supra taxavi-
awriten beon gefẏllede to nihtsange   þa ẏlcan sealmas
mus   impleantur ;   Ad completorium vero.   idem   psalmi
beon geedleehte   þæt is se feower 7 hundnigenteoða sealm.
repetantur.   cotidie id est quartus.   nonagesimus.

gedihtere [e.]   [b.]
et centesimus et trigesimus tertius ;   Disposito ergo

endebẏrdnesse [c.] sealmsangas [e.] godcundlice [d.] ealle [f.]
ordine   psalmodie   divine.   reliqui 5
ða oðre [f.] sealmas [f.] þa þa [g.] tolafe sẏnt [g.] gelice [h.]
omnes   psalmi   qui   supersunt   aequaliter
beon *godælede [a.] ætforan nihta [m.] uhtsangum [l.] dælende [i.]
dividantur   septem noctium   vigiliis   parciendo
gewistlice [k.] þa þa [n.] beotwux [p.] heom længran [o.]
scilicet   qui   inter   eos   prolixiores
sẏnt [n.] *salmos [q.] 7 twelf [r.] iond [s.] æghwilce [s.] 7 beon ge-
sunt.   psalmi.   et duodecim per unamquamque   consti-
sette [q.] nihte þæt [b.] healicost [c.] mẏndigende [a.] þæt [d.]
tuantur noctem ;   Hoc   precipue   commonentes.   ut   10
gif [f.] wenunge [e.]   [g.] þis todal [g.] sealma [b.] ænigum
si cui   forte   haec distributio   psalmorum   displi-
mislicað [f.] hegeendebẏrde [d.] gif [l.] bett elles [k.] dem [i.]
cuerit   ordinet   si melius   aliter   judicaverit.
þonne [m.] bid mid eallum [o.] gemettum [o.] þæt [n.]
dum omnibus   modis   id
be iẏmð [m.] þæt beon [p.] an ælcere [q.] wucan [q.] saltere [r.]
attendatur.   ut omni ebdomada   psalterium
of ansundan [ſ.] getele [s.] hunteontig [t.] 7 fiftig [t.]
ex integro numero   centum   quinquaginta 15
sealma [t.] gesungenne [p.] 7 [u.] on sunnandæge [ẏ.] [ẏ]
psalmorum   psallatur.   et   dominico   die
æfre [x.] fram [z.] anginne [x.] si geedleht to uhtsangum et
semper   a   capite   repetatur ad vigilias.

---

1. *imnis.* Is the *s* of this Latin word perhaps a remnant of the plural ending *-as* which may have originally stood over *ẏmni*? See 54. 2. *versus* supplied by glossator. *scripsimus* in glossator's hand, the gloss to which, as well as to *taxavimus*, is *awriten* in l. 2. 7. *godœlede*, read *gedœlede* or *todœlede.* 9. *salmos*, scribe's eye caught by Latin ending. See note to Latin, l. 9. 11. Erasure before *pis.* 13. *bid* or *bið* ? 15. *getele, te* above line. 17. *et* added by glossator.

9. *psalmi*, MS. *psalmos.*

forðam [a.] swiðe [c.] cræftleasne * estfulnesses heora [d.] þeowdom
quia *nimis* *iners* *devotionis* *sue* *servitium*

þe atiwað [a.] munecas [b.] þa þa [e.] læs [f.] sealmsanges [g.]
ostendunt *monachi* *qui* *minus* *psalterio*

[h.] mid lofsange [h.] mid gewunelicum [h.] iond [i.]
cum *canticis* *consuetudinariis* *per*

þære [k.] ụwucan emrene [i.] singað [l.] buton þonne [l.]
septimane *circulum* *psallunt.* *dum* *quando*

weræduð [l.] ure halige [m.] fæderas [n.] [m.] on anum [q.]
5 *legamus* *sanctos* *patres* *nostros uno*

dæge þæt [o.] hrædlice gefýllan [n.] þæt [r.] eala [r.] sleawe
die *hoc* *strenue* *implevisse.* *quod* *nos* *tepidi.*

gif ge | ucan [t.] on ansundre [t.] læstan [r.]
utinam | *septimana* *integra* *persolvamus.* (137 b.)

DE DISCIPLINA PSALLENDI. (CAP. XIX.)

æighwære [c.] we gelýfað [a.] godcundlice [d.] beon andweard-
UBIQUE *CREDIMUS* *DIVINAM* *ESSE PRE-*

nýsse [d.] [e.] eagan [f.] drihtnes [f.] on ælcere [g.] stowe [g.]
10 *SENtiam.* *et* *oculos* *domini* *in* *omni* *loco*

besceawian [e.] þagodan 7 þa ýfelan [d.] swyðest [b.] þeah-
speculari *bonos* *et* *malos.* *Maxime* *tamen*

hwæðere þæt [c.] butan ælcere [e.] twýnung [e.] þa gelýfað [a.]
hoc *sine* *aliq*ua *dubitatione* *credamus.*

þonne [f.] æt þam godcundlicum [g.] weorce [g.] we ætstandað
cum *ad opus divinu*m *assistimus.*

forði [c.] æfre [b.] [d.] gemýndige we beon [a.] þæt sæde
Ideo *semper* *memores* *simus ;* *quod ait prophet*a;

þeowiað on æge 7 eft singað wislice [a.] 7 on
15 *Servite domino in timore ; Et iteru*m *Psallite sapienter ; Et in*

gesýhðe engla 7 ic singa [a.] þe [b.] [b.] utan foresceawian
conspectu angelorum *psallam* *tibi.* *Ergo* *consideremus*

hu hit [c.] gedafenige [c.] [e.] on his gesihðe [e.] godcundnesse [f.]
qualiter *oporteat* *in* *conspectu.* *divinitatis*

---

1. *estfulnesses*, see note to Latin, l. 1.   4. *u* before *wucan* underdotted,
probably to be regarded as the wrong beginning of *ucan* instead of *wucan*.
11. [e.] not quite clear.

---

1. *devotionis*, MS. *devotioni*. An *s*, which is wanting here, is superfluous
in the gloss *estfulnesses*. May we suppose that an *s* written above the line was
wrongly transcribed as belonging to the gloss instead of to the lemma?
7. *septimāna* in MS.   8. *De* above line. *PSALLENDI*, I is cut away.

7 [g.] on ængla   his [g.]   beon [d.]   7   [h.]   uton standan to
et   angelorum   ejus   esse   et   sic   stemus   ad

singanne þæt [k.] ure [l.]   mod   [l.]   geþwærlice [k.] ure [m.]
psallendum.   ut.   mens   nostra   concordet   voci

stefne [m.]
nostre.

DE REVERENTIA ORATIONIS.   (CAP. XX.)

gif   mid rican mannan   we   wẏllað   sum   þinc
SI   CUM   HOMINIBUS POTENTIBUS   VOLUMUS   aliqua   5

tihtan   we na [a.] gedẏrstlæcan [a.] buton mid eadmodnesse
· suggerere.   non   presumimus   nisi   cum   humilitate

7 arwurðnessa 7 hu micele swiðor   gode ealra þingan
et   reverentia. ·   quantomagis   domino deo universorum.

mid ealre ead   7 clænnesse mid estfulnesse is to halsi-
cum omni humilitate et puritatis   devotione   supplicandum

genne 7   na on mænifealdre spræce ac on clænnesse
est.   Et non in multiloquio   sed in puritate   cordis

7 on bẏrdnesse   teara   we ne beon gehẏrede witon   7 forði
et conjunctione lacrimarum. nos   exaudiri   sciamus. Et ideo 10

scort sceal   7 clæna gebed buton wenunge of   lufe
brevis debet esse et pura oratio. nisi   forte   ex affectu

eþunge   godcundlicere gife hit beo gelend on gegaderunge
(138 a.) inspirationis   divine gratie | protendatur; In   conventu

eallunga * sescẏrð gebed 7 gewordenre tacne fram
tamen   omnino   brevietur oratio; Et   facto   signo   a

þam ealdran ealle ætgædere hi arisan.
priore.   omnes pariter   surgant.

DE DECANIS MONASTERII.   (CAP. XXI.)   15

gif mare bið   gegæderung beon gecorene of ðam sẏlfan
SI   MAJOR FUERIT   CONGREGATIO   ELIGANTUR   DE   IPSIS

gebroðran goddra gecẏðnesse 7 haligre 7 * liredrohtnunge 7 beon
fratribus boni   testimonii. et sancte   conversationis.   et con-

---

7. swiðor, w nearly effaced.   12. gelend for gelengd.   13. sescẏrð, read
si gescẏrð?   17. 7 haligre 7 liredrohtnunge. I think lire must be a
remnant of (ha)ligre, as gloss to sancte, and afterwards haligre has been
again put in.

---

6. suggerere, MS. suggere.   8. humilitate, an e over first i.

gesette   hohfolnesse   þa don   ofor   heora wican
stituantur decani ; qui sollicitudinem gerant super   *deca-*
heora decánhades on eallum þingum efter godes bebodum godes
nias   suas in omnibus secundum mandata   *dei*
7 bebodu abbodes heores *þu *decanis þẏllice beon gecorene
et *precepta. abbatis sui.   Qui decani tales   eligantur*
on ðam he todælð orsorh se abbod swẏrige hẏs bẏrðena 7 hi na beon
in   quibus securus   abba   partiat honera sua. Et non eli-
gecorene endebẏrdnesse ac æfter earnungum lifes   7
5 *gantur.   per ordinem. sed   secundum   vite meritum* et
wisdomes 7 lare   þæt   ænig   of ðam on sumere færunga
sapientiae doctrinam. Quod si quisque ex eis   aliqua   forte
to * bæd modignesse gif ge bið met ́ teallic   geþreat   ære
inflatus superbia repertus fuerit reprehensibilis. correptus semel.
7   eft   7 þriddan siðe gif he nele gebetan   he si ut-
et *iterum. Átque tertio. si non   emendare voluerit dei-*
adræfed   on his stẏde   se ðe is wẏrðe
ciatur. et alter   in   loco eius   qui   dignus est
7 efterfilige beðam ut pravoste þæt ẏlce 7 we gesettað
10 *succedat ; Et de preposito   eadem   constituimus.*

QUOMOÐO DORMIUNT MONACHI. (CAP. XXII.)

ænlepige geond ænlepige bedd   hi slapan   beddreaf
SINGULI   PER SINGULA   LECTA   DORMIANT; LECTIsternia
for gemede drohtnunge æfter gesetnesse. oððe dihtinge abbodes
pro modo conversationis   secundum dispositionem   abbatis
heora under hig gif hit mæg   ealle on anre stowe hi slapan
sui accipiant. si potest fieri. omnes in uno loco dormiant;
gif   meniu   ne geþafeð tẏnfealdum oððe twentifealdum
15 *Si autem multitudo non sinit   deni aut viceni*
mid   ealdrum þa ofer hig hohfulle beon hi gerestan candel
cum | senioribus qui super eos solliciti sint   pausent; Candela (138 b.)
æfre on ðam ẏlcan huse bẏrne   oð   merien gescridde
jugiter in   eadem cella ardeat usque mane ;   Vestiti
hi slapan 7 begẏrde gẏrdelsum oððe strængum 7 seax
dormiant. et cincti cingulis   aut funibus et cultellos

---

3. *þu*, read *þa*.   *decanis*, see note to 51. 1.   4. *swẏrige*, see note.
7. *tobæd*, read *tobræd*.   *gif ge bið met*, read *gif bið ge met*.   12. *ænlepige*
(twice) and in line 13. *forgemede* ; in these three cases *e* seems to be corrected
from *i*.

heora æt sidan 7 hi nabban þonne hi slapaðʒ   þurh
suos ad latus non habeant.   dum dormiunt ne forte per
swefn þelæs þe hi wýrðan oððe gewundode
somnium   vulnerentur   dormientes ; Et
   ah þæt hi beon   gewordenem tacne
*ut   parati   sint monachi semp*er. et   *facto signo*
buton ýldinge 7 a·hi arisænde 7 hi eˀstæn heom betwýna fora-
absque mora   surgentes.   festinent   se   invicem pre-
hradian godes weorce mid ealre swa ðeah * stæfnýsse 7 mid
venire ad opus dei. Cum omni tamen   gravitate et mo- 5
metfæstnýsse   þaginran gebroðra wýð hi sýlfe hi nabban
*destia.   A dolescentiores frat*res *juxta se   non habeant*
bed ah gemengede mid ealdrum   arisende soðlice to godes
lecta. sed   permixti cum senioribus ; Surgentes vero ad opus
weorce   gemedlice tihtan oððe laran   slac-
*dei.   invicem se moderate   cohortent   prop*ter *somnolen-*
fulran for beladunge
torum excusationes ;

DE EXCOMMUNICATIONE CULPARUM. (CAP. XXIII.)   :0

             to þunden
SI QUIS FRATER CONTUMAX AUT INOBEDIENS. *aut super*bus. *aut*
cýrigende oððe on ænigan þingan wiðerweard [ý] wunigende
murmurans. vel in   aliquo   contrarius   existens
þam haligon regole 7 bebodu heora ealdra forhicgend 7
sancte   regule. et preceptis seniorum suorum contemptor et
gif bið gemed   þes æfter bebode
*repert*us   *fuerit. híc secundum   domini nostri preceptum*
sý gemýnegod æne 7 oðersiðan dihlice fram his ealdrum
*ammoneat*ur *semel* et · *secund*o · *secrete a   senioribus suis;* 15
gif he hit na gebet he si geþread openlice toforan eallum
Si non emendaverit. objurgetur. publice coram omnibus ;
       gif he hit swa he bið geþread gýf he understent
Si vero   neque sic se correxerit.   si   intelligit

---

2. *oððe*, see note.   4. *a*, gloss to *semper* in l. 3 ?   5. *stæfnýsse*, read
stæpinýsse.   12. [ý.] not clear.

---

3. *sint* corrected in the MS. from *sunt* by underdotting the *u*, and writing an
i over it.   13. *et* not in other texts ; redundant.

hwylc wite sig amansumunge   he underhnige elles
qualis   pena   sit.   *excommunicationi   subjaceat ;* | *Sin   autem* (139 a.)
wiðercoren he is lichamlicere   wrace   7 he sig underþeod
improbus   est.   *vindicte   corporali* et   *subdatur ;*

QUALIS DEBEAT ESSE MODUS EXCOMMUNICATIONIS.
(CAP. XXIIII.)

æfter gemete   gyltas   amansumunge   oððe lare. styre
5 SECUNDUM MODUM. CULPE. EXCOMMUNICATIONIS *vel   discipline*
sceal beon aþenod   gemet   þæt   gylta
debet   extendi   mensura ; Qui culparum modus in abbatis
hangige oððe stande on dome   þeahhwæðere   on
pendeat judicio ;   *si quis   tamen   frater in*
leohtum gyltum gif bið *gemedemod fram *heode dælnimunge
levioribus culpis   invenitur.   a   mense participatione
si gesyndrod * asyndrodest   fram meosan oððe fram geferæ-
privetur ;   Privati   autem a   mense   consortio. ista
dene þis beo gescead   on cyrican   sealm   oððe   antemp
10 *erit   ratio.   ut in oratorio psalmum aut antiphonam*
þæt he na onginne na he na nurædinge recce oððe fulre dæd-
non imponat   neque lectionem recitet. usque ad satisfac-
bode gereordunge   æfter   gereordunge ana
tionem ; Refectionem autem *cibi post fratrum refectionem solus*
he under þæt swilce hic swacweðe   hegereordige to middæges
accipiat ut.   si verbi gratia fratres   reficiant sexta hora
se broðor to nonas   he on æfen oððæt he be mid
ille frater nona, si fratres nona. ille vespera. usque   dum
dædbote fulre þæslicere forgifennesse   gite
15 *satisfactione congrua   veniam   consequatur ;*

DE GRAVIORIBUS CULPIS. (CAP.) XXV.

se   broðer   hefolices gyltes mid dara   si
IS AUTEM FRATER QUI GRAVIORIS CULPE NOXA *teneatur. sus-*

---

2. *wiðercoren,* second *e* above the line ; probably to be read *wiðercora.*
8. *gemedemod,* read *gemet ;* see note. *heode,* read *beode.*   9. *asyndrodest,*
read *asyndrodes.*   11. *nu,* wrongly transcribed for *na ?* *dædbode,* the third
d has been corrected either from or into *t,* probably the latter.   13. *he*
under, fill up *-fo.* *hic* for *ic ;* the *h* has afterwards been underdotted.

---

2. *et,* cf. p. 55, l. 13 (note).   3. MODUS, MS. MODUM. EXCOMMUNICATIONIS,
MS. EXCOMMUNICATIONE.   5. EXCOMMUNICATIONIS, MS. EXCOMMUNICATIONES.
14. *respora,* corr. into *vespera.*

framadon fram beode samod 7 fram cýrcean ænig him gebroðra
pendatur   a   mensa. *simul et ab oratorio; Nullus ei fratrum*
on ænigre na si geþeod geferrædcne   ne   on   spræce   ana
in   ullo   jungatur consortio   neque in colloquio ; Solus
to weorce   to betæhtum   þurhwunigende behreowsunge
sit ad opus sibi   injunctum.   persistens in poenitentie
on heofunge witende þone egeslican   cwide   secgendes
luctu. sciens illam   terribilem apostoli sententiam dicentis.

betæhtne   þýllicne   manna   þam sceoccan   on   feorwýrde
(139 b.) *tradi | tum   hujusmodi   hominem   satane   in   interitum* 5
lichaman   þæt he halsie   .   on drihtnes dæge metes
carnis. ut spiritus   salvus   sit in die domini ;   Cibi
     gereordung ana   he underfo   gemet   oððe on tida   on
autem refectionem solus   percipiat. mensura   vel hora.   qua
ðære þe forsceawiað   him   feccan   ne he ne sige fram
     previderit   abba ei   competere ;   Nec   a
ænigum farendum · bletsod   men   na mete se þe bið him
     quoquam   benedicatur transeunte. nec cibus qui   ei
geseald   10
datur ;

DE IS QUI SINE IUSSIONE ABBATIS JUNGUNTUR EXCOMMUNICATIS.

(CAP. XXVI.)

gif hwýlc broðer   gedýrstlæcð   butan   hæse   abbotes   þam
Si QUIS FRATER PRESUMPSERIT   sine jussione abbatis. fratri
amansumedan breðer mid ænigum gemete   geþeondan gelice
excommunicato   quolibet modo   se   jungere. similem
he gehleote   amansumunge   wrace
sortiatur   excommunicationis vindictam.   15

QUALITER DEBEAT ABBA ESSE SOLLICITUS ET CIRCA

EXCOMMUNICATIONES. (CAP. XXVII.)

ealre   hohfolnesse   gýmene   do   abutan þa agiltendan
OMNI SOLLICITUDINE CURAM GERAT ABBAS circa delinquentes
broðra forþam þe nis   neode þam halum   læce   ah þam
fratres.   quia   non est opus   sanis   medicus.   sed

---

2. *sprœce, œ* or *a*?   5. *feorwyrde, y* of peculiar form   8, 9. *na he sige
fram œnigum farendum bletsod men*, understand *na he si. f. œ. f. men
gebletsod.*   9. *fa:endum, n* indistinct.   14. *geþeondan, i.* e. *geþeodan.*

untruman o𝛿𝛿e ẏfel habbendum 7 forþi he brucan he sceal
    male habentibus; Et ideo uti debet

mid eallum gemete swa swa   wis   læce   ˙onasændan swilce
omni modo   ut   sapiens medicus.   immittere quasi

dihle   frofra   þa ealdan   swẏlce
*occultos; Senpectas. id est   seniores   sapientes fr*atres. *qui quasi*

digelice þa gefrefran gesewene   bro𝛿or   7   hi tihta
*secrete   consolentur   frat*rem *fluctua*ntem. et *provocent   eum*

to fuleadmodnesse   dædbote   7   hi gefrefrian hine mid
5 *ad   humilitatis   satisfactionem.* et *consolentur   eum   ne*

maran   unrotnessa þæt he ne si fornumen ac swa swa
habundantiori   tristitia   absorbeatur.   sed.   sicut

sæde   si getrimed on him so𝛿 lufe 7 si gebeden
ait idem apostolus; confirmetur in   eo karitas; et   *oretur*

*fram heom fram eallum gebro𝛿rum þearle swi𝛿e   scel
pro   eo   ab   omnibus.   Magno | pere enim débet* (140 a.)

mid hohfulnesse   don   se abbod 7 mid ealre glæwnesse mid
sollicitudinem   gerere   abbas. et *omni   sagacitate* et

forwitolnesse 7 gelacnian   ænig   of befæstum sceapum him
10 *industria curare.   ne aliquam de   ovibus   sibi creditis*

sẏlfum þæt he na forlure   he   cunne   *untruwa
perdat;   Noverit enim   se infirmarum curam

underfon   sawla   na ofor þa halan   wælreow o𝛿𝛿e re𝛿e
suscepisse animarum.   non super   sanas   tirannidem;

7 heondræde   egesunge   þurh þone he sæig𝛿
Et   metuat   prophete comminationem per quem   dicit

    þæt þæt ge   fæt   sawon   ge underfengon 7
deus;   Quod   crassum videbatis   assumebatis;   et

þæt wanhal wæs 7 gewi𝛿socan 7 he geafæn godes hẏrdas
15 *quod debile   erat proicebatis;   Et   pastoris boni*

ærfæste læce bẏsene   forlætenum nẏgon 7 hundnigonti
pium   imitetur exemplum qui   relictis nonaginta

sceapum on dunum se 𝛿e gode   þæt þe dwelede
novem   in montibus   abiit   unam ovem   que   erraverat

---

1. *uti* in glossator's hand.   4. *gesewene,* see note.   5. *fuleadmodnesse
dædbote,* for *eadmodnesse ful(re)dædbote.*   8. *fram,* read *fore.*   11. *untruwa,*
read *untrumra.*   15. *geafæn* belongs to *læce* in line 16.   16. Erasure after
hundnigonti?   17. *gode* for *geode.*

---

3. *Senpectas,* MS. *senpecta.*   7. *oretur,* MS. *orietur.*   9. *gerere,* MS.
gegere.   MS. *sagacizate.*   17. Most of the other texts have *novem ovibus,*
which may have been in ours, as the gloss *sceapum* is there.

secan   untrumnesse swa midlum he besargode oð̃e mænde
querere ; Cujus   infirmitate   in   tantum   compassus est.

hit   on   his   halgum   eaxlum   þæt   he   gemedemode
ut eam in   sacris humeris   suis   dignaretur
onasettan 7 ægen bringan *to* heorde
imponere. et sic reportare ad gregem.

DE IS QUI SEPIUS CORREPTI NON EMENDAVERINT.

(CAP. XXVIII.)

forgehwilcum gilte
SI QUIS FRATER FREQUENTER CORREPTUS PRO   *qualibet   culpa.* 5

þeah þe he   amansumad   hit ne gebet   teartere
etiam   si excommunicatus non emendaverit acrior ei

genealæce þræiungan þæt is   swincla wrace on him þæt
accedat   correptio   id est ut verberum vindicta in eum

forð stepð þæt gif he   he swang bið geþread oð̃e
procedat ;   Quod   si nec   ita correxit   aut

wenunge þæt næfre ne gewyrð̃e on modinyssa oð̃e upahafan
forte   quod absit   in superbiam   elatus

bewerian oð̃e gif he wile his weorc þon*n*e   swa swa
defendere voluerit   opera sua. tunc abba faciet quod 10

wis   læce gif he gegearcað swoð̃unga smyrunga oð̃e |
(140 b.) *sapiens medicus ; Si   exhibuit fomenta. si unguenta ad-* |

lara   læcedomas gewrita   godcundra æt nextan
hortationum. si medicamina scripturarum divinarum si ad ultimum

berned   amansumunge oð̃e wita   girda
ustionem excommunicationis. vel plagas virgarum : etiam si

his * foran nahtswyrian glæwnesse he gearcie soð̃lice
viderit nihil   suam prevalere   industriam. adhibeat etiam

þæt mare is his gebed 7 ealra gebroð̃ra   for him
quod majus est   suam   et   omnium   fratrum pro eo 15

se ð̃e ealle þinc mæig þæt wyrce
orationem : ut dominus qui omnia potest. operetur salutem

embe þone untruman breð̃er   þæt gif he na forð̃am mid þisum
circa infirmum   fratrem ; Quod si   nec isto modo

---

3. *to ; t* corr. from *g.*   14. *foran nahtswyrian, naht,* gloss to *nihil ;*
see note.

---

gemete bi∂ gehæled þonne eallunga se abbod bruce isene
sanatus fuerit.   *tunc   jam   abba   utatur   ferro*

ofkẏrfes   eal swa sæde   afẏrsia∂ þone ẏfelan fram
abscisionis   ut ait   apostolus ; Auferte   malum   ex

eow 7   eft   swa ungeleafulla gif he aweig aweg gewite
vobis ; Et iterum.   *Infidelis   si   discedit   discedat.*

þæt na anadli   sceap   ealle heorde   besmite
ne   una ovis   morbida. omnem gregem contaminet.

5 SI DEBEANT ITERUM RECEPI FRATRES EXEUNTES DE MONASTERIO.

(CAP. XXVIIII.)

            for agenum leahtrum qui se∂e utgæ∂ o∂∂e bi∂ uta-
FRATER QUI   PROPRIO VITIO EGREDITUR   AUT PROICI-

dræfæd   gecẏrran gif he wile   behate   ær
Tur   de monasterio. si reverti   voluerit.   spondeat. prius

      ealle bote   for∂am þe he utferde   on ∂ære
omnem emendationem vitii   pro quo egressus   est. et sic

  ẏtemestan stæpe   hi si underfangen þæt of þam his
10 *in ultimo   gradu   recipiatur.   ut   ex hoc ejus*

eadmodnẏsse si gefandod . þæt gif he o∂er si∂an utfær∂ o∂∂e
humilitas comprobetur ; Quod si   denuo exierit.   us-

þriddan si∂e he si underfangen   so∂lice sẏ∂∂an he wite ælcne
que   tertio ita recipiatur.   Jam vero postea ; sciat omnem

him sẏlfum gecẏrrednẏsse færeld beon forwẏrned
sibi   reversionis   aditum   denegari.

DE PUERIS MINORI AETATE QUOMODO CORRIPIANTUR. (CAP. XXX.)

  ælc   *ẏ∂   andgit   agenge met sceal habban
15 OMNIS AETAS VEL INTELLECTUS *proprias debet habere mensuras :*

forþig swa oft cildra   o∂∂e ginran   ẏlde o∂∂e þa þe
Ideoque quoties pueri. vel *adolescentiores aetate aut qui*

læs understandan swa magun humicel þæt wita is amansu-
minus intellegere   possunt   quanta pena sit excommuni-

munge þas þẏlice þonne hi agilta∂ o∂∂e mid swi∂licum
ca | tionis. hi tales   dum delinquunt.   aut   jejuniis   (141 a.)

---

2. *kẏrfes*, *r* corrected from *f*.   7. *qui* repeated by glossator.   8. *ær*
indistinct, might be *ier*.   15. *ẏ∂*, read *ẏld*. *agenge* nearly erased.   It
was probably the intention to erase *gemet* so as to put it over *mensuram*.

---

8. *spondeat*, MS. *sponde*.   11. *humilitas*, two letters erased between *a*
and *s*. *denuo*, *o* above line.   14. PUERIS, MS. PUEROS. QUOMODO, Q̊ in the
MS.   15. MS. *mensuram*.

fæstenum hi beon geswencte oððe mid * tearum swinglum hi
nimiis   affligantur   aut   acribus   verberibus co-
beon geþreade þæt hi beon gehealdenne
erceantur ;   ut sanentur.

DE CELLARARIO MONASTERII QUALIS DEBEAT ESSE. (CAP. XXXI.)

hordere   si gecoren of   gegæderunge   wis
CELLARIUS MONASTERII ELIGATUR DE CONGREGATIONE. *sapiens.*

on geripedum * wea   sifre   na   mycel   æte   na upahafen
maturis   moribus. sobrius. non multum aedax: non elatus. 5

   drefende   .teonful.   sæne   na   cystig   ac
non turbulentus non injuriosus. non tardus. non prodigus sed

atodrædenne   se ealra gegaderunga si swa swa
timens   deum : Qui omni congregationi sit   sicut   pater ;

gimene hedo be eallon þingan butan   hæse   naht
curam gerat de   omnibus :   Sine jussione abbatis nihil

he nado þa þinc þe beoð bebodene he gehealde   he na
faciat ;   Que   jubentur custodiat ;   fratres non

dræfa   gif hwilc broðor fram him færunga æni þing
contristet ; Si   quis   frater   ab   eo   forte   aliqua 10

ongesceadwislice   bitt   forseonde hine he ne gedrefe
inrationabiliter   postulat. non spernendo   eum   contristet.

gesceadwislice   mid eadmodnesse   yfel biddendum ac he
sed rationabiliter   cum   humilitate   male   petenti   dene-
forwyrne   his lif   he gehealde gemyndig æfre þæs apostolican
get ;   Animam suam custodiat : memor semper illius apostolici
bebodes forðam seðe wel   þenað   stepe godne him sylfum
precepti quia   qui bene ministraverit. gradum bonum   sibi
he begit   untruma   cildra   cumena   7 þearfena mid
adquirit ; Infirmorum. infantium. ospitum.   pauperumque cum 15
ealre   hohfulnesse   he do   buton twyn þæt he
omni sollicitudine curam gerat. sciens sine dubio. quia pro
foreallum þisum   sceall agyldan   ealle
his omnibus   in die judicii rationem redditurus est ; Omnia

---

1. *tearum,* read *teartum.*   2. *gehealdenne,* see note.   5. *wea,* read
þea, for *þeawum.*   7. *atodrædenne* in the MS., but *o* looks like *d.*
This points to a gloss : *god drædenne,* which the lemma would make us
suspect.   13. *lif, ·f* corrected from *w,* and indistinct.

---

1. *acribus,* MS. *acris.*   3. MONASTERII, MS. MONASTERIO.   6. MS.
juriosus.   13. *apostolici,* MS. *apostoli.*   15. *ospitum,* MS. *inospitum.*

andluman   7 ealle   æhte   swẏlce weouedes
vasa   *monasterii. cunctamque substantiam. ac si altaris*

halige fatu he besceawige naht he ne getelle *gunlæslices ne
vasa sacrata conspiciat; Nihil ducat neglegendum. nec

gitsung he ne hogige na he na si cẏstig   oððe mẏrrent
avaritie studeat. neque prodigus sit; aut stirpator

æhte   ac ealle þinc gemetlice   7
substan | tie monasterii: sed omnia mensurate faciat : et (141 b.)

efter   hæse   ætforan eallum
5 *secundum jussionem abbatis ; Humilitatem ante omnia*

*þinga he hæbbe þær þær þam nenẏs   scðe foregifen
habeat et *cui substantia non est que tribuatur.*

spræc andsweras 7 si gereht god   seo gode
sermo responsionis porrigatur bonus. ut scriptum est ; Sermo

spræce ofor þa selestan sẏlene ealle þinc þe þe him betæht
bonus : super datum optimum ; Omnia que ei injunxerit

þa sẏlfan he hæbbe under his gimena fram þam him
abbas ipsa habeat sub cura sua ; A quibus eum

þe beoð beboden he ne gedẏrstlæce   forasetne *bitleofan
10 *proibuerit. non presumat ; Fratribus constitutam annonam*

buton ænigre * or hiunge oððe ẏldinga he sẏlle þæt hine beon
sine aliquo typo vel *mora offerat ; ut non scan-*

geaswicode   sit godcundre spræce hwæt gegearnige se þe
delizentur memor divini eloquii. quid mereatur qui

geaswicað ænne of ðisum lẏtlingum gif gaderung mare
scandalizaverit unum de pusillis. Si congregatio major

bið frofras him beon gesealde fram þam he sẏlf gefultumiað
fuerit ; solacia ei dentur. a quibus adjutus et

mid efnum mode gefẏlle þenunge him sẏlfan betæhte
15 *ipse aequo animo impleat officium sibi commissum ; Horis*

ongedafenlicum tidum beon gesealde þa þinc þe sint to sillanne
competentibus dentur que danda sunt

7 beon gebedene þa þinc þe sin tobiddanne þæt nan ne sig
et *petantur que petenda sunt. ut nemo*

todræfd ne ne sig geunrotsaded on drihtnes huse.
perturbetur. neque contristetur in domo domini.

---

2. *gunlæslices,* read *gimlæslices.*   6. *þinga,* read *þingum.*   10. *bitleofan,*
read *bigleofan.*   11. *or,* read *on.*   12. *sit,* Latin added by glossator.

---

4. *mensurate, n* corr. from *m* by erasure.   13. *scandalizaverit,* MS.
scandalizave.

DE FERRAMENTIS VEL REBUS MONASTERII.   (CAP. XXXII.)

æhta   oððe reafum oððe mid-
SUBSTANTIA MONASTERII IN FERRAMENTIS VEL *vestibus seu quibus-*
sumum þingum foresceawige   be life þara   7
licet   rebus   prevideat   abba fratres de quorum vita et
þeawum orsorh he sig 7 heom ænlepige be ðam nitwyrðlice þe
moribus securus sit et eis *singula   ut   utile   ju-*
he demð betæce þa gehealdennelicun 7 þa gelohgenlican of
dicaverit consignet   custodienda   atque recolligenda; Ex 5
       þam   [b.]   gewrit [a.] tohealde þæt [e.] æfter þonne him
(142 a.) *quibus | abbas brevem   teneat   ut dum   sibi*
sylfan   betahtum þingum [e.] stundmælum   fylian
in   ipsa   assignata   · fratres   vicissim   succedunt.
[e.] he wite hwæt he sylle 7 hwæt he underfo [b.] gyf hwylc
sciat   quid dat.   et   quid recipit.   Si   quis
       fullice [c.] oððe gimleslice þinc mynstres hrepað si ge-
autem sordide   aut neglegenter res monasterii tractaverit cor-
þread   gif hit [f.] na gebett   steore   regolicere he under-
ripiatur.   si non emendaverit discipline regulari   sub- 10
þeodde
jaceat ;

SI QUID DEBEAD MONACHUS PROPRIUM HABERE.

(CAP. XXXIII.)

healicost þes leahter grundlungæ is of todonne is
Precipue hoc vitium   radicitus   amputandum est. de monas-
þæt ne gedyrstlæce æni þinc syllan oððe underfon buton
terio. ne quis   presumat   aliquid dare   aut accipere sine 15
hæse þæs abbotes ne   nabban sinderlice   ne
jussione   abbatis ; Neque aliquid habere proprium ; neque
nan þinc ealles   na boc   na weaxbredu   ne græf
nullam omnino rem; neque codicem. neque tabulas. neque gravium
ah na þinc   witodlice forþam ne habban his agenne
sed   nihil   omnino ; Quippe quibus nec corpora   sua

---

5. *gehealdennelicun,* read *gehealdenlican.*   14. Not clear whether *heoli-*
cost or *healicost* ; *grundlungæ,* or *grundlunga.*

---

5. *recolligenda, lig* above line, in glossator's hand ?

9

lichaman willan alȳfed habban agenum anwealde ealle
nec voluntates. *licet habere in propria voluntate; Omnia vero*
neodbehæfnȳssa   hihtan   ne ne si æni þinc
necessaria; a patre sperare monasterii; Nec quicquam
gelȳfed habban þæt þæt   ne sealde oððe ne geþafað
liceat habere quod abbas non *dederit aut non permis-*
 he ealle þinc eallum beon gemæne swa swa hit is awriten
*erit; Omnia*que *omnibus sint communia; ut scriptum est;*
ne ne secge ænig his æni þinc   oððe gedyrstlæce þæt
5 *nec quisquam suum aliquid dicat vel presumat; Quod*
gif bið þisum wȳrstan leahtre arasod   beon gelust-
si quisquam huic nequissimo vitio deprehensus fuerit   delec-
fullod sȳ he gemȳnegod æne 7 eft   gif hit na gebett
tari. ammonitus semel. et *iterum ; Si non emendaverit ;*
þræiunge he under*rhige*
correptioni subjaceat;

Sɪ ᴏᴍɴᴇs ᴀᴇǫᴜᴀʟɪᴛᴇʀ ᴅᴇʙᴇɴᴛ ɴᴇᴄᴇssᴀʀɪᴀ ᴀᴄᴄɪᴘᴇʀᴇ. | (142 b.)

10   (Cᴀᴘ. XXXIIII.)

                 wæs todæled ænlepigum þam þe wæs
Sɪᴄᴜᴛ ꜱᴄʀɪᴘᴛᴜᴍ ᴇꜱᴛ ˙ ᴅɪᴠɪᴅᴇʙᴀᴛᴜʀ ꜱɪɴɢᴜʟɪꜱ   *pro ut*
gehwȳlcum neod þe wæs þær we na secað   hada   þæt
cuique opus erat ; Ubi non dicimus ut personarum quod
forsig onfangennisse   untrumnȳssa ah forasceawung þær
absit acceptio sit. sed *infirmitatum consideratio; Ubi*
hedo se ðe læs hofað he do   7 he na si geeadmod
qui minus indiget agad deo gratias et *non contristetur;*
    mare   he si geadmet for untrumnesse 7
15 *qui vero plus* et *non indiget. humilietur pro infirmitate;* et
he na si upahafen for mildheortnessa   ealle liman 7 beon
non extollatur pro misericordia; et ita omnia membra erunt
on sibbe ætforan eallum þingum   murcnuncge ȳfel for
in pace. Ante omnia ammonemus ne murmurationis malum. pro

---

1. *anwealde,* see note.   8. *underrhige,* first *r* corrected from *n,*
second *r* corrected by erasure into *n,* the whole evidently meant for
underhnige.   14. *na si, na* above the line; *n* before and *a* after the *s.*

---

7. MS. *emendaverint.*   8. *correptioni,* MS. *correptionem.*   14. *agad,*
MS. *aga.*   15. *indiget,* corr. from *indigetus* by underdotting the *us.*

gehwẏlcum intingan   on   ænigum gehwilcum   worde intingan
   qualicumque   *causa in aliquo qualicumque*
on ænigum gehwilcum worde   oðða to getacnunge þæt he
causa in aliquo qualicumque verbo vel   significatione   ap-
na ætiwe   þæt gif bið arasod ænig   hefelicor steore
pareat : Quod si deprehensus qui fuerit :   districtiori
stẏðlicor stire he si underþeod
   discipline   *subdatur.*

DE SEPTIMANARIIS COQUINE. (CAP. XXXV.)   5

     heom betwẏnan þenian þæt nan ne si belaðod fram
FRATRES SIBI INVICEM SERVIANT ET NULLUS EXCU*setur*   *a*
cicene þenunge [b.] oðða mettrumnesse oðða on intingan hefigran
coquine officio nisi aut   egritudine aut in causa gravis
      ænig buton he si gebisgod [b.]   for þanon
utilitatis quis   occupatus fuerit.   quia exinde major
mede 7 soðlufu þam þe bið beiẏten þam wacmodum
merces. et caritas   adquiritur.   Inbecillibus   autem
* þe onforsceawunge helpas   mid unrotnessa þæt
   procurentur   solacia ; ut   non cum tristitia hoc 10
he nado ahhi habban ealle frofras   æfter gemete gegæder-
faciant : sed habeant omnes solacia. secundum modum congre-
unge oðða gesetnẏssa stowe gif mare gegaderung   bið
gationis aut positionem loci ; Si major congregatio fuerit.
hordere si belaðod fram   oðða gif hwẏlce swa swa
cellararius excusetur   a   coquina vel si qui   ut
we sædon mid marum nẏtwẏrdnẏssum bẏð gebẏsgode oðre him
diximus   majoribus   utilitatibus   occupantur :   ceteri
sẏlfan undre soðre lufe heom betwẏnan * þeniant se ðe is ut to-
(143 a.) *sibi | sub karitate   invicem   serviant ; Egres-* 15
foranne on ðære ucan on sæternes dæg clænsunga   do
surus de septimana ;   sabbato   munditias faciat ;

---

1. *worde, intingan,* both in very black ink. 10. *onforsceawunge, unge*
has been corrected into *ode,* by underdotting *unge,* and writing *ode* over it,
in the same hand, read *beon forsceawode.* 15. *þeniant, t* owing to the
scribe's eye being caught by the ending of *serviant.*

---

1. *causa in aliquo qualicumque,* with its gloss, is repeated in the MS.
5. MS. SEPTIMANARIS.

[b.] wæterclað mid [c.] þam þe heom sylfan [u.]   handa
Linthea   cum   quibus   sibi   fratres manus.

oððe fet * clipað [a.] he þwea [c.] fett soðlice ge se   se ðe
aut pedes tergunt.   lavet;   Pedes   vero tum ipse qui

utgæð   ge se   se þe is in tofarenne [e.] eallum
egreditur quam ille   qui intraturus   est; omnibus

hi þwean fata þenunge his clæna 7 hale [eb.] hordere he
lavent; Vasa ministerii sui munda et sana cellarario re-

betæce [a.] betæce se hordere eft into farenne dum he
5 *consignet; Qui cellararius iterum   intranti   con-*

betæce þæt he wite hwæt he sylð oððe hwæt he underfo [c.] þa
signet. ut sciat   quid dat aut   quid   recipit; sep-

wucan þegnas [b.] ær   anre [d.] tide gereordunge * mman
timanarii autem   ante unam horam refectionis. accipiant

[d.] forgesetne bileofan [d.] ænlepige [e.] drencas [e.]   [f.]
super statutam annonam   singulos   biberes et panem;

on tide gereordunge buton   ge 7 hefigum geswince
ut hora refectionis sine murmuratione et gravi labore

[g.] þæt hi þenian heora gebroðrum on simbel swa þeah
10   *serviant   fratribus suis; In diebus tamen*

dagum * oððe mæssan hi þolian. abidan [b.] þa in-
solemnibus; usque ad missas   sustineant;   In-

farendan   [c.] 7 þa utfarendan [b.] ucuþena on gebedhuse
trantes autem et   exeuntes   ebdomodarii in oratorio

þarrihtes merigenlicum geendedum on sunnandæge betyridum
mox   matutinis   finitis   dominica   provolutis

cneowum ætforan þam weofode   [f.]   [a.] biddan for hi beon
genibus coram altare ab omnibus postulent pro se

gebedene þa utgangendum   on þære ucan secgan þis
15 *orari; Egredientes   autem de septimana: dicant hunc*

fers gebletsod þu eart eala þu drihten god þu fultumodest
versum; Benedictus es   domine deus qui   adjuvasti

7 þu gefrefredest me þam [c.] gecwedenum þriddan siðan.
me; et consolatus es me;   Quod dicto tertio.

---

2. *clipað*, read *wipað*?   4. *þwean*, there is possibly an *i* between *w*
and *e*, although this is probably part of the *g* of *egreditur* just above it.
5. *ce* of second *betæce* indistinct. *dum*, Latin in glossator's hand. 7. *mman*,
read *niman*. 11. *oððe*, read *oð*.

---

3. *quam*, MS. *quo*.   4. *lavent*, MS. *avet*.   8. *statutam*, MS. *sta-turam*.

hi [a.] underfon [b.] bletsunge utgangende æfter fýlian
*accipiant   benedictionem egredientes ; Subsequunt*ur *aute*m

þa ingangende 7 hi secgan god mine fultum   beiẏm
ingredientes et *dicant;* Deus *in adjutorium meu*m *intende*

eala þu drihte*n* to gehelpanne   efes*ð*   *þæt* sẏlf þriddan si*ð*e

(143 b.)   *domine   ad adjuvandum me festina ; | Et hoc idem tertio*

7 si geedleht fram eallum   afangenre bletsunge 7 he
repetatur   ab omnibus et   *accepta   benedictione ingredi-*

ingan :
antur ;   5

DE INFIRMIS FRATRIBUS. (CAP. XXXVI.)

[c.] untruma[b.] gimen[d.] ætforan eallon þingan. 7 ofer ealle þinc
INFIRMORUM   CURA   ANTE   OMNIA   ET SUPER   OMNIA

is to gearcienna   so*ð*lice   swa þæt sigeþenod
adhibenda est. ut sicut revera christo ita ei serviatur.

forþam þe hesẏlf sæde untruman ic wæs 7 gegeneosodan me
Quia   ipse dixit; infirmus fui; et *visitastis me;*

þæt þæt gedẏdon anum   me hit gedẏdon
Et quod fecistis uni de ís minimis meis mihi fecistis;   10

ah þa sẏlfan untruman   sceawien on wur*ð*mente godes hecm
Sed et *ipsi infirmi   considerent in honorem dei*

sẏlfum beon geþenod 7 mid heora oferflowednesse 7 hine ge-
sibi   serviri; et   *non superfluitate sua contris-*

drefan. heora gebro*ð*ra þeowiende hecm sẏlfan þa swa þeah
*tent fra*tres *suos; servientes sibí; Qui   tamen*

geþẏldelice sind to cepanne forþam swẏlcum genihtsumere
patienter   portandi sunt: quia   de talibus copiosior

med [d.] he bi*ð* beiẏten   [b.] seo mæsta gimen * sit
merces   adquiritur; Ergo   cura maxima   sit 15

þam abbode ænigre gimeleaste þæt hi na þolian þa untru-
*abbati ; ne aliqua*m *neglegentiam   patiantur ;   Quibus*

man gebro*ð*ra   sig hus. cẏte ofer hi betæht 7 þen
*fra*tribus *infirm*is sit *cella super se deputata ; et servitor·*

---

11. *untruman*, first stroke of second *u* probably corr. from *e*.   15. *sit, t*
copied from Latin, read *sig.*

---

4. *repetatur*, MS. *reperetur.   benedictione*, MS. *benedictio.*   7. INFIR-
MORUM, I is forgotten by rubricator. *super*, MS. *supe.*   9. *visitustis*, MS.
visitatis.   11. Erasure before *ipsi.*   14. *quia, i* above line.   17. *infirmis*,
corr. from *infirmus* by erasure. *sit*, corr. from *scit.*

? ★

adrædende   7 lufiænde ac he fulfremed   baða brice
timens   deum. et *diligens ac   sollicitus.   Balnearum usus ;*
þa untruman swa oft swa hit fremeð sigeboden þam halum 7
infirmis   quoties expedit offeratur ;   Sanis autem et
swyðest 7 geonclicum lætlicor si geunnen [a.]   flæsca
maxime   juvenibus   tardius   concedatur ;   Sed et *carnium*
*bæt þam untruman eallunga   þam wanhalum forhæle   ac si
*esus   infirm*is   *omnino debilibus*que *pro reparatione con-*
geseald *þæt onne hi beoð *gebeorode fram flæsclicum midgewune-
5 *cedat*ur *: Ac ubi mel`orati fuerint ;   a   carnibus more solido*
lic þeaw ealle 7 hi forhabban [c.] þa mæsta [b.] gimene habbe
omnes abstineant ;   Curam autem maximam habeat
se abbod fram þam horderum oððe fram þenum þæt ne beo for-
abbas   ne a cellarariis   aut a servitoribus neglegantur
gimeleaste þam untruman forþam to him þehitlocað swa swa
infirmi | quia ad ipsum respicit.   quic- (144 a.)
hwæt fram leornincnihtum swa bið agýld.
quid   a   discipulis   delinquitur.

10   DE SENIBUS VEL INFANTIBUS. (CAP. XXXVII.)

þeah þesig þa sýlfe mænnisnesse gecind [c.]   [e.]
LICET   IPSA   HUMANA   NATURA   TRAHATUR
[f.] to mildheortnesse on þisum ýldum ealdra   7
AD   MISERicordiam ;   in   is aetatibus   senum   videlicet et
cildra þeahhwæðere [c.] regules ealldordomlicnýss heom
infantum ;   tamen et *regule   auctoritas eis*
besceawige si foresceawod æfre wacmodnýss nateshwon
*prospiciad ;   Consideretur   sempe*r *inbecillitas.* et *nullatenus*
heom stiðnis regoles 7 na si gehealdan on   fotum   ac sig
15 *eis   districtio   regule   teneatur   in alimentis ; sed sit*
on heom arfæst foresceawung 7 hi forahrædian minsterlice
in   eis   pia   consideratio : et   *preveniant horas*
tide.
canonicas.

---

4. *bæt*, probably *b* is a 'paving' letter.   5. MS. *þonne*=*þæt* onne ; read
þonne.   gebeorode, read *gebetrode.*   11. *mænnisnesse*, cf. Introd., Ch. V,
§ 67.   15. *fotum*, cf. ib., § 54.

---

3. *juvenibus*, MS. *invenibus.*   4. *infirmis*, corr. from —*us.*   12. *aetatibus*,
MS. *eatatibus.*   15. *teneatur*, MS. *teneat.*   17. MS. *canonicis.*

DE EBDOMEDARIO LECTORE. (CAP. XXXVIII.)

meosan etenda * gebroðrum rædinc wana beon na scell ne
MENSIS FRATRUM EDENTIUM LECT:O DEESSE NON debet ; ne
he on færlicum gelimpe se ðe gelæcð boc rædan
fortuitu casu qui arripuerit codicem legere

negedýrstlæce þæra seðe rædan sceall ealra þæra wucan on þam
audeat ibi. sed lecturus tota ebdomada dominico

drihtenlicandæge ah inga se bidde ingangende æfter mæssan
die ingrediatur ; Qui ingrediens ; post missas 5

7 gemænsumunge oððe huselgange fram eall. m for hi
et communionem petat ab omnibus pro se

beon gebeden þæt awende fra him g modignisse 7
orari ; ut avertat ab ipso deus spiritum elationis ; Et

sigesæd þis færs on cýrican þriddan siðe fram eallum
dicatur hic versus in oratorio tertio ab omnibus.

him sýlf swa þeah frum anginne mine lippan
ipso tamen incipiente. Domine labia mea

þu geopena 7 min muð 7 kýð lof þin [a.] [b.]
aperies : et os meum adnuntiabit laudem tuam Et sic 10

afangenre bletsunge 7 he inga to rædenne healic * smegen
accepta benedictione. ingrediatur ad legendum ; Summumque

7 beo [b.] [c.] æt meosan þæt na æniges * drenc
fiat silentium ad mensam ut nullius musitatio

oððe stefn [h.] buton þæs anes ræderes þær si gehired. |
(144 b.) vel vox : nisi solius legentis ibi audiatur |

[f.] þa þinc [b.] neodbeheofe sind etendum 7 drincendum
Que vero necessaria sunt comedentibus et bibentibus ;

heom sýlf stundmælum þenian [c.] ænig þæt ne behofige
sic sibi vicissim ministrent fratres ut nullus indigeat 15

biddan ænig þinc gif hwilc neod beoð mid býcnunge
petere aliquid. Si quid tamen opus fuerit sonitu

sumes tacnes swiðor sigebeden þonne mid stefne na he ne
cujuscumque signi otius petatur quam voce : Nec pre-

---

2. gebroðrum, through influence of Latin ending for gebroðra. 7. g =
god? 9. frum anginne, see note. first n of anginne above the line.
11. smegen, read swigen. 12. drenc, see note. 13. stefn, e corr. from some
other letter. 16. býcnunge, g corr. from some other letter, c ?

---

3. casu, MS. causu. 4. lecturus, MS. lecturis. 8. versus, MS. vers.
oratorio, MS. oratorii. 12. musitatio, corr. in MS. from musitatione by
the underdotting of ne. 13. legentis, MS. legentes, the e of es being
changed in the MS. from i.

gedýrstlæce þara ænig be þære sýlfan   oððe elles hwanone
sumat   ibi aliquis de   ipsa   lectione aut   aliunde

ænig þing smæigan þæt ne si geseald iŋtingan buton wenunge
quicquam requirere :   ne   detur   occasio ;   nisi   forte

se ealdor fore lare oððe fram trimminge wýlle   ænig þing
prior   pro   aedificatione   voluerit aliquid

scortlice secgan broðor   seo wuca þen nime snædinge
breviter dicere ; Frater autem ebdomedarius accipiat mixtum

ær þan þe he aginne rædan forþam halgum gesumunge   [f.]
5 priusquam incipiat legere. propter   communionem sanctam :

7 þæt na sig   healic   him fæsten forþýldian ·sýððan
et ne   forte   grave sit ei jejunium sustinere ; Postea

             cicenen. mid þam wucuþenum 7   þenum
autem cum coquine   ebdomedariis ;   et servitoribus.

hi gereordiað [c.]   na be endebýrdnesse rædan oððe
reficiat ; Fratres autem non per ordinem legant aut

singan ac þa getrimman þa gehýrandan
cantent sed qui edificent audientes ;

10   DE MENSURA CIBORUM. (CAP. XXXVIIII.)

genihtsumian we gelýfað to dægþerlicere reordunge [c.] gemid
SUFFICERE   CREDIMUS AD REFECTIONEM COTIDIANam :   tam

dæges   ge   nones eallum   monðum twa gesodene sýflian
sexte   quam none omnibus   mensibus   cocta   duo

sanda [g.]   for   mistlicora untrumnessa wenunge
pulmentaria. propter diversorum infirmitates.   ut forte   qui

of anum seðe mæg, etan of oðrum þæt he si gereord þonne
ex uno non potuerit edere ex alio   reficiatur ; · Ergo

twa sanda [i.]   [h.]   [n.]   genihtsumiað 7 gif
15 duo pulmentaria cocta omnibus fratribus sufficiant. Et si

beoð ac hwanone æpla oððe acennedlicu ofetu [g.] asigeglið
fuerint unde poma aut nascentia leguminum addatur

swilce þæt þridde. an pund   awegen   genihtsumige on
et tertium ; Panis libera una propensa   sufficiat | in (145 a.)

dege swa hwæðer [g.] swa [f.] [f.] ðu sig on gereordunge oððe
die.   sive   una sit   refectio.   sive

4. seo wuca þen, see note. 16. asigeglið, I do not understand this gloss.

4. ebdomedarius, MS. ebdomedariis. 6. eĩ, sic in MS. ; in glossator's
handwriting. 14. potuerit, u above line. 16. poma, MS. pomi.

gereordunge 7 æfenþenunge þæt gif hi sceolan on æfen
prandii   et   *cene ;*   *Quod si cenaturi*
gereordian of þam sylfan punde se þridda [c.] fram þam hordere
sunt. *de eadem   libra tertia. pars a   cellarario*
si gehealden to agifenne on æfenþenung*um* [f.] geswinc   [f.]
reservetur. reddanda cinaturis   Quod si labor forte factus
[f.] [g.] mare oncyre [d.]   de [e.] hitbeo gif hit fremað
fuerit major. in arbitrio et potestate abbatis erit si   expediat

[k.] ycan asyndrode toforan eallum þingum oferfylle
aliquid augere remota   pre   omnibus crapula 5
þæt næfre ne undersmæge [m.] þam munece oferæt forþam
ut numquam subripiat   monacho indigeries. quia   nihil
swa wiðerweard þen is   swa swa oferfylle   [s.]
sic contrarium est omni christiano quomodo   crapula :
swa swa sæde ure drihten warniað þæt ne beon geheofogode
sicut ait dom'nus noster. Videte   ne   graventur
[c.] [c.] on oforfull cildum [g.] onginran ylde [h.] seo ylce
corda vestra in crapula. Pueris vero minore   aetate. non eadem
ne si gehealdan micelness ah læsse þonne þam yldrum
servetur quantitas.   sed minor quam   majoribus 10
gehealdanra [m.]   [l.]   * fiðer   * feteflæsð
servata in omnibus parcitate. Carnium vero quadrupedum omnino
[c.]   si * forhæmed   butan wanhalum   7
ab omnibus abstineatur commestio. preter omnino   debiles et
þa * metrunian
aegrotos ;

DE MENSURA POTUS. (CAP. XL.)

anra gehwylc [b.] synderlice [a.] hæfð sylene of gode sume
Unus quisque   proprium   habet donum ex deo *alius* 15

---

3. *æfenþenungum*, corrected from *æfenþenunge*, probably not contemporary.
10. *ne*, the *n* has a stroke through it.   11. *fiðer* over *carnium*, and *feteflæsð*
over *quadrupedum*, probably ought to be partially transposed. Read *flæsca*
(instead of *flæsð*) over *carnium*, and *fiðer fete* over *quadrupedum*.   12. *forhæmed*, read *forhæbben*.   13. *þa metrunian*, read *metruman* (for *med-
truman*).

---

1. *cenaturi*, MS. *cenatur*.   5. *remota*, MS. *premota*.   *omnibus crapula*, *ibus cra* on erasure, MS. *crapuli*.   15. DONUM, a letter erased
between D and O; E ?

soðlice   [a.] [n.] mid sumum   ingehýda
summe sic alius vero   sic. Et ideo cum aliqua scrupulositate.

fram us   7 gemett bigleofa   córa   7 is geðett swa þeah
a nobis mensura   victus   aliorum constituitur :   Tamen

untrumera   [g.]   wacmodnesse   wegelýfað [d.]   gemet
infirmorum contuentes imbecillitatem :   credimus   eminam

wines geonden ænlepige genihtsumian   geon dæg þam þe sýlð
vini   per sinjulos   sufficere   per diem ;   Quibus

       [f.] geþýld [h.]   forhæfednesse   agene   he
5 *autem donat | deus   tolerantiam abstinentie   propriam   se* (145 b.)

silfe   mede   hi witan þæt gif   stowe neodþearfnesse
habituros mercedem sciant ; Quod si aut loci   necessitas

oððe geswinc   [h.]   sumeres oððe swiðlic hæte þæt gif
aut labor   aut ardor aestatis   amplius   popos-

bitt [d.] [b.]   on dome ealdres oððe hi wunige   [i.]   on
cerit   in   arbitrio prioris consistans.   considerans in

eallum þingum na þæt undersmege oferfýlle oððe druncennesse
omnibus   ne   subrepat   satietas aut ebrietas licet

þe we radan eallunga * windred   muneca   beon getiht
10 *legamus   omnino   vinum monachorum persuaderi   non*

[a.] huru þinga huru þinga [g.] þæt   [f.]   þæt þena
potest : saltem vel   hoc consentiamus. ut   non usque

oð oferfýlle drincan   [k.] ac hwoulicor forþam * windrend
ad satietatem libamus sed   parcius.   quia   vinum

wiðersacan þedeð   þa witen · þar þar   neodþearfnessa
apostatare facit etiam sapientes. Ubi   autem   necessitas

stowe   bitt   [d.]   þæt forasædegemed oððe forawritene beon
loci exposcit ut   ne   suprascripta mensura in-

gemett þæt fur ðonne mage ah micel .   [h.] mid ealle
15 *veniri   possit. sed   multo   minus :   aut ex   toto*

naht bletsian god þara   eardiað 7   hi na cýrian
nihil benedicant deum qui ibi habitant et non murmurarent ;

: 7. *hæte* is gloss to *ardor.*   10. **windred**, read *windrenc,* i. e. *windrēc.*
11. *þena*, read *we na,* or more probably read *þe* as belonging to the preceding *þæt.*   12. *windrend*, read *windrenc.*

---

2. *victus*, MS. *victis.*   6. MS. *mercedam.* MS. *necessitate,* corrected
into *necessitas.*   7. MS. *aestas.*   9. *aerietas* in the MS. for *ebrietas.*
10. Before *persuaderi,* the words *non esse, sed quia nostris temporibus id
monachis,* found in the other texts, are omitted.   13. MS. *sapientis.*
16. *deum*, MS. evidently by mistake has *dominum* (*dūm,* for *dm̄*).

þæt　　　minigende　　buton ceorunge þæt hi na
Hoc ante omnia ammonentes. ut absque murmuratione
beon
sint ;

QUIBUS HORIS REFICIUNT FRATRES.　(CAP. XLI.)

fram　þære　haligan　eastran [d.]　　[d.]　　to middæges
A *SANCTO PASCHA USQUE AD PENTECOSTEN AD* SEX*tam*
hi gereordian　　　　　to æfenne 7 hi gereordian fram pente-
reficiant fratres. et *ad seram* cenent ;　A *pente-* 5
costen　　　on eallum sumera geswinc　felda　gif hi nabbað
costen autem tota estate : si labores agrorum non habent
munecas swiðlicnesse sumeras oððe ne gedefð on wodness [c.]
monachi. aut nimietas estatis non perturbat. quarta. et
[b.] dæg [a.] hi fæsten　oð non　　on odrum dagum
(146 a.) *sexta feria jejunent usque ad nonam :* reliquis |
dagum to middæge hi gereordian þa gereordunga to mid
diebus ad sextam prandeant ; Que prandii sexta :
weorcum on æcerum gif hi habbað　sumeres　swiðlic hæte
si opera in agris habuerint. aut aestatis fervor 10
　　　bið to *belippendan bið þæs abbotes hit si on fora-
nimius fuerit : continuanda erit. et *in abbatis sit provi-*
scawunga　　　7 he gemetige ealle þinc and he gedihte
dentia. Et sic temperet omnia atque disponat
　　　saula　　　þæt þæt [c.] hi doð [c.] gebroðra
qualiter et *anime salventur ; Et quod faciunt fratres.*
butan [d.] [d.] ælcere ceorunge 7 don fram anginnum [d.]
absque ulla murmuratione faciant ; A b idibus
　　[e.]　　oð andgin fæstenes [f.]　to nonas
autem septembris usque ad capud quadragesime ad nonam 15
[b.] hi gereordian on lænctene fæsten [b.] oð eastran
semper reficiant. In quadragesima vero usque (in) pasca :

---

4. *middæ* nearly quite erased.　7. *gedefð, ð* very pale ink, read *gedrefð.*
11. *belippendan,* see note.

---

1. MS. *murmurationis.*　5. *fratres, fr* erased, then added at the top, where it is again partially erased.　7. *nimietas, e* add. later, in very pale ink.　9. *prandii, ii* above line, by way of correction to *-eant.* The MS. had originally *prandeant.*　12. MS. *temperit* ; *utque* ; *disponit.*　16. *reficient* in MS.　There is an erasure before *pasca* in the MS. ; of *in* ?

on æfæn   hi gereordian se sẏlfa   æfen   si gedon
ad vesperam   reficiant;   Ipsa   autem vespera sic agatur:
   leoht leohtfætes þæt hine behofian gereordgende mid leohte
*ut lum*en   *lucern*e   *non indigeant reficientes.   sed luce*
˙þagit dæges ealle þinc ah beon gefẏllede ac on ælcere   tide
adhuc diei   omnia   consummentur;   sed et omni tempore
swa æfen þenunge   .   oððe on tỉde swa þus gemedemod [g.]
sive sit cene sive refectionis   hora. sic   temperatur.   ut
mid dæg þæt gewẏrdan ealle þing.
5 *cum luce   fiant   omnia.*

UT POST COMPLETORIUM NEMO LOQUATUR. (CAP. XLII.)

on ælcere tide   swigen   sceolan healdan   munecas swẏðost
Omni tempore   silentium debent   studere   monachi.   maxime
þehhwæðere on nihtlicum tidum 7 forði on ælcere tide sit
tamen   nocturnis   horis. Et ideo omni tempore sive
fæstenes sit gereordung g tima   gif hit bið gereordunge sona
jejunii. sive prandii: si tempus   fuerit   prandii.   mox
þæt hi arisað fram æfen þenunge 7 hi sittan ealle togædere
10 *ut surrexerint a cena.   sedeant   omnes in unu*m.
7 ræde an *þurhtogenes race oððe on ealdfædera lifa oððe
et legat unus   collationes.   vel   vitas patrum.   aut
soðes sum ðinc þæt getȝẏmme þa gehẏrendum
*certe aliquid quod edific*et   *audientes; Non autem epta-*
           forðam untrumum andgitum þena bið
*ticum aut reg*um. | *quia   infirmis   intellectibus non   erit* (146 b.)
nẏtwẏrðlic on ðære tida   þis   gewrit gehẏran on oðrum
utile   illa   hora   hanc   scripturam audire. aliis vero
tidum [c.] beon gerædde gif beoð fæstenes dagas   [a.]
15 *horis   legantur;   Si autem jejunii dies   fuerint.*
gesungenum æfensanga betwux lẏtlum fæce sona hi gan to
dicta   vespera.   parvo   intervallo mox accedant ad
rædinge race oððe recednesse swa swa we bufon sædon 7
lectionem.   collationum   ut diximus.   et

8, 9. *sit, sit,* read *sig*? *sig*? *g tima*, very slight traces of erasure between
g and *tima*; read *gif*?   11. *þurhtogɛnes, s* owing to the influence of Latin
ending? read *þurhtogene.*

---

12. *autem,* corr. from *aurero* by writing *tem* over *vɛro,* and *o* (= *idem*)
over *au.*   15. *legantur, a* corr. from *u.*

geræddum feower oððe fif leafum [p.] [p.]
lectis quattuor. aut quinque foliis vel quantum hora

[q.] eallum becumen togædere [q.] þurh þas
permittit; omnibus in unum occurrentibus per hanc

ẏldinge rædinc gif ænig wenunge on ðam sẏlfum
moram lectionis; Si quis forte in assignato

betæhtum him sẏlfum þingum beon ænig bið gebisgod he
sibi commisso fuerit occupatus oc-

becume ealle togædere gesette hi gefẏllan 7 utgan-
currat; Omnes ergo in unum positi compleant; Et ex- 5

gende fram nihtsangum ænig 7 nasi leaf sẏððan ænigum
euntes a completoriis nulla sit licentia denuo cuiquam

spræcon ænig þing þæt gif bẏð gemett funden [a.] ænig
loqui aliquid; Quod si inventus fuerit quisquam

þisne forgæian stilnesse mid þearfnesse cumena
hanc prevaricari taciturnitatis regulam. si necessitas hospidum

gif ofor becimð wenunga ænigum ænig þinc oððe hate
supervenerit: aut forte abba alicui aliquid jusseret

þæt [a.] beon 7 swẏlce mid healicum gedreoge 7 gemetegunge
Quod tamen et ipsum cum summa gravitate et moderatione 10

arwurðlicor þæt beo
honestissime fiat.

De his qui ad opus dei et admensam tarde

veniunt. (Cap. XLIII.)

to tide godcundre þenunge sona ' þonne bið gehẏred swa
Ad horam divini officii mox ut auditum *fuerit*

beoð tacen eallum forlætenum [h.] swa hwẏlce þinc
signum: relictis omnibus que libet fuerint 15

on handum mid hælicum ofoste [b.] si becumen mid
in manibus summa cum festinatione curratur: cum

gedreoge þeahhwæðere þæt ne ge higeleas mete tender
gravitate tamen. ut non scurilitas inveniat fomitem;

---

2. *becumen,* gloss to *occurrentibus*; read *becumendum.* 17. *higeleas,*
probably the subst. *higeleast* was originally there.

3. *lectionis,* second *i* erased. *in assignato,* MS. *in* has *signato.* 8. *regulam,* not in the MS.; *sine cessitas* in MS. Before these words a line (*regulam
graviori vindicte subjaceat excepto*) has been left out. 9. *aut forte,* MS. *aut-
ferte* in one word, and *t* added above line in the MS. 12. *QVI* not in the MS.

　　　naht goJes weorce na si forasett þæt gif b.ð　　　　to
Ergo nihil　　operi dei　　preponatur;　|　Quod si　　quis　ad (147 a.)
nihtlicum　uhtsangum [o.]　[q.]　[p.]　þas feower and hund-
nocturnas　　vigilias　　post gloriam　　psalmi nonagesimi
nigenteoðan sealmas þane　forþi　　eallunga　teoṅde
　　　quarti　　　quem propter hoc omnino protrahendo et
latlicē we wẏllað beon gesæd　begimð　na　stande on ændebẏrd-
morose volumus　　dici　　occurrerit. non　stet　in　ordine
nesse [b.]　on choro　ac　hæftemæst　ealra　stande oððe on
5　*suo　　in choro.　sed　ultimus　omnium　stet;　aut　in*
stowe þe þe swẏlcum gimelesum　　　[k.]　　asundran geset
loco　　quem　　talibus　neglegentibus seorsum　con-
　　　se abbod þæt he sigewarnod fram him　oððe fram
stituerit　abba.　ut　videatur　ab ipso:　vel　ab
eallum　oððe [o.]　gefẏlledum weorce　　　　mid fulre
omnibus　usque du n　completo　opere　dei publica　satis-
dædbote he behreowsige for þi　[b.]　hi on ðam ẏtemestan stẏde
factione　peniteat;　Ideo autem eos in　　ultimo aut
on sundran we demdon scẏlan standan þæt gesawene fram
10　*seorsum judicavimus.　debere　stare　ut　visi　ab*
eallum　oððe for ðære sẏlfan scame　　he beon gebette [a.]
omnibus. vel pro ipsa verecundia sua emendentur;　Nam
wið utan　on cẏrican gif hi beoð lifað bẏð færunga þẏlc
si foris　oratorio　remaneant:　erit　forte　talis qui
　　　7　he slape　oððe gewislice hi sette him sẏlfan
se aut collocet et *dormiat:　aut　certe　sedeat sibi foris:*
þærute spellungum * geænigtigað 7　beon geseald intinga þam
　　　vel *fabulis　　vacet;　* et　*detur　　occasio*
awẏridan deofle　　　ah ingá　wið innan þæt he forþam
15　*maligno;　Sed ingrediat*ur　*intro.　ut　nec totum*
ne forleose 7　be ðam oðrum hi si gebet on dægðerlicum
　　　*perdat　　* et　*de　reliquo emendetur;　Diurnis*

　2. [o.] [q.] [p.] are partly pasted over.　　3. *teonde, eo* quite indistinct.
4. *lallicē,* sic in MS., but the stroke may be the remnant of a letter
erased after *quarti. begimð,* i. e. *becimð.*　6. *gimelesum, le* not quite
clear, probably *gimeœsum* was in the MS. first, then *l* was added through
the *œ,* making it into *gimelesum.*　14. *geœnigtigað* or *geœmgtigað;* read
geœmtigað.

　2. *vigiliis* in MS.　　3. *i* erased after *quarti.*　　4. *morose, r* corr. from
another letter.　　6. *talibus,* MS. *alibus.*　　8. MS. *ominibus. satis-,*
MS. *sitis-.*　　11. *sua,* put in later.　　15. *intro, t* added above line.
16. *relinquo, ēĕ* (= *esse*) *mendetur* in the MS.

tidum [o.]   [d.]   [c.]
autem horis qui   ad   opus dei post versum et gloriam

þæs forman sealmas þe   biðgesungen se ðe na
primi   psalmi   qui post   versum · dicitur   non occur-

becymð [d.] on æ onðære þe we bufan sædon   on
rerit.   lege   ,   qua supra   diximus in

ðære ýtemestan stowe he stande ne he negedýrstlæce beon
ultimo stet :   nec   presumat

gefærlæht   sin   oð fulre dædbote   buton
sociari choro psallentium   usque ad   satisfactionem. nisi 5

            leafe   sýlle be his þafunge [x.] [y.] [z.]
forte abbas licentiam dederit permissionem suam : ita tamen :

        þæt he gebete scýldig þanonforð |
(147 b.) *ut satisfaciat   reus ex hoc ;   Ad mensam | autem qui ante*

        se de ne becýmð þæt he sette   singan   7
versum   non ocurrerit :   ut   simul omves dicant versum et

hi gebiddan 7 hi under anum ealle genea!æcan to meosan þurh
orent.   et ,   sub   uno omnes accedant ad mensam : qui

his gýmeleaste   oððe leahtor se ðe ne becýmð oð
per neglegentiam suam aut vitium   non   occurrerit : usque 10

oþre siðe [c.]   for þisum leahtre he si geþread [a.]   eft
ad secundam vicem   pro   hoc   corripiatur ; Si denuo

gif he hit na gebet   [c.]   gemenelicere meosan
non emendaverit   non permittatur   ad mense   communis

to dælniminge ac he geasindrod [h.] fram geferıædene   [k.]
participationem :   sed sequestratus   a consortio   omnium

reordige ana ætbrodenum his dæle [n.] of wine   [p.]
reficiat solus :   sublata   ei portione sua de vino : usque ad

oð fulre   dædbote   swa gelice [b.] he þolie se ðe na
satisfactionem ét emendationem ; Similiter autem patiatur. qui 15

        ættan ferse [d.]   bið andwerd þæt bið æfter mete
ad illum versum non fuerit presens : qui   post cibum

gesungen ne ne gedýrst quam læce þare forasetan̄ tide
dicitur ;   Nec quis presumat   ante   statutam   horam :

---

1. [d.] not quite clear.   16. *ættan* for *æt þam.*   17. *ne ne gedýrst quam
læce*; read *ne ne gedýrstlæce*; *quam*, though belonging to *quis*, is in the
hand of our glossator.

---

14. *de vino*, MS. *divino.*   16. *ad*, MS. *et.*

oðð̇e æfter syð̇ð̇an ænig þing metes ge sægde drencg underfon
aut   postea   quicquam   cibi   ait   potus presumere ;
ahhe gif enigum bið bebedum æni þing fram þam ealdre
Sed   si   cui   offertur   aliquid   a priore

7 underfon 7 he wið sæcð on tide þæt on þare þe he gewilnað
et   accipere   renuntierit.   hora   qua   desideraverit.

[d.] þæt he þæt æfte þæt þæt he wið soc oðð̇e   eallunga
hoc   quod   prius   recusavit.   aut aliud omnino

naht na underfon   æt fulre dædbote gecwemlice
5 *nihil   accipiat :   usque ad emendationem congruam ;*

DE HIS QUI EXCOMMUNICANTUR QUOMODO SATIS FACIANT.

(CAP. XLIIII.)

for healicum gylte fram gebedhuse 7 *fram* beode se þe bÿð
QUI PROGRAVI CULPA AB ORATORIO *et   mensa   excom-*
amansumad on tide on þæt godes weorc on cyrcean þær bið wurðod
municatur: hora   qua   opus   dei   in oratorio percelebratur :
ætforan dyran   aþreht alinge naht secgende buton þæt an
10 *ante foras oratorii prostratus jaceat nihil dicens : nisi tantum*
ahyldum on eorðan heafde pro afered eadmod ealra of
posito   in   terram capite: Stratus   pronus omnium de
cyrcean utgangendre mid fotum 7 þæt swa lange do
oratorio exeuntium   pedibus Et hoc tam diu faciat :
oðð̇æt [s.]   deme   fullice gebed   se þonne
usque   dum abbas | judicaverit satisfactum esse ; Qui dum (148 a.)
he gehaten fram   cÿmð abetyrne þam sylfan
jussus   ab   abbate. venerit : volvat se ipsius abbatis
fotum syð̇ð̇an eallra fotswaþum broðra þæt hi gebiddan
15 *pedibus. deinde omnium vestigiis fratrum : ut   orent*
for him 7 þonne gif hæt   he si underfangen on chore
pro ipso: Et tunc si jusserit abba ; recipiatur in choro
oðð̇e on eddebÿrdnysse þar þar   gement swa *vel* plane
vel in   ordine :   quo   abba decreverit : ita sane

---

1. *underfon, f* corr. from *r.*   2. *bebedum, bo* above the line ; read *beboden.*   8. *fram* (second). The MS. has *fr̃a.*   10. *ætforan, ran* seems to be blotted. *apreht,* for *astreht. alinge,* originally *alincge,* for *alicge.* 11. *pro* in glossator's hand.   14. *abetyrne, a* ' paving' letter?

---

1. *cibi,* MS. *ubi. ait* must be a very old mistake for *aut,* since a glossator, meaningless, has provided it with the gloss *sægde.*   11. *pronus* added by glossator. *de* corrected from two other letters.   13. *satisfuctum, t* corr. from another letter by erasure.   14. *ab* omitted in the MS.   16. *si, i* corrected from *e.*

sealm   oð̄ð̄e   antemn   oð̄ð̄e   rædinge   oð̄ð̄e   hwæt   æni   þing
ut psalmum.   ut antiphonam   seu   lectionem   vel   aliud   quid

ne gedẏrstlæce on gebedhuse aginnan   buton eft se abbod
non presumat   in oratorio   imponere: nisi   iterum   abba:

hate   7   on eallon tidum þænne þe bið̄ gefylled godes weorc
jubeat   Et omnibus   oris   dum   completur   opus   dei

nið̄er   alenge hine sẏlfne on eorþan on stowe on þam ð̄e
proiciat   se   in terram in loco   quo

stẏnd   7   swaful gebete 7 *hihtt oð̄ð̄æt   him hate eft
stat.   et sic   satisfaciat   usque dum   ei jubeat iterum 5

    þæt he geswice eallunga fulredædbote fram þissere
abba ;   ut   quiescat jam   ab hac satisfactione ;   Qui

fram leohtum gẏltum þa ð̄e beoð̄ amansumode þæt an fram
vero pro   levibus culpis   excommunicantur   tantum   a

meosan on cẏrican hit gebeta oð̄hige   hæse   þæt abbotes
mensa : in oratorio satisfaciant : usque ad jussionem   habbatis

þæt fremman   oð̄ð̄e   bletsige 7 he secge genohhit is.
Hoc perficiant usquedum beneficiat et   dicat   sufficit ;

DE HIS QUI FALLUNTUR IN MONASTERIO. (CAP. XLV.)   10

gif ænig þonne   he aginð̄   sealm   repse   oð̄ð̄e an-
Si quis dum pronuntiat psalmum responsorium. aut anti-

temp   leogð̄   rædinge butan þurh fulre dædbote
phonam.   vel fallitur   lectionem   nisi   per   satisfactionem

þara toforan   eallum   geadmet   he beo   mare wrace
ibi coram omnibus   humiliatus   fuerit :   majori   vindicte

he underhnige witodlice se ð̄e nolde mid eadmodnesse þreagian
subjaceat :   quippe   qui noluit   humilitate   corrigere :

þæt þæt he agelte mid gimeleaste   cildra
quod   neglegentia   deliquid ; Infantes autem 15

for swilcum gẏlta * beimbeswugen.
pro tali culpa   vapulent ;

---

4. *alenge,* cf. 78. 10 ; originally *alencge,* for *ale·ge.*   5. 7 *hihtt,* quid ?
13. *ge admet,* erasure of one letter (*e* ?) after *ge-*.   15. *he* above line.
16. *be imbeswugen,* or *beon beswugen* ? Indistinct.   Understand : *beon*
beswungen.

---

9. *Hoc,* corrected from *non* in the MS.   10. MONASTERIO.   All the
other texts have ORATORIO (cf. Schröer, W. V., p. 94 ; Schmidt, p. 49).
12. *fallitur.* Above *ll* there is the sign of contraction for *ur*. It has
been torn asunder by the stretching of the MS. consequent upon and
necessitated by the MS. being pasted up after the fire.

DE HIS QUI IN LEVIBUS REBUS DELINQUUNTUR. (CAP. XLVI.)

gif   * spinð on ænigum geswince innon cicena on hederne
SI QUIS DUM IN LABORE   QUOVIS IN COQUINA IN   CELLARIO.   (148 b.)
on þenunge on bæcerne   on orcerde on ænigum cræfte
in ministerio, in pistrino ; in orto   in arte aliqua.   dum
     oððe on swa hwilcere stowe æni þing he agild oððe
laborat. vel in quocumque loco aliquid   deliquerit ut aut
tobrýt   ænig þinc   oððe forlýsð gif
5 regerit quippiam.   aut perdiderit sive aliud quid excesserit
þær ubi 7 hesýlf cumende þærrihte toforan þam abbode
ibi   et   non veniens continuo ante abbatem.

oððe to gegaderunge hit na sýlf willes gebete 7 he gefremmað
vel congregationem ipse ultro satisfecerit et prodiderit
    his gilt   þonne he þurh oðerne   cuð   hit bið
delictum suum :   dum per alium   cognitum   fuerit
maran bote underhnige   saule [m.] sýnne
    majori   subjaceat emendationi ; Si anime vero peccati
intinga gif beoð lettinge þæt an þam abbude oððe gastlicum
10 causa fuerit latens.   tantum   abbati   aut spiritalibus
ealdrum   he geswutelige   þa cunnan gelacnian heora
senioribus patefaciat.   qui   sciant   curare   sua :
ælfremeda wunda   na abarian 7 geswutelian
et aliena vulnera non detegere aut publicare ;

(DE SIGNIFICANDA HORA OPERIS DEI.) (CAP. XLVII.)

           godes   dæges 7 nihtes sig caru þæs
NUNTIANDA HORA OPERIS DEI DIE NOCTUQUE SIT cura
abbotes oððe hesýlf cýðan oðrum   hohfullum breðer
15 abbatis : aut ipse nuntiare : aut tali solicito fratri
oððe betæce þas gimene þæt þæt   · ongedafenlicum timan
injungat hanc curam : ut   omnia horis competentibus

---

2. spinð, read swinð, for swincð, and take it as gloss to laborat in l. 4.
3. in orto in glossator's hand.   6. ubi written by glossator.   11. Erasure
after geswutelige.

---

2. COUINA in MS.   3. aliqua, MS. aliquo.   6. veniens, MS. invens.
7. prodiderit, MS. perdiderit.   10. MS. fuerint. tantum, tantem
in MS., but the correction is indicated by writing u over e.   12. After
aliena, vulnera is written above the line, possibly by glossator.   detegerœ in
MS. et instead of aut.   13. The title of Chapter XLVII not being found
in our MS., it has been supplied from the other MSS.   16. injungat, MS.
injugat.

beon gefẏllede sealmas soðlice oððe antiphonas æfter þam abbode
compleantur; Psalmos autem vel *antiphonas post   abbatem*
be heora ændebẏrdnesse þam þe b.ð gehaten hi aginnan singan
ordine suo quibus jussum fuerit   inponant; Cantare

7 rædan ne ne gedẏrstlæce buton se ðe mæg þa sẏlfan
autem et legere non presumat: nisi   qui potest ipsum
þenunge welgefullan þæt beon getimbrode þa gehẏrendum þæt
officium bene implere. ut   aedificentur   audientes;   Quod

7 mid ege beo 7 þam þe hæt.
cum humilitate: et gravitate: et tremore fiat: cui jusserit 5

abbas;

De opere manuum cotidiano. (Cap. XLVIII.)

idelnes feond is sawle 7 forþi ongewissum tidum
Otiositas inimica est anime; et ideo   certis *temporibus*
beon gebisgode scealan   on geswince handa   onge-
(149 a.) *occupari   debent fratres in labore manuum:* | *certis*
wissum eft tidum on godgundre rædinge 7 forþi þissere
iterum horis in   lectione divina.   Ideoque   hac 10
we gelẏfað æiwheþera tida beon geendebẏrde
dispositione credimus utraque tempora   ordinari.   id est
oðclẏpunge þæs nigeþan monþas on ærne utgangende
a pascha   usque ad kalendas octobris   mane   exeuntes
fram primsange oððe fullan feorðan tida   hi swican
a   prima: usque ad horam pene quartam: laborent
þæt þæt beoð nẏdbehefe   fram tide   þære feorðan
quod   necessarium   fuerit; ab hora autem   quarta
oðða sẏxtan tide   hi æmtian æfter þære sẏxtan
usque ad horam sextam lectioni vacent;   Post sextam 15
tida arisende   hi geresten on heora beddum mid
autem surgentes a mensa   pausent in lectis suis cum
eallum swige oððe wenunga se ðe wẏle him sẏlfan rædan
omni silentio: aut forte qui voluerit sibi   legere.
swa ræde þæt oðer he ne gedrefe sigedon   gemetlicor
sic legat ut alium non inquietet; Agatur nona temperius

10. *godgundre,* second *g* corr. from *t.*   13. *fallan,* gloss as if the lemma
were *plene.*

1. *Psalmus* in MS.   2. *jussum, jussus* in the MS., and the first *u*
added later.

G

midwengendum þære ehta tide   þæt þæt eis towýrcanne
mediante   octava hora : et iterum   quod faciendum

hi wýrcan oððe æfan   [a.] [b.] neodbehefnes
est operentur usque ad   vesperum ; Si autem   necessitas

stowe oððe *þearflices giforcrafað   wæsmas togegaderigenne
loci aut paupertas   exegerit ut ad fruges   colligendas

þurh hi þæt hi beon gebisgode hi na beon gedrefede forþam
per   se occupentur   non contristentur :   quia

þonne soðan munecas   þurh *gespinð heora handa
5. *tunc veri   monachi sunt ; si   labore manuum suarum*

gif hi libbað swa swa   ure fæderes
vivunt.   sicut et patres nostri et apostoli ; Omnia tamen

gemetelice beon forþam wac modum   fram clýpunge
mensurate fiant : propter pusillanimes ; A   calendis autem

oð anginn længtenfæsten on þa oðran fulran tide
octobribus usque ad caput quadragesime :   usque   in horam

rædinge hi æmtian se oðer tida on ðære ucan s'gedon
secundam plenam lectioni vacent ; Hora   secunda   agatur

undern   on heora weorc 7 hi geswican
10 *tertia ; et usque ad nonam omnes in opus suum   laborent*

þæt bið   betæht   gewordenum   forecnýll þære
quod eis injungitur ;   Facto   autem primo signo hore

nontide hi geðeodan fram heora weorce ænlepie 7 hi beon
none : disjungant se ab opere suo   singuli. et sint

gearwe þonne þone oðerne cnýll   cnýlð æfter gereordunge
parati : dum secundum signum | pulsaverit ; Post refectionem (149 b.)

hi æmtian heora rædingum   oððe on sealmum
autem vacent   lectionibus suis aut psalmis ; In

længtenes fæstenes   on dagum fram ærne merien oð ðære
15 *quadragesime vero   diebus a   mane usque   ad*

þriddan tide   emtian *heorædingum   oðða
tertiam   plenam vacent lectionibus suis. et usque ad

---

1. *midwengendum*? *n* may be *r*; perhaps read *midligendum*. *eis*, Latin,
or *e* 'paving letter'? 3. *þearflices*, i. e. *þearflicnes*. *giforcrafað*, see note.
5. *gespinð*, read *geswinð*. 7. *clypunge*, *l* above line. 8. *on*, *n* corr. from
other letter: *ð*? 11. *forecnýll*, read probably *forme cnyll*. 12. *heora*, *h*
indistinct. 15. *længtenes*, *læng* not quite clear. 16. *heorædingum*, read
heora rædingum.

---

1. MS. *faciendam*. 3. *exierit* in the MS. 4. MS. *occupaentur*.
5. *labore*, MS. *labores*. 6. MS. *viunt*. 9. *secundam*, MS. *secundum*.
16. *lectionibus*, MS. *lectiones*.

fullan teoðan tida   hi wýrcan þæt heom beoð betæht
*decimam horam plena*m operentur   quod   eis injungitur.

on þam dagum lænctenfæsten * hiderfan ealle ænlepige
*In quibus diebu*s quadragesime. accipiant omnes singulos

bec of boc cýstan þa hi be endebýrdnesse eall abutan
codices de bibliotheca quos per   ordinem   ex integro

rædan þa bec sýnd to sýllanne on anginne   fæsten
legant ;   Qui codices :   in caput quadragesime dandi

toforan eallum þingan   wislice si betæht an oððe
sunt ;   Ante omnia   autem sane deputetur unus aut 5

twegen ealdres þa emfaran   mýnster on tidum þam hi
duo seniores: qui cýrcumeant monasterium · horis   quibus

gcæmtian   ræding 7 hi gewarnian þe læs þe si gemet
vacant fratres lectioni. et videant.   ne forte inveniatur

asolcen   se ge emtige idelnesse oððe spellingum 7
frater accidiosus :   qui vacet   otioso   aut fabulis   et

he nis   geornfull   7 he nis þæt an him unnýt wurðe
non est intentus lectioni : et non solum   sibi inutilis est.

ac he   oðre upahefð þes þýllice   þæt feorsi gif he bið
sed etiam alios extollit : hic talis si quod absit   reper- 10

gemet   si geþread æne 7 oðre side þæt an gif he hit
tus fuerit. corripiatur semel et secundo ;   si non emen-

na gebett regollicere þreaiunge   be þam elles swa
daverit correptioni regulari subjaceat :   et taliter

þæt oðre þæt ondıædað ne ne   to breðer
ut ceteri   timeant ; Neque frater ad fratrem jungatur :

on ungedafenlicum tidum on þam drihtelicum dæge rædinge
*horis incompetentibu*s: Dominico die   lectioni

hi emtian ealle asindrodum þisum   mislicum þenungum
vacent   omnes   exceptis his   qui variis   officiis 15

þa þe sýnd betæhte gif ænig soðlice   gimeleas oððe asolcen
deputati   sunt : Si quis vero ita neglegens et desidiosus

bið þæt nele   oððe ne mage smægan oððe an
fuerit : ut non velit ;   aut non possit meditari aut legere.

---

2. *hiderfan*, read *hi underfan*.   9. *þæt*, *þ* corrected from or into *ð*.
14. *on*, indistinct.   17. *an*, merely ending of *(ræd)an* to denote infinitive.

---

1. *injungitur*, MS. *ingungitur*.   3. *quos*, MS. *quas*.   4. *Qui*, MS. *quia*.
7. *inveniatur*, MS. *inveniat*.   13. *timeant*, MS. *timcat*.   15. *vacent*,
MS. *veacent*.   17. *velit*, MS. *fuelit*.

si betæht him   weorc þæt   he do   þæt he ne ge æmtige
injungatur   ei   opus   quod faciat :   ut non vacet. | (150 a.)
þa [c.] untruman [b.] gebroðran [c.] oððe [d.] estfullum
*Fratrib*us *autem.*   *infirmis.*   *aut   delicatis :*
swýlcum [c.] weorca oððe ... æft oððe si geþeoda þæt [f.] hi
talis   opera   aut   ars   injungatur :   ut nec
forðanne idele   na hina mid stiðnessa geswing beon [i.] of-
otiosi   sint.   nec   violentia   laboris   oppri-
sette   þæt [f.] hi beon aflingede þara   * wacmodes fram
5 *mantur :   ut effugentur ;   Quorum inbecillitas   ab*
þam abbote is to forsceawiende
abbate   consideranda   est ;

DE QUADRAGESIME OBSERVATIONE. (CAP. XLVIIII.)

[l.] þeh þe on ælcere [q.]   lif [m.] munecas lænctenfæstenes
LICET   OMNI   TEMPORE VITA MONACHI QUADRAGESIME
sceale 7 gehealdsumnesse [p.] [o.] forþam þe is forþam feawera
debeat   observationem   habere.   tamen   quia   paucorum
þe is þeos miht [a.] we atihtað on [b.] þisum dagum læncten-
10 *est ista virtus.   ideo suademus   istis diebus   quadra-*
fæstenes [c.] [f.] on ælcere clænnesse heora lif [e.]
gesime.   omni   puritate   vitam   suam
[d.]   [h.] 7 ealra   heora gimeleasnesse [c.] [h.]
custodire :   et   omnes pariter   neglegentias   suas
          oðra tida on þisum halgum dagum adlian þæt [a.]
aliorum temporum   his   diebus sanctis diluere ; Quod
[b.] wýrðlice bið [a.] gif fram eallum leahtrum [e.]   [d.]
tunc   digne sit :   si ab   omnibus   vitiis temperemus ;
7 gebede [d.] mid wopum [f.] 7 onbrýrdnesse [g.] [h.]
15 *Orationi   cum fletibus lectioni et compunctioni cordis*
7 [a.] forhæfædnesse [g.] gimene uton [a.] sýllan on þisum
atque abstinentie   operam demus ;   Ergo his diebus
uton don   sum þinc ![d.] gewunelicne [c.]   gafol
augeamus   nobis   aliquid   ad solitum   pensum

---

3. ... *æft*, nearly illegible, read *cræft*. 5. *aflingede*, *n* under the line ;
cf. Introd., V. § 70. *wacmodes*, read *wacmodnes*. 9. *forþam þe*, dittography.
11. [c.] or [i.] ? 17. [c.] not quite clear ; may be part of *d* (of *adsolitum*).

5. *effugentur*, MS. *effugatur*. 7. The title in the MS. is DE XL*
OBSERVATIONE. 9. *paucorum*, MS. *paveorum*. 13. *sanctis*, possibly in
glossator's hand. *diluere*, MS. *defluere*. 16. *operam*, MS. *operum*. *his*
added by glossator. 17. *augeamus* in glossator's hand ; its gloss, *uton don*,
would make us think that the glossator has read *agamus*.

ures þeowdomes [f.]   sinderlices gebedu [g.]   [g.]
　　servitutis　　　　*nostre.*　　　　*Orationes*　　　*peculiares.*

metta　7　drencas [h.] for hæfednesse [i.] 7　anra gehwylc
ciborum et *potus*　　*abstinentiam ;*　　*Et*　*unusquisque*　*super*

　　　　him sylfum on þam foresædan gemette sum þinc
mensuram　　　　*sibi indictam :*　　　　　　*aliquid*

mid agenum [s.] willa [r.]　mid gefean [o.]　þæs halgan gastes
　propria　　*voluntate*　*cum gaudio*　　*sancti spiritus*

ofrige gode　　　　he ætbrede his lichaman　　of mette 7 of
offerat deo ; id est　*subtrahat*　　*corpori*　*suo de cibo :　de* 5

drencu of slæpe　7　of spræce　7 of higeleaste 7 [a.] he and [c.]
potu :　de somno. de loquacitate : de scurilitate :　　et　　*cum*

gastlicere gewilnunge mid gefean [c.] mid blisse haligum [b.]
spiritalis　desiderii　　　　*gaudio*　　　　*sanctum*

eastran bidige [a.]　[b.] þæt sylfe [b.]　þeahwære [c.]　þæt [d.]
pascha exspectat ;　*Hoc*　*ipsum*　　*tamen*　　*quod*

anra　　[e.]　beode his [f.] abbode [f.]　he tihte　7 hit beo [g.]
unusquisque offert ;　*abbati*　*suo suggeret ;*　　et　　*cum*

mid his gebede [g.]　bene [g.]　7 [i.]　　[i.]　　forþam þæt [m.]
(150 b.)　*eius*　　*fiat*　　*oratione*　et　*voluntate ;*　*quia | quod*　10

buton [n.] willan [e.]　buton gastlices fæderes þe he bið [n.]
　sine　　　　　　*patris spiritalis*　*fiat voluntate.*

dyrstignesse þe biþ geteald　7　na ideles [p.] wuldres [q.] buton
presumtioni deputabitur :　et　*vane*　　*glorie*　*non*

wið [p.] meten　　mid　willan　þæs abbodes ealle þinc
　mercedi ;　*Ergo cum voluntate*　*abbatis*　　*omnia*

sind to donne
agenda sunt ;

DE FRATRIBUS QUI LONGE AB ORATORIO LABORANT AUT　15
IN VIA SUNT. (CAP. L.)

[b.]　[i.] þa eallunga [k.] feor synd on geswince [m.] 7 hi na
FRATRES　QUI OMNINO LONGE SUNT IN　LABORE　et *non*

magon ongenbecuman [p.] ongedafenlicere [q.] tide to [p.] mynstre
possunt occurrere　　*hora*　　*competenti*　*ad*

---

6. *he and, and* belongs to the *bidige* of l. 8.　8. *bidige* ; see note to l. 6.
di above the line.　　13. *meten,* a mistake for *mede ?*

---

2. *potus,* MS. *potius,* but *i* underdotted.　　5. *de cibo,* MS. *decimo.*
7. *desiderii,* MS. *desiderio.*　　15. MS. GONGE, AD.

[r.] se abbod [s.] þæt [r.] andgit þæt þæt swa is
oratorium et *abbas* *hoc* *perpendit* *quia* *ita est:*
[a.] don þærrihte godes [d.] weorc [d.], [e.] þar þar hi [n.]
agant *ibidem* *opus* *dei* *ubi ope-*
wýrcan[e.] [f.] ege mid godcundum bigænge [g.][h.]*cwuwa
rantur *cum tremore* *div:no* *flectentes* *genua;*
[a.] swa gelice [b.] þa þa on [b.] gange [c.] sýnd [b.] asende [b.]
Similiter *qui* *in* *itinere* *sunt* *directi;*
*hid hi [e.] na for gimeleasian [p.] on gesettere tide [c.] ahhi [h.]
5 *non eos* *pretereant* *hore* *constitute:* *sed*
swa swa hi [k.] magon don [h.] heom sýlfum [l.] 7 [o.] þeow-
ut *possunt* *agant* *sibi* et *servi-*
domes [o.] gafol [n.] hi na forgimeleasað agýldan.
tutis *pensum* *non neglegant* *reddere;*

DE FRATRIBUS QUI NON LONGE SATIS PROFICISCENTUR. (CAP. LI.)

[b.] þa for ænigre andsware þa beoð afarenne
FRATRES QUI PRO QUOVIS RESPONSO PROFICISCUNTUR
7 on þam sýlfan dæge hi hihton gecýrran to mýnstre
10 ET EA *die* *sperant* *reverti* *ad monasterium;*
hina gedýrstlæcan wið utan [d.] etan [c.] [e.] þeah þe
Non presumant. *foris* *manducare:* *etiam*
[e.] beon fram ænigum [f.] men gebedene buton hit sig beboden
si *a* *quovis rogentur:* *nisi*
wununga [i.] fram heora [k.] abbude [k.] heom [g.]
forte *ab* *abbate* *suo* *eis* *precipiatur;*
þæt [b.] gif hi elles doð [b.] hi beon * amsumude.
Quod *si* *aliter* *fecerint:* *excommunicentur;*

15 ## DE ORATORIO MONASTERII. (CAP. LII.)

gebedhus [c.] [b.] þæt sig [a.] þæt hit is [d.] gecweden [d.] ne ne
Oratorium *hoc* *sit* *quod* *dicitur:* *nec*
þær ænig þincg ælles si ge don [d.] oððe [e.] gelod
ibi *quicquam* *aliud* *geratur* *aut* *condatur*

---

3. *bigænge*, see note. *cwuwa*, read *cnuwa*. 5. *hid*, probably *d* is a
paving letter and *hi* dittography. 14. *amsumude*, read *amansumude*.
16. *gebedhus*, *h* above line. 17. *egelod*, see note.

6. *agant*, MS. *agans*, *s* being underdotted, and *t* written over it. 8. SATIS,
MS. STATIS. PROFICISCENTUR, MS. PROFICISCE. 10. MS. *sperantur*.
15. ORATORIO, MS. ORATORII. 16. *Oratorium*, MS. *Ooratorium*.

gefẏlledum weorce [c.]   mid healicum [d.] swige   [b.]
Expleto   opere   dei : cum   summo   silentio

hi utgan 7 si gesungen mid arwẏrðnẏsse [f.] þæt [g.] [b.]
exeant : et agatur   reverentia   deo   ut   frater

[l.] færunga heom sẏlfan [n.] sẏnderlice [m.] se þe wile [m.]
(151 a.) *qui   forte   sibi   peculialiter   vult | orare:*

[g.] na si gele*d*t oðres mid onhrope [a.] 7 gif wile [a.]
non impediatur alterius inprobitate ; Sed et si   aliter

him [g.] sẏlfum wenunga [k.] digelicor gebiddan [i.] andfealdlice
vult   sibi   forte   secretius   orare :   simpliciter 5

ah he inga 7 he gebidde [b.] na mid hludre [d.] stefne [d.]
intret et   oret.   non in   clamosa   voce :

ac on tearum 7 onbrẏrdnesse [f.] heortan [g.] [b.] se þe
sed in lacrimis et   intentione   cordis ;   Ergo qui

gelice weorc na deþ he na si geþafod gefẏlledum [f.] weorce [f.]
simile opus non facit : non permittatur   explicito   opere

bæftan belifan [e.] eallswa hit is geræd   oðer
dei remorari in oratorio   sicut dictum   est. ne alius

lettincge þæt he na þolige.
impedimentum patiatur ;   10

DE HOSPITIBUS SUSCIPIENDIS. (CAP. LIII.)

[b] ealle ofer becumendlicum [b.] cuman [b.] swa swa crist [c.]
OMNES SUPERVENIENTES   HOSPITES :   TAMQUAM

[c.]   forþam [d.] þe his to cweðenne [d.] [e.]
christus suscipiantur.   quia ipse   dicturus   est :

cuma [b.] ic wæs 7 geunderfangenne [c.] [d.] [a.] 7 eallum
hospes   fui : et   suscepistis   me ; Et omnibus

þæslic [b.] wurð menð [b.] 7 si gegearcod [a.] swẏþest [c.]
congruus   honor   exibeatur :   maxime 15

hiwcuðum [d.] geleafan 7 ælþeodigum [f.] [g.] þonne bið
domesticis   fidei   et   peregrinis ;   Ut ergo   nun-

gecẏged [g.] cuma [h.] [a.] si becumen [b.] fram þam ealdre
tiatus   fuerit hospes :   occurratur   ei   a   priore

---

4. *geledt, d* corr. from other letter, *o* ? *onhrope, e* indistinct.   17. *gecẏged.*
In the MS. *ged* is crossed out, and *dd* written over it.

7. *lacrimis,* MS. *lacrimo* ; but *o* underdotted, and *is* written over it.
13. *suscipiantur,* MS. *suspiciantur.*   14. *hospes,* MS. *hos spes. suscepistis,*
MS. *suscepistist,* but the latter *t* underdotted.   16. *peregrinis,* MS. *pere-grinus.*

oð̄ð̄e fram [d.] gebroð̄rum [d.] mid ealre [e.] þenunga [e.]   soð̄re
vel   a   fratrilus :   cum omni   officio kari-
lufe [a.] 7 ærest [b.] hi gebidan [a.] eac samod [c.] 7 swa hi beon [d.]
tatis;   Et   primitus   horent   pariter :   et   sic sibi
gefærlæhte [d.] on sibbe þæt [a.] na sig geboden sibbe   cost
socientur   in pace ;   Quod   pacis   osculum
[a.]   buton þam foresædan   gebeda   for deoflum [f.]
non offeratur ;   nisi   oratione   premissa.   propter
swicunegum [f.]   [f.]   [c.] on ð̄ære sylfan gretinge [c.]
5 illusiones   diabolicas ;   In ipsa   autem   salutatione :
ælc [b.] si [a.] gegearcod ei him   mæð̄   eallum [e.] aweg
omnis   exibeatur.   humanitas ;   Omnibus
cð̄ð̄e cumende [e.] [f.] gewitendum [f.]   cuman   sit [g.] ahyltum
venientibus   sive   discedentibus hospitibus.   inclinato
heafde [g.] [h.]   [h.]   eallum   lichaman   on corð̄an [k.]
capite.   vel   prostrato   omni   corpore ;   in   terram
[b.] crist on [c.] heom si gebeden [a.] se ð̄e bið̄ underfangen
christus   in   eis   adoretur :   Qui et suscipitur ;
underfangenum [b.] [i.] cuman [g.]   beon [a.] gelædde [c.]
10   Susceptis   hospites   ducantur   ad
to gebede 7 sið̄ð̄an [h.] 7 sitte [e.]   ealdor [h.]
orationem. et   postea   sedeat   cum eis prior aut cui
[h.]   [h.] si geræd [a.] ætforan þam cuman seo [c.]
jusserit ipse ; | legatur   coram   ospite   lex   (151 b.)
godcunde lage [c.] þæt [d.] beon getrymede   [e.] 7 æfter þisan
divina   ut edificetur   et post
ælc [f.] him gearcod mæð̄ [f.]   [h.] fæsten fram ealdre
hec omnis ei exhibeatur humanitas ; jejunium   a   priore
si tobroden for [d.] cuman [d.] buton wenunga [f.] healic [g.]
15 frangatur   propter hospitem :   nisi   forte   preci-
dæg [e.] sig [g.] fæstenes se na mage beon * gewænmed [c.]
puus sit dies jejunii qui non possit   violari ;   Fratres
[b.]   [d.] gewunan fæstena [e.]   fylian   wæter [c.]
autem : consuetudinibus jejuniorum prosequantur ;   Aquam in

6. ei, Latin in glossator's hand, under him. mað̄, see note. aweg belongs
to gewitendum in l. 7.   7. sit, Latin, or a misreading for sig, belonging
to si gebeden (l. 9).   10. [c.] or [e.]?   12. [c.] not clear.   14. [h.]?
or [k.]? or hc = autem ?   16. gewænmed, read gewæmmed.

9. adortur, MS. adorietur. suscipitur, MS. suspicitur.   10. Susceptis
in the MS. (read suscepti); a very old mistake, which has been glossed
accordingly.   14. jejunium, MS. junium.   15, 16. precipuus, MS. precipius.

on handum [d.] [b.] [a.]   cumum   sylle [a.] fete [g.]   [f.]
manibus   abba   hospitibus   det ;   Pedes   vero

[h.]   eallum cuman ge se abbod ge eall seo gæderunga [k.]
hospitibus   omnibus   tam abba   quam   cuncta

[k.]   þwea [e.] þam geþwagenum [c.]   þis fers   [b.]
congregatio   lavet ;   Quibus   lotis :   hunc   versum

hi seccan we underfengan   on mideweardan
dicant.   suscepimus   deus misericordiam tuam in   medio

[f.] þearfena 7 * eall þeodscipa swyðest underfangenra
templi tui ; Pauperum et peregrinorum   maxime susceptionum 5

giman [h.] hohfullice [a.]   si gegearcod forðam   on   heom
cura   sollicitate   exhibeatur.   quia   in   ipsis

swiðor [k.]   [g.]   scdes [a.] bið   [h.]
magis   christus suscipitur ;   Nam   divitum terror :

[b.] him sylfan [a.]   [a.] wurðment cicena [b.] þæs abbodes 7
ipse   sibi   exigit honorem ; coquina   abbatis   et

cuman [d.] ofer [e.] hig [e.] sig [a.] 7 ongewissum tidum ofer
ospitum   super   se sit :   ut   incertis   horis

[h.] becumenlice [h.]   [h.] þam þe næfre ne ateriað   [k.]
supervenientes   hospites   qui numquam   desunt 10

[l.] minstre þæt hina gedræfan gebroðra on þa cicenan [c.]
monasterio :   non   inquietent fratres ; In   quam

[c.]   to eare [d.] ingan [a.] twegen [b.] gebroðra
coquinam   ad   annum   ingrediantur   duo   fratres :

þa [e.] sylfum þenunge [g.]   [g.]   [f.] bene   [e.]
qui   ipsum   officium   bene   impleant.

þam [k.] behofiað þæt hi helpan [k.] beon [h.] geþenode [l.]
quilus   ut   indigent solacia ministrentur.   ut

buton ælcere [m.] ceorunge [m.] þæt hi [l.] þeowian. [n.] [o.]
absque murmuratione   serviant ;   et iterum 15

þonne hi habbað læssan * gemysgunge [t.]   [t.]   [s.]
quando   occupationem   minorem   habent :

7 hi utgan [n.] þar [p.] þar [q.] bið [p.] beboden on
exeant   ubi   eis   imperatur   in

---

5. *eall þeodscipa = ællþeodscipa*, glossed as if the lemma were *peregrina-
tionum.*   7. Over *suscipitur* there is a 'paving' letter, which is either
two *f*'s above each other, or *f* over *x*.   10. *ateriað*, a dot or a small *c* over
er ; possibly an *o*, making it into *ateoriað.*   13. *bene*, copied from the Latin.
16. *gemysgunge*, read *gebysgunge.*

---

7. *suscipitur*, MS. *suspicitur.*   9. *horis*, MS. *horet*, but *et* underdotted,
and *is* written over it.

weorce 7 na þæt an [c.] [c.]   on heom [e.] ah on eallum [e.]
opera ;   Et   non solum in ipsis :   sed in omni-
þenungum [e.]   mýnstres [b.]   sig [a.] þeos foresceawunga [b.]
 bus   officiis mona | sterii ista   sit   considerat'o.   (152 a.)
þæt þonne hi behofiað · [i.]   helpas   beon befæste
ut   quando   indigent : solacia accommodentur eis :
[k.]   [l.]   þonne hi [n.] æmtiað [n.] 7 hi hirsumiað bebo-
et iterum   quando   vacant   obediant   imper-
denum [c.] [d.] [e.]   cumena [f.] habbe betæht hus [b.]
5 anti; Item et cellam   hospitum   abeat asignatam frater.

þæs   sawle godes [h.]   ege [h.]   he geahnige þar beon
cuius anima   timor   dei   possidet ;   ubi sint

bedreaf   genihtsumlice [m.] [n.] [n.] fram wissum mannum
lecti strati sufficienter.   et domus dei a   sapientibus

wislice 7 si geþenode [m.]   cuman   [b.] þam þe na bið
sapienter amministretur ;   Hospitibus autem cui non pre-

bebcden nateshwon na sigefærlæht ne ne sig   gesprecan
cipitur : nullatenus   societur   neque   conloquatur.

7 gif he agen   cýmð   oððe he gesihð gegrettum [l.] swa
10 sed et si   obviaverit aut   viderit :   salutatis humi-

swa hit [m.] is her bufan gesæd [m.]   gebedenra [k.]
 liter   quod dictum   est :   et petita

bletsunga [k.] ah he ga [i.] [n.] [p.] na beon alifæd
benedictione   peitranseat dicens sibi   non   licere

samod spræcon mid cuman
conloqui   cum hospite.

VT NON DEBEAT MONACHUS LITTERAS VEL ELOGIAS

15   SUSCIPERE. (CAP. LIV.)

 naht   na si alifed þam   nafram his magum
Nullatenus   liceat   monacho neque a parentibus suis :

nafrom ænigum mannan   heom betweona
 neque quoquam hominum : nec sibi invicem litteras. eulogias :

oððe ænige   lac   underfon oððe syllan buton bebode
vel quelibet munuscula accipere aut dare sine precepto

3. accommodentur, MS. accommedentur.   6. anima, MS. animor.
sint, added by glossator.   8. sapienter, MS. sipienter. hospitibus, MS.
hospotibus.   10. obriaverit, ve above line.   15. suscipere, MS. suscipe.
18. munuscula, MS. munusculpa.

þæs abbodes þæt gif bi𝆑 eac swýlce fram his   magum
abbatis.   Quod   si   etiam   a   parentibus suis

him ænig þinc gesend   he na gedýrstlæce underfon þæt
ei quicquam directum fuerit : non presumat suscipere illud. nisi

ærest buton hit beo geꞅæd þam abbode þæt gif he hæd
prius indicatum fuerit   abbati ;   Qucd si   juserit

beon underfangen   sig on * anfealde þam þe he þæt
suscipi.   in abbatis sit   potestate.   cui   illud

hæt sýllan 7 he na si gedræfed   þam þe hit bi𝆑
jubead dare :   et   *non contristetur* frater *cui   forte* 5

gesent   þæt na si geseald intingu þam deofle ꞅe 𝆑e ge-
directum fuerat   ut non detur   occasio   diabolo ;   Quia

dýrstlæc𝆑 elles   regolicere   stire   he
(162 b.) *autem   aliter | presumserit   discipline   regulari sub-*

underfon
jaceat ;

  be hrægel þenum 7 sceoh þenum gebro𝆑ra
DE VESTIARIIS ET CALCIARIIS FRATRUM. (CAP. LV.)

[b.] reaf   [c.]   [d.] æft*er* stowa [e.] gehwýlcnýsse [d.] þær
Vestimenta fratribus secundum   locorum   qualitatem   10

þær hi eardia𝆑   beon gesealde for𝆑am on cealdum
ubi abitant. vel aerum temperiem   dentur.   quia in frigidis

eardum [l.]   swý𝆑or þe behofa𝆑 on wærmum [n.] læs   [a.]
regionibus amplius indigetur. in   calidis vero minus ; Haec

þeos foresceawung [a.]   mid þam abbude is   [a.]   [b.]
ergo consideratio :   *penes abbatem est ;   Nos tamen*

on medenlicum stowum [e.] genihtsumian [c.]   [c.]   munecum
mediocribus   locis   sufficere   credimus monachis

geond ænlepige [f.]   * culam 7 tonican   * culam on wintre
per   singulos   cucullam et tonicam ; Cucullam in hieme 15

þicce [h.]   on sumere þinne   [k.] o𝆑𝆑e   ealdnesse   7
villosam.   in   estate   puram.   aut   vetustatem : et

scapularian for   weorcum [o.] * fiandreaf [b.]   fota
scapulare   propter   opera ;   Indumenta   pedum.

---

3. *hæd, d* or *t.*   4. *anfealde,* read *anwealde.*   13. *foresccawung, f*
might be *r.*   15. *culam,* read *culan* (twice).   17. *fiandreaf,* see note.

5. *jubead dare,* MS. *jube ad dare.*   9. LV. In the MS. this is found
before *vestimenta.*   9. CALCIARIIS, MS. CALCIARIS.   11. *temperiem,*
MS. *temperium.*   16. *vetustatem,* MS. *vetustantem.* The other texts
have *vetustam* for which *vetusta(n)tem* is an old mistake, having been
glossed as though a substantive.

soccas 7 hosan [e.]   þara þinga   eullra be bleo
pedules et caligas;   De quarum rerum omnino de colore
ne oððe gretnȳsse [d.] na   cidan   [b.]   ah swa swilce
aut   grossitudine   non causentur monachi.   sed quales

swa magan beon gefundene   [f.]   on scira [h.]   on þam þe hi
inveniri possunt   in provincia   qua habi-
wuniað oððe swa hwæt swa waclicor [m.] beon wiðmetene mæg
tant. aut   quod   vilius   comparari   potest ;

[c.]   [b.]   be gemete   foresceawige þæt na beon [e.]
5 Abbas autem de mensura   prevideat   ut non   sint
gescȳrte þa sȳlfan   reaf   brucendas hi ah   gemetlice
curta   ipsa   vestimenta utentibus. ea sed mensurata ;

nimende niwe þa ealdan [b.] hi agifan on andwerdum to
Accipientes nova   vetera semper reddant in presenti loco re-
geleohgenne on rægel huse   for   þearfan genoh bið
ponenda   in   vestiario.   propter pauperes ; Sufficit

[b.] munece twa tunican 7 twa   cuflan habban
enim monacho duos tonicas. et duas cucullas habere

for   nihtum   7   for   þweale   þæt   þæt
10 propter noctes.   et propter lavationem. Jam quod

to lafe bið   beon ofadon   [a.]   7 meon
supra fuerit superfluum est. amputare decet ; Et pedules :

7 swa hwæt swa his   eald   [b.]   7 hi agildan þonne
et quodcumque est vetustum : semper   reddant
hi underfoð þonne hi underfað niwe   . rec   þas þa þa
dum | accipiunt novum ; Femuralia hi qui in (153 a.)

[f.] beoð asende on hrægelhuse niman þa hi gecȳrrende
via diriguntur de vestiario accipiant qui revertentes
geþwagenu þara agenbringan [b.] cuflan [a.] 7 tonican [c.]
15   lota ibi restituant ;   Cuculle et   tonice
beon oðerhwilen sȳnd gewunede sunt habban æthwigan beteran
sint aliquanto   solito   quas habent modice meliores ;

8. geleohgenne, h above line. 13. underfoð (a dittographical gloss to
accipiunt), o or a? . rec, one letter not clear, probably b ; this would make it
brec. 15. geþwagenum, w corr. from r. cuflan, see note. 16. sunt in
hand of glossator.

1. colore, MS. calore. de? cf. note to 10. 7. 2. aut, MS. uit. causentur,
MS. causenter, with a u over the er. 7. Accipientes, MS. Accipiens.
loco in none of the other texts ; the MS. has loce. 11. decet, MS. dedet.
13. dum, the MS. has dirine dum. novum, MS. novem, but e corr. into u.
16. solito, MS. solitis.

*þamman utgangende   þonne hi underfon of hrægelhuse
  quas   *exeuntes* *in viam*   *accipiant*   *de vestiario.*

7 gecyrrende 7 hi agenbringan bedreaf   [b.]   bedda geniht-
et   *revertentes restituant ;*   *Stramenta* autem *lectorum :*   *suf-
sumiaõ [e.] 7 hwitel 7 wesline 7 heafudrægel þa   bed
ficiant matta et *sagum.*   *lena*   et *capitulœ.*   *Que tamen lecta*

ofer rædlice [a.]   sind to smeagenne   for   weorc
frequenter   ab abbate   *scrutanda*   *sunt : propter   opus*

sindor   þæt hine si gemett 7 gif ænigum   gett   byõ
peculiare   ne inveniatur ;   Et si   cui   inventum fuerit 5

fram þam abbude   he ne underfehõ þære healicosta stire [b.]
quod   ab   abbate non acceperit: gravissime   discipline

he underþeodde 7 þæt sig þisne leahtor sinderlices *grimþionge
subjaceat ;   et   *ut   hoc vitium peculiare   radicitus*

ofadon beon gesealde [c.]   [b.] þa þe sýnd nydbehefe
amputetur ; Dentur ab   abbate omnia   que   sunt necessaria.

þæt is cufle [g.] tanecan [h.] meon hosan earmslife   sex
id est cuculla.   tonica.   pedules. calige.   bracile.   cultellus.

græf [m.] nædl [u.] mýshrægel [p.] wexbreda [q.] þæt ælc [q.]
gravium.   acus.   mappula.   tabule.   ut   omnis 10

si gefýrsod neþearfnesse beladung [q.] from þam [c.]   [c.]
auferatur   necessitatis.   excusatio ;   A   quo   tamen abbate

[b.] [a.] si foresceawod se cwýde dæda þæra apostola
semper   consideretur   illa sententia actuum   apostolorum :

for þam þe wæs *geald ænlepium beõam þe gehwýlcum [i.]
quia   dabatur   singulis prout   cuique

neod weorc   7 [a.] se [a.] foresceawige untrum
opus   erat ; Ita et   abba   consideret   infirmitates

beþyrfendra na ýfelne   wýllan   niõfulra. andigendra
indigentium.   non   malam   voluntatem   invidentium ; 15

---

1. *þamman*, probably *þa niman*, as gloss to *accipiant.*   7. *grimþionge*,
read *grundlonge.*   9. *tanecan*, a corr. from *o*? probably it was intended
to be corrected into *u.*   11. *neþearfnesse*, for *nedþearfnesse.*   13. *geald*,
read *geseald*   14. *se* over *et*; I think it is meant for *se* (*abbod*) over *abba.*
untrum for *untrumnessa.*

---

2. *reverlentes*, MS. *reverentes.*   5. *inventum*, the MS. has *iurenta*, *ũ*
written over *a*, and after that *inve* crossed out.   6. Second *b* of *abbate* above
line.   7. The MS. has *peculiares.* The other texts have partly *peculiaris*,
partly *peculiare*, which latter would seem to be right from a Latin stand-
point; but the gloss points to a genitive.   11. *necessitatis*, MS. *necestatis.*
15. *malam*. MS. *malum.*

on   eallum   [b.]   his domum   [c.]   godes   edlean
In omnibus   tamen   judiciis   suis;   dei   retributionem
he þence
cogitet ;

DE MENSA ABBATIS. (CAP. LVI.) | (153 b.)

. . nisan [c.]   mid ælþeodigum   7   [e.] cuman * sȳð
MENSA   ABBATIS   CUM   PEREGRINIS   ET   HOSPITIBUS   *sit*
simble   swa of swa   þeahhwæðere   læs [i.]   sint [g.]   [h.] gȳstes
5 *semper ;   Quoties   tamen   minus   sint   hospites :*
ða þa he wile   of gebroþrum   [b.] geclȳpian   his   sig
quos vult   de fratrilus   vocare   in   ipsius   sit
on * anfealdre   ealdres   [b.]   ænne oððe twegen   æfre   mid
potestate ;   Seniores tamen   unum   aut   duos   semper   cum
gebroðrum   to forlætene   for   lare oððe stire
fratribus   dimittendum propter   disciplinam ;

DE ARTIFICIBUS MONASTERII. (CAP. LVII.)

* cræfican [b.] gif sind on   mȳnstre   mid   ealre   eadmod-
10 ARTIFICES   SI SUNT IN MONASTERIO :   CUM   OMNI   *humili-*
nesse hi don   þa sylfan cræftas   gif   geþafað   se abbud
tate faciant   ipsas artes.   si   permiserit   abba ;
þæt [a.] gif við   ænig [a.] [b.]   upahafan [a.] for ingehide
Quod   si aliquis   ex eis   extollitur   pro scientia
his cræftes   þeah þe he beogæsæwen sum þinc þurhteon
artis   sue eo   quod videatur   aliquid   conferre
on minstre   þes swylce   si upahræred   fram þam sylfan cræfte
monasterio.   hic talis   erigatur   ab   ipsa   arte
7 oðer siðan þurh hine   he na fare   buton wenunge geead-
15 *et   denuo   per eam   non transeat.   nisi   forte   humi-*
mettum   [p.]   hatte gif hwæt [a.]   [b.] of weorcum
liato ei iterum abba   jubeat ;   Si   quid   vero ex operibus

---

4. Erasure before . . . *nisan,* read *misin. sȳð,* read *sȳg* or *bȳð.*   5. *of,*
for *oft.*   7. *anfealdre,* read *anwealde.*   10. Read *cræftican.*   13. *beo-*
gæsæwen, sæ under the rest, a contemporary addition.

3. LVI. in the MS. before *mensa,* in line 4.   6. *ipsius,* MS. *ipsis.*
8. *dimittendum,* MS. *dimittendo.* The word *procuret* of the other texts
completing ours is omitted in the MS.   9. ARTIFICIBUS, MS. ARTICIBUS.
LVII before *Artifices* in l. 10.   12. *ex eis* in glossator's handwriting.

wẏrhtena is to sillanne   warnian hi sẏlfe þurh
artificum venundandum est ;   *videant ipsi per*

ðara handa þe sẏnd to sẏllanne   þæt hina gedẏrstlæcan
quorum manus transigenda sunt   *ne aliquam*

ænig facen [k.]   on gebringan   hi gemunon   æfre
fraudem presumant inferre.   *Memorentur semper*

      þæt hine [e.] [f.] þe hi   on lichaman
annanie. et saphire ne forte mortem quam illi in corpore

þolodan [f.]   þas [h.]   oððe ealle   ænig facen   [l.]   of
peitulerunt : hanc isti vel omnes qui aliquam fraudem de 5

þingum mẏnstres   þaðedoþ   [d.]   þolian [c.]   on
rebus ; monasterii fecerint in anima patiantur ; In

þam sẏlfum [b.]   sceattum ne undersmuge gitsunge ẏfel
ipsis autem pretiis non subripiat avaritie malum.

ah sige   æthwega   waclicor seald þonne fram oðrum
sed semper aliquantu'um vilius detur quam ab aliis

woruldlicum þingum þæt sig eallum gewuldrod gode
(154 a.)   *secularibus | ut in omnibus glorificetur deus ;*

DE DISCIPLINA SUSCIPIENDORUM FRATRUM. (CAP. LVIII.)   10

niwan [f.] cumenne ænig to .gecẏrrednesse ne si him eðelic [b.]
NOVITER VENIENS QUIS AD CONVERSIONEM. *non ei facilis*

forgifen in færeld [c.] ac [i.] swa swa sæde   [i.]   [k.]fandiað
tribuatur ingressus. sed sicut ait : apostolus. probate

gastes gif hi of gode sind [m.]   [a.]   cumende gif he þurh-
spiritus si ex deo sunt. Ergo si veniens persevera-

wunað cnuciende 7 gif he on gebrohtum teonum 7 unfrodnẏssa
verit pulsans et inlatas sibi injurias. et difficultatem

inagan [l.]   æfter feowerdagum   [m.]   [m.] 7   bið
ingressus post quattuor aut quinque dies   15

gesawen [n.]   [d.] geþẏldelice beran 7 þurhwunian his bene [t.]
visus fuerit patienter portare. et persistere petitioni

[q.] [m.] si forgifen in agan in færeld   [r.] on huse mid-
sue : annuatur ei ingressus : et sit in cella hos-

---

9. *gode, g* partly erased, instead of *e*, which was most likely intended to be
erased.

---

1. *ipsi*, added by glossator.   10. SUSCIPIENDORUM FRATRUM, MS. AD S. F.,
which may also indicate that AD SUSCIPIENDOS FRATRES was in the original.
LVIII in the MS. before *Noviter*.   12. *ait*, MS. *ut*.   13. *veniens*, MS.
inveniens.

cumendre on feawum dagum sẏðð̈an [e.] [b.] sig on huse
pitum   paucis   diebus;   Postea   autem *sit in cella*

nicumendra þær he smæge [g.] 7 he ete   7 he slæpe [i] [a.]
novitiorum: ubi meditetur   et *manducet* et   *dormiat ;*

[a.] ealdor him [b.] swilc 7 si betæhte se sig [d.] gelimlic [e.]
Et senior   ei   talis deputetur :   quia   aptus

[f.] to gestɪ́ynenne [f.] sauwla [g.] [h.] [i.] ofer [i.] him ne [l.]
sit ad   lucrandas   animas :   qui   super   eum

eallunga [k.] geornlice si begeme 7 hohful [m.]
5 *omnino   curiose   intendat;* et *sollicitus sit. revera deum*

[q.] [r.]   to godes weorce to gehẏrsumnesse [t.]
querit si solicitus est ad   opus dei :   ad   oboedientiam :

7 to hospa beon gebodenne ealra heardnessa [c.] [c.] 7
ad obprobria ; Predicentur   ei omnia   dura. et

stiðnissa [d.] þurh þæt he si gefaren to gode [a.] 7 gif he behæt
aspera   per que itur   ad deum ; Et si promiserit

be his staþolfæstnessa [c.] [c.]   anrædnessa æfter twegra
de   stabilitate   sua perseverentiam : post   du-

monð̈um [d.] onbrine [a.] si geræd [b.] him [c.] þes
10 *orum   mensium   circulum   legatur   cui   hec*

regol be endebẏrdnessa [d.] 7 si gesæd him efne her is
regula per   *ordinem :*   et *dicatur ei ecce lex :*

under þære þeowian þu wilt gif [c.] þu·miht [i.] gehealdan [k.]
sub qua militare vis ;   Si   potes   observare

infaran gif þu na miht [n.]   [m.] [q.] frige [p] aweggewit
ingredere. si   vero   non potes. liber   discede ;

gif [e.] þa git [f.] he stint þonne *he* si gelæd on þam fore-
Si   adhuc   steterit. tunc | ducatur in   supra- (154 b.)

sædan [c.] huse [c.] nicumenra 7 he si fandod [q.]
15 *dictam   cellam   novitiorum :* et   *iterum prcbetur*

on eallum geþẏlde 7 æfter sẏx monð̈a [e.] embrine 7 si ofor-
in omni patientia ; Et post sex mensium circulum rele-

ræd him regol [c.] þæt he wite to þan ingange [g.] 7 gif
gatur ei   regula,   ut sciat ad quod ingreditur ; Et si

---

5. *si* (Latin), *i* corr. from *e*.   10. *on brine,* read *embrine.*   14. Second *he*
not clear.   15. *fandod* stands so close upon margin that something before
it may have been cut away.

---

2. *meditetur,* MS. *medicetur.*   5. *revera deum querit,* MS. *reverendum
quem.*   8. *per que itur,* MS. *persequentur.*   13. *discede,* MS. *disscede.*
14. *ducatur, d* cut away.   15. The contraction for *pre* stands over *pro*
of *probetur* in glossator's hand as if he wished to correct it thus.

he þa git stýnt   eft si geræd him
adhuc stat: *post quattuor menses iteru*m *legatur* *ei*

se ýlca regol 7 gif * habban * ðretioðinge   he be
eadem regula; Et si habita   secum deliberatione pro-

hæt hene ealle þinc gehealdan 7 ealle bebeodenlice
miserit se   omnia   custodire: et cuncta   sibi

þinc 7 gehealdan 7 he si underfangen on gegæderunge
imperata servare;   tunc suscipiatur in congregatione

witende under lage regolas   * gescendne 7 þæt ne sig
sciens se sub lege   regule constitutum: et quod   5

        gelýfed   utgan of minstre nato swýran
ei ex illa die non liceat egredi de monasterio nec collum

sceacan under geoce regoles þæt si under swa langsumum
excutere de sub jugo regule: quam   sub tam morosa

frigedome gelifed wið sacan oððe underfon se underfonlica
deliberatione. licuit ei excusare: aut suscipere. Suscipiendus

[b.] on cýrican [a.] toforan eallum gebroðrum behate be his
*aute*m *in oratorio: coram   omnibu*s : *promittat de*

staðolfæstnessa [f.] 7 drohtnunge heora þeowa 7 gehýrsum-
stabilitate sua. et conversatione morum suorum: et oboedien- 10

nesse toforan gode 7 his halgum   þæt gif he deþ æt
*tia   coram deo et   sancti*s *eius: ut si ali-*

sumum cýrre elles [q.]   [o.]   hine sýlfne fordemed
*quando   aliter fecerit: a   deo   se damnandu*m

[b.] he wite hwæne he gebýsmrige be þam his behate [c.] [c.]
sciat   quem   irridet; De qua promissione sua

he do [a.] [b.] gewrit [d.] 7 naman halgena þare lafe þe sind
faciat petitionem ad nomen sanctorum   quorum re-

halidomas þara sind 7 þæs andweardes abbodes þæt gewrite
*liquie ibi sunt: et   abbatis presentis; Qua*m *petitione*m 15

mid his agenre hand he awrite oððe soðes gif he na can
manu sua scribat;   aut certe si non scit

stafas oðer fram him [h.] gebeden [g.] write 7 se nicumena [b.]
litteras. alter ab eo rogatus   scribat; Et   ille novitius

---

2. *habban ðretioðinge*, see note. 5. *gescendne*, read *gesætne* ? 6. *nato*,
to is part of gloss to *excutere* in l. 7. 7. *regoles*, *o* corr. from *u* contemporarily.
8. *frigedome*, as if the lemma were *liberatione* ?

---

4. *imperata*, MS. *imperate*. 5. *sciens*, MS. *siens*. *sub* not found in the
MS., but necessitated by the gloss. 6. *illa*, MS. *illi*. 8. *excusare*, MS.
excusere. 10. MS. *conversione*. 12. *se*, MS. *sed*. 16. *scit*, omitted
by Latin scribe.

mearce do 7 mid his handa hit ofor þam weofode
signum faciat: et *manu sua eam super altare*

he lecge þæt gewrit þonne he læigd agenne se nicumena sona
ponat; Quam dam posuerit. | incipiat ipse novitius mox (155 a.)

þis fers : [b.] [c.] [c.] æfter þinre [d.] spræce
hunc versum ; Suscipe me, domine *secundum eloquium*

[d.] 7 ic libbe na gescýnd þu me fram minre anbidunge
tuum et *vivam :* et *ne confundas me ab expectatione*

[h.] þæt fers eall sco gæderung þriddan siðan
5·*mea ;* Quem *versum omnis congregatio tertio respondeat*

to geþeodenne mid [f.] [b.] se nicumena broðor [e.] si
adjungentes. gloria patri ; Tunc ipse frater novitius proster-

aþreht ænlepigra [d.] fotum þæt hi biddan for him [a.]
natur singulorum pedibus ut orent pro eo ; Etiam

of þære tide on gegæderunge he si geteld gif he hwýlce
ex illa hora in congregatione reputetur. Res si quas

þinc hæfð þæt heiaspendæ [c.] ær þearfum [d.] oððe geworden
habet : aut eroget prius pauperibus. aut facta

simbollice sýlene he forgife minstre [k.] him sýlfum
10 *solempniter donatione conferat monasterio. nihil sibi*

na healdende of eallum witodlice se ðe of þam dæge [q.] neto
reservans ex omnibus. quippe qui ex illa die nec

*ontigenum lichaman *andfealde wite sana [b.] on cýrican
proprii corporis potestatem sciat; Mox ergo in oratorio

he si unscrýd agenum þingan Mid þam þe wælgescrýd [e.] 7
exuatur rebus propriis quibus vestitus est : et

he si gescrid mid þingum minstres þa [b.] reaf [b.]
induatur rebus monasterii ; Illa autem vestimenta

mid þam þe he wæs unscrid beon gelogodre on rægelhuse
15 *quibus exutus est reponantur in vestiario*

to gehealdenna æt suman cýrre tihtendum deofle gif he þafe
conservanda : ut si aliquando suadente diabolo consen-

þafað þæt he utga of minstre unscrýd
serit, ut egrediatur de monasterio quod absit : tunc exutus

---

8. *of, o* crossed, perhaps corrected from *e*. 11. *neto,* see note. 12. *onti-*
genum, see note. *andfealde,* read *anwealde.* 15. *gelogodre,* see note.
16, 17. *gif he þafe þafað,* read *gif he þafað.*

---

8. *quas,* MS. *quod.* 13. *exuatur rebus,* MS. *exuaturebus.* 14. *Illa,*
MS. *Illi.*

þingum [r.] he si ut adræfed þæt þehhwæþere
rebus monasterii proiciatur ; Illam tamen

gewrit [c.] his þæt he nam uppan [f.] þan weofode [f.] [g.]
petitionem eius quam super altari abbas

underfond he na underfo [h.] ac hit si gehealden
tulit non recipiat sed in monasterio reservetur ;

DE FILIIS NOBILIUM AUT PAUPERUM QUI OFFERUNTUR.
(CAP. LVIIII.) 5

gif hwa [d.] [b.] of æðelborenum offrað ꞇ dat his *earn
SI QUIS FORTE DE NOBILIBUS *offert filium suum*

gode on minster gif he þæt sylfe cild on iunre ylde
(155 b.) *deo in monasterio : si ipse puer | minori*

is his magas don gewritt swa swa we bufan
aetate est. parentes eius faciant petitionem quam supra

mid ofrunge þæt gewrit hand
diximus. et cum oblatione ipsam petitionem. et manum

cildes 7 he be fealde on weofodsceatan
pueri involvant in palla altaris. et sic eum 10

7 hi geofrian of heora æhtum oððe on andweardum
offerant ; De rebus autem suis : aut in presenti

gewrite hi behatað under aðsware þæt hi næfre ne þurh
petitionem promittant sub jurejurando ; quia numquam

hi sylfe ne þurh gewenedne had ne mid nanum
per se : numquam per suffectam personam : nec quo-

gemett him æt ænigon cirre æni þinc syllan oððe hi
libet modo ei aliquando aliquit dent. nec tri-

forgifan intingan to habbenne oððe sopes þæt don
buant occasionem habendi ; Vel certe si hoc facere 15

gif hi nellað 7 ænigþincg offrian 7 hi wyllað to ælmæssan
noluerint : et quid offerre voluerint in elemosina

on minstre for heora mede hi don of þingum þa þe hi
monasterio pro mercede sua : faciant ex rebus quas

willað syllan mynstre sylene gehealdenum
dare volunt monasterio donationem. reservato

2, 3. nam, gloss to *tulit* (l. 3) ; *underfond*, originally marginal note to *he*
underfo ꞇ 6. ꞇ *dat* in hand of glossator. *earn*, a letter blotted before it ;
read *bearn*. 13. *gewenedne*, see note. 14. *gemett* or *gemete* ꞏ

---

4. MS. OFFERUNT DE F. N. A. P. QUI. 6. SI, erasure between S and I.
nobilibus, second *i* corrected from *u* by erasure. 7. *in* omitted by Latin
scribe. 12. MS. *promittat*. 13. *suffectam*, see note. 18. *donationem*,
m corrected from two other letters.

11★ H 2

him sýlfan   swa gif hi willað   landare   7 beon * behýdda
sibi.   si ita   voluerint, usufructuario;   Atque ita
ealle þinc   * dedre   þæt ænig to hopa na belife þam cilde
omnia   obstruantur ut nulla suspicio remaneat   puero
þurh   þa bepæhð losian he mage þæt feor sig þæt mid afun-
þer quam deceptus perire possit quod absit ; quod experi-
dennesse welleorniaþ swa gelice soðlice swýlce þa þearflicran
mento   didicimus ; Similiter autem :   et pauperiores
don gif   mid ealle hi naht nabbað   anfealdlice
5 faciant ; Si qui vero ex toto   nihil habent :   simpliciter
gewrit   hidon   mid ofrunge 7 hi ofriað heora cildra ætforan
petitionem faciant. et oblationem   offerant filium suum coram
gewitnessum
testibus ;

DE SACERDOTIBUS QUI VOLUERINT IN MONASTERIIS HABITARE.

(CAP. LX.)

gif hwilc be endebýrdnesse * mæssepreostrum on   minstre
10 SI QUIS DE ORDINE   SACERDOTUM in monasterium se
beon underfangen   [e.]   [a.] ne sig   [b.]   hrædlice
suscipi   rogaverit :   non   quidem | ei citius (156 a.)
geþafod   [b.] gif eallunga he þurhwunað   [c.] on þissere
assentiant ; Tamen si omnino perstiterit. in hac   suppli-
halsunge he wite ealle lare regules þeahfæstnýsse to healdenne
catione.   sciat se omnem regule disciplinam   servaturum ;
nene ænig þinc   si forgifen þæt hesig swa swa hit awriten
Nec aliquid ei relaxabitur ut sit   sicut   scriptum
is eala þu freond to hwam comeþu sý geunnen him
15 est ;   Amice. ad quod venisti ; Concedatur ei tamen
æfter þam abbote standan 7 bletsian oððe mæssen healden
post   abbatem stare. et benedicere · aut missas tenere.
gif [b.] hæt [g.] hi him * hellas [a.] nateshwon he nege-
si tamen jusserit ei abba ; Sin alias nullatenus   pre-

1, 2. *behýdda ealle þinc dedre, behýdda* and *dedre* probably belong together,
and read, *behýddedre,* thus eliminating the consequences of a partial dittography ; see p. 98. 15.   4. *welleorniaþ,* i. e. *we leorniaþ.*   10. *mæsse-*
preostrum, read *mæssepreostra* ; see note.   13. *þeahfæstnýsse,* read *þeaw-*
fæstnýsse, h corrected from other letter, possibly *w.*   17. *hellas,* read *he*
elles.

1. *voluerint, n* corr. from *ti.*   6. *offerant,* MS. *offreat.*   8. MS.
VOLERINT.   11. *ei citius,* MS. *excitius.*

dŷrstlæce ænig þing [d.] hine regolicere stire underþeodne
sumat　aliqua　　　　sciens　se discipline regulari　subditum :

7 swiðor eadmodnesse bŷsna eallum he sÿlle 7 gif wenunge
et magis humilitatis exempla omnibus det ; Et si forte

hades hadunge oððe æniges þinges　　intingan bið on
ordinationis aut　alicujus　　rei　causa　fuerit in

minstre þa stowe þæne stÿde 7 he begime on þære þe he
monasterio.　illum　locum　　attendat :　　quando

inferde [c.]　[c.] on minstre [d.] ne þæne se þe for
ingressus　est　in monasterium non illum qui ei pro 5

arwŷrðnesse preosthades þæs geunnen is　preosta　gif
reverentia　sacerdotii　concessus　est ; Clericorum autem si

hwÿlce þære ÿlcan gewilnunge on minstre beon gefærlæhte
qui　eodem　desiderio　monasterio　　sociari

willað on medomlicere stowe [a.]　[c.] 7 hi [d.]
voluerint :　loco　mediocri　collocentur.　et　ipsi

[f.] gif hi behatað behealdsumnesse regoles oððe agenre
tamen si promittunt de observatione regule vel propria

staþolfæstnessa :
stabilitate ;　　　　　　　　　　　　　　　　　　　　　10

DE MONACHIS PEREGRINIS. (CAP. LXI.)

gif ænig　　　of ælþeodigum mannum of fŷrlænum scirum
SI QUIS MONACHUS PEREGRINUS DE LONGINQUIS

　　　becimð gif forcuman he wile wunian on
provinciis supervenerit : si pro hospite voluerit habitare in

minstre 7 geþæf 7 he bið on gewunan [u.]
monasterio et contentus fuerit consuetudine loci quam

[u.] [q.] [o.]　　mid his oferflowodlicnÿsse [q.] [q.]
invenerit et non forte　　superfluitate　　sua 15

7 he ne gedrefð minster ahh lice geþeef is
(156 b.)　perturbat monasterium. sed | simpliciter contentus est

þæt þæt þæt he gemet he si underfangen on swa langre
quod invenerit.　suscipiatur　　quanto

---

9. behadað or behatað.　14. Over the words . . . tudine loci quam
invenerit et non forte, the gloss has probably been erased.　16. ahh .., a
letter erased ?　17. Three times þæt, thus the MS.

5. ei above line.　6. Clericorum, MS. clerfcum.　8. MS. collocetur.　9. de,
MS. ded.　11. PEREGRINIS, MS. PEREGRINIO.　16. perturbat, MS. perturbet,
with a written over e of ending.

tide   swa he gewilnað gif he   gewistlice   gesceadwislice 7
tempore   *cupit ;*   *Si qua*   *sane*   *rationabiliter* et
mid eadmodnesse soðre lufe hwylce þinc repað oððe geswutalað
cum humilitate   karitatis   reprehendit   aut   ostendit.

smæge [b.] snotorlice þe læs forþan sylfan þingan hine
tractet abbas prudenter ne forte   pro   hoc   ipso   eum

[e.] sænde gif he wile syððan [o.] his staðolfæstnesse
dominus direxerit. Si   vero   postea voluerit   stabilitatem

[d.] getrýmman na si forwýrned swýlc   willa   7 swiðest
5 *suam firmare.   non renuatur   talis voluntas. et maxime*

forþan   cumliðnesse þe mihte his lif [h.] beon acnawan
quia tempore hospitalitatis potuit   eius vita   dignosci.

þæt gif bið gemet oferflowende oððe leahterfull [g.]   [g.]
Quod si superfluus   aut   vitiosus inventus fuerit

on tide   [g.]   [b.] þæt an [b.] hena scel beon gefærlæht gefer-
tempore hospitalitatis: non solum non debet   sociari   cor-

reddene mýnstres ac eac swýlce   si gesæd arwýrðlice þæt he
pori monasterii.   verum etiam dicatur ei honeste   ut

aweggewite [p.] mid [r.] his ýrmða [r.]   cðre [q.] [p.]
10 *discedat :   ne   eius   miseria etiam   alii vitientur.*

þæt gif he na bið   swýlc geearnige   beon ut adræfæd
Quod si non . fuerit talis qui mereatur   proici

þæt an gif he bitt he si underfangen gegæderunge
non   solum   si petierit suscipiatur   congregationi

to geferlætenne ac eac swýlce he si gelæred þæt he stande [p.]
sociandus   verum etiam   suadeatur ut stet   ut

mid his bisne oððre beon gelærede 7 sig on ælcere stowe
eius exemplo alii erudiantur ; Et quia in omni   loco

anum drihtne þæt geþeowod anum cinge 7 si gecampod
15 *uni domino servitur ;   uni regi   militatur ; Quem*

gif [k.] þýline beon besceawiað [h.] sigelifed him on
si etiam talem esse perspexerit abba. liceat eum in

uferan æthwega [d.] gesettan stide [n.] [o.] [o.]
superiorem aliquantulum constitueret. locum. non solum autem

---

10. *ýrmða, a* of much larger size than the other characters.

---

4. *direxerit,* MS. *dixerint.*   6. MS. *hospitalis.*   9. *monasterii,* MS.
monasterio, but last *o* underdotted, and *i* written over it.   11. *proici,*
MS. *projiciunt.*   15. *servitur,* MS. *serviatur.*   17. *autem,* MS. *aut.*

[p.]	ah	[q.]	of	þam	foresædum	gradum	[s.]
*monachum.	sed	etiam	de	superscriptis	gradibus	sacerdotum.*

oðᷝe	preosta	gestaþolfæstan	mæg	[x.]	on maran whænue
(157 a.)	*vel	clericorum	stabilire	potest abbas	in | maiori	quam*

incode	stede gif	he hig	besceawad	þæt lif	[w.]	wærnige
*ingreditur	loco	si	ejus talem	perspexerit	vitam.	esse.	Caveat*

[b.]	[c.]	þæt	æhwænne	of	oðrum	cuðum	mýnstre
*autem	abba	ne	aliquando	de	alio.	noto	monasterio*

[e.]		to wunigenne	he ne underfo	buton	geþafunge
*monachum	ad	habitandum	suscipiat :	sine	consensu* 5

abbotes	his	[i.]	stafum	oðᷝe	gegretlicum	forþam	þe hit is
*abbatis	ejus	aut	litteris	commendaciis ;	Quia	scrip-*

awriten		þæt þæt	þe sylfan	þu nilt	beon ne du oðrum
*tum	est ;	Quod	tibi	non	vis fieri.	alii	ne*

feceris ;

DE SACERDOTIBUS MONASTERII.	(CAP. LXII.)

gif ænig	[b.]	him	sylfan	mæssepreost	oðᷝe	[l.]	diacon
SI QUIS ABBAS	SIBI		PRESBITERUM	VEL	DIACONEM. 10

beon gehadod	geornð	of his geceose	se wýrðe	sýg preosthade
*Ordinari	petierit ;	de suis	eligat	qui dignus sit	sacerdotio*

brucan	se gehadoda	[b.]	warnige upahafennesse	7	modig-
*fungi ;	Ordinatus	autem	careat	elationem.	at*que super-

nesse	ne he ne ge ænig þing dýrstlæce	butan	þæt þe him
*biam ;	Nec quicquam presumat :		nisi	quod ei*

fram	þam abbode bið beboden witende	' micele swýðor	stýre
*ab	abbate precipitur :	Sciens se multo	magis	discipline*

regollicere	underþeodne	[a.]	intingan preost	ne he na for-
*regulari	subditum ;	Nec occasione	sacerdotii	oblivisca-* 15

gimeleasne	regoles gehýrsumnesse	7	þeawfæstnesse ac	swiðor
*tur	regule	oboedientiam	et	disciplinam :	sed magis*

7 swiðor	on	gode	he geþeo	stede	þæne	[b.]	[c.]
*hac magis	in	deum	proficiat ;	Locum	vero	illum	sem*per

he begýme	on þam þe he in * neode	[d.]	on mýnstre	toforan
*attendat	quo	ingressus	est in	monasterium ;	preter*

3. *besceawad*, a indistinet.	15, 16. *forgimeleasne*, read *forgimcleasie*.
18. *in neode*, read *inn eode*.

2. *clericorum*. MS. *declericorum*.	10. *presbiterum*, MS. *presbiteri*.
14. *ab abbate precipitur*, MS. *abba tepreecpitur*, and *i* written over second *e*
of *precepitur*.	17. *vero*, MS. *vera*.	18. *monasterium*, *u* corrected from *a.*

þenunge weofodes oððe gif _wile_ gecorenes   gæderunge   7
officium   altaris ;   Aut   si   forte   electio   congragationis et

willa   þæs abbodes   lifes forgearnunge him wendan oððe
voluntas   abbatis   pro vite   merito   eum   promovere

stiran [a.]   se   [l.]   regol   fram decanum oððe fram
voluerit   qui   tamen   regulam   a   decanis   vel   pre-

pravostum him sylfan gesetne   gehealden [i.]   wite þæt gif
positis sibi constitutam   servare sciat ;   Quod si

he elles gedyrstlæcð na sacerdos ac hwiðercora ac beo geme-
5 _aliter presumpserit : non sacerdos sed   rebellio   judice-_

demod [a.]   gelome geminegod   gif he ne bið geþreadd   [b.]
tur ;   Et sepe ammonitus   si non correxerit.   etiam

[b.]   si gegearcod   [d.]   on gewitnesse þæt [a.] gif he hit
episcopus | adhibeatur   in   testimonium ;   Quod si nec   (157 b.)

swa [a.] ne ge bett [a.]   [d.]   he si utadræfed
sic emendaverit :   clarescentibus culpis   proiciatur

[c.]   gif hwilc [h.]   bið his toþundennessa [g] þæt
de monasterio : si tamen talis fuerit ejus   contumacia   ut

he beon underþeod oððe gehyrsumian þam regole nele.
10 _subdi   aut   obedire   regule nolit ;_

DE ORDINE QUO CONGREGATUR. (CAP. LXIII.)

heora endebyrdnesse   [d.]   swa hi gehealden swa swa
ORDINES SUOS   IN MONASTERIO ITA CONSERVENT   _ut con-_

gecyrrednesse   tima   [g.]   earnunge swa swa asyndrað
versiones   tempus   et vite meritum   discernit.

7 swa swa se abbod   hit gesette   sene [a.]   abbod [a.]   ge-
utque abbas   constituerit :   Qui   abbas   non

drefe [a.] befæste him sylfum   heorde   ne swilcum freolicum
15 _conturb_et _gregem   sibi   commissam : nec quasi   libera_

brucenne * anfealde unrihtlice he ne gedihte   [e.]   ac he þænce
_utens   potestate   injuste   disponat   aliquit   sed cogit_et

---

1. _wile, w_ above line. _gecorenes,_ i. e. _gecorenness._   5. _sacerdos._ The
scribe wrote _sacerdos_ by mistake; corrected _o_ into _h,_ put _o_ over _s,_ and _de_
under it; the whole is meant for _sacerdhades._   5. _beo, b_ corr. from _g._
5, 6. _gemedemod,_ probably _gedemed_ is the original reading.   16. _anfealde,_
read _anwealde._

---

2. _vite,_ MS. _ivvite._   3. MS. _propositis._   7. _si nec,_ MS. _sinet._
11. QUO not in the MS., nor in any other Latin texts. These read: DE
ORDINE CONGREGATIONIS.   13. _et vite meritum,_ MS. _ut vi temeritum._
15. _commissam,_ MS. _commissim._   16. _utens,_ MS. _ut nos._

simle þæt he be eallum his *domumum 7 weorcum be his
semper quia de omnibus judiciis et operibus suis
is to gildanne [b.] [d.] [m.] æfter endebýrdnesse
redditurus est deo rationem. Ergo secundum ordines
[i.] þa þa he gesette oðða þa þa habbað þa sýlfan gebroðran
quos constituerit. vel quos habuerint ipsi fratres
hi ne genealæcan [b.] to huselgange to on sealmum
si accedant ad pacem. ad communionem. ad psalmum
ginnende on choro standende 7 [e.] [o.] eallunga
imponendum : in choro standum; Et in omnibus omnino 5
[e.] ýld na si gesindrod on endebýrdnesse ne he ne foredeme
locis etas non discernatur in ordine nec prejudicet.
forþam [g.] [h.] [h.] cnihtas preostas þe demdon [b.]
quia samuel et daniel pueri presbiteros judicaverunt ; Ergo
þisum asindrodum þa þa ge swa swa we bufon sædon mid
exceptis his quos ut diximus altiori
maran ræde [h.] recð oðða [l.] of gewissum
consilio abbas pretulerit. vel degradaverit certis
intingan ealle þa oðre swa swa hi beoþ gecýrde swa
ex causis. reliqui omnes ut convertuntur ita 10
beon swilce ic swa cwæða seþe æt þære oðran tide cýmð to
sint. ut verbi gratia. qui secunda hora diei venerit in
minstre ginran hine hecunne his beon seþe [x.] [ý.]
monasterium juniorem se noverit illius esse qui prima
on þære forman tide swa hwýlcere ýlde oðða wurðscipe
(158 a.) hora venerit diei cujus | libet aetatis. aut dignitatis
hesi cildra [b.] geond ealle þing fram eallum gebroðrum stýr
sit. Pueris vero per omnia ab omnibus disciplina
si gehealden þa ginran iornostlice heora ýldran arwurþian
teneatur ; Juniores igitur : priores suos honorent ; priores 15
lufian on þære sýlfan clýpunge namena
minores suos diligant. In ipsa autem apellatione nominum :
ænigum na si gelefed mid agenum naman genan ac þa ýldran
nulli non liceat alium puro nomine apellare sed priores

---

1. domumum, read domum. 4, 5. on in l. 4 belongs to ginnende in l. 5.
5, choro, Latin influence. 17. na in the margin. genan, beginning of
genamian.

---

6. A letter erased before ordine. In ordine, i has been corr. from
a or u. 10. reliqui, MS. relinqui, but n nearly erased. 12. juniorem,
MS. juniorum. 13. venerit, MS. venirit. aetatis, MS. cecitatis. dignitatus
in MS. 16. minores not in MS.

heora ginran nemnan þa ginran þa ỹldran
juniores *suos fratres nominent juniores autem priores suos*
arwurðe hi gecian þæt bið to understandenne mid fæderlicere
nonnos vocent ; quod intellegitur paterna
arwurðnesse [d.] for þam ðe þa spellunga is gelỹfed
reverentia ; Abbas autem quia vices christi creditur
don . si genemned na mid his underfangennes
agere dominus et abbas vocetur ; non sua assumtione.
ac on wurðmente 7 mid *christes* lufan he sỹlf þence
5 set *honore* et *amore christi. ipse autem cogitet et*
hine 7 he gearcie weorðe þæt he si swilcum wurðmente
sic se exhibeat. ut dignus ut dignus sit. tali honore.
swa swa ongeancumað se ginra fram þam ealdre
Ubicumque autem sibi obviant fratres junior a priore bene-
bletsunge bidde se læssa aris 7 he sỹlla
dictionem petat. Transeunte majore. minor surgat : et det ei
rỹmet to sittenne ne ne gedỹrstlæce se ginra sittan buton
locum sedendi ; Nec presumat junior consedere nisi ei
hate his ealdor þæt beo on wurðmente
10 *precipiat senior suus ut fiat quod scriptum est honore*
* foahrædigende geongra cildra oððe ginran
invicem prevenientes. Pueri parvi vel adolescentes
oððe æt meosan mid þeawfæstnessa heora endebỹrd-
in oratorio. vel ad mensas. cum disciplina ordines
nesse fỹlian wiðutan hi beon oþ þæt hi heordrædene
*suas consequantur foris autem vel ubicum*que *custodiam*
hi habban 7 to lare oððæt hi to andgitfullere ỹlde
*habeant : et disciplina*m *us*que *ad intellegibilem etatem*
becumen
15 *perveniant :*

DE ORDINANDO ABBATI. (CAP. LXIIII.)

þæs abbodes on hadunge þæt [b.] si forasceawod gescend
In abbatis ordinatione illa semper consideretur | ratio. (158 b.)
her þæt si gesæd þone þe him sỹlfum eal seo gesibsum
ut hic constituatur. quem sibi omnis

---

11. *foahrædigende*, read *forahrædigende.*

5. *christi*, MS. *episcopi* (the scribe read *Epi* for *Xpi*). *amore*, MS, *amor.*
6. *ut dignus*, repeated thus in MS. 9. *presumat*, MS. *presumant.*

gegæderung   [æ.]   æfter   godes   ege   sit oððe
concors   congregatio   secundum   timorem   dei :   sive
eac swýlce þeah þe he gehwæde dæl gegæderunga mid ge-
etiam. pars quamvis parva congregationis saniori
wissum geþeahte gecýsð   be iarnunge 7 wisdomes
consilio elegerit; Vite autem merito : et sapientiae
lare he si gecoren se þe is tohadgenne   þeah æfter
doctrina elegatur qui ordinandus est : etiam si ultimus
þe he beo on endebýrdnesse gegæderunge þæt
fuerit in ordine congregationis; Quod si etiam 5
   for his leahtrum þæt feor   * sit
omnis congregatio vitiis suis quod qu em absit
geþafienne had mid gelicum geþeahte gif gecýsð 7
consentientem personam pari consilio elegerit :   et
þa sýlfan leahtras æthwega on cýðe biscopis becumon to
vitia ipsa aliquatenus in notitiam episcopi pervenerint ad
þæs scir þegena gebýrað seo stow oððe to
cujus diocessim pertinet locus ipse vel ad
abboddum oððe þa cristenan nýhgeburum geswuteliað hi for-
abbates aut christianos vicinos claruerint. pro- 10
beodan þwýrlicra swýþrian geþafiunge ah * hwiwræddene
hibeant pravorum prevalere consensum sed domui dei
wurðe gesetton dihtneran witende for þi hi to under-
dignum constituant dispensatorem. scientes pro hoc se recep-
fonne méde [b.] gode gýf þæt clænlice 7 mid ande don hi
turos mercedem bonam. si illud caste et zelo dei faciant :
eall swa þær togenes synna gýf ' hi forgæwað gehadod
sicut e contrario peccatum si neglegant ; Ordinatus
soðlice he þence æfre hwilce byrdena he underfeng 7
autem abba cogitet semper quale honus suscepit : et 15
hwam he is to agendenne gescad his gerefsciran 7 wite he
cui redditurus est rationem villicationis suæ Sciatque
him sýlfan o gedafenian fremian swiðor þonne derian him gebýrað
sibi oportere prodesse : magis quam preesse ; Oportet

---

1. *oððe, o* corr. from *e.*   6. *sit,* read *sig.*   9. *þegena,* i. e. *þegnunga?*
10. *geswuteliað, t* corrected from *l?*   11. *hwiwrædenne,* read *hiwrædenne.*
12. *underfonne, o* corr. from *u* or *n.*   14. *togenes,* first *e* corr. into *æ.*
forgæwað, see note.   15. *byrdena, d* corr. from some other letter?
17. *gedafenian, a* corr. from *c.* I cannot account for the *o.*

2. *pars, r* above line. *saniori,* MS. *samori,* but *m* is dotted under the second stroke, so as to indicate the reading *saniori.*   8. *notitiam,* MS. *notetiam.* *perrenerint,* MS. *perreniam.*   10. *vicinos,* M°. *ricinis.*   11. *dei* above line.

soðlice hine beon gelæred on godcundlicra æ þæt he wite 7 he
ergo eum esse doctum lege divina : ut sciat et sit

si hwanon he forð teo niwe 7 ealde clæne [ɴ.] sefre
unde proferat nova et vetera ; Castum. sobrium.

mildheortnesse 7 æfre he upahebbe on
*misericordem | et semper superexaltet misericordia*m   (159 ᴀ)

dome þæt he þæt ylce begyte hatige he lehtras
judicium ut idem ipse consequatur. Oderit vitia

lufige he gebroðra on þare sylfre soðlice þreatinge snotorlice
5 *diligat fratres; In ipsa autem correptione prudenter*

he det 7 nan þing ofer swiðe þæt he na to swiðe ne gewilnige
agat. et ne quid nimis. ne dum nimis cupit

upawyrtlian rust oððe om si tobrocen fæt 7 his tydder-
eradere eruginem. frangatur vas : suamque fragi-

nysse æfre ge. em. hydi sy 7 geþence reod forþrest
litatem semper suspectus sit. memineritque calamum quassatum

ne sy to bryd on þam we ne secgað þæt w beon for-
non conterendum. In quibus non dicimus, ut permittat

lætanne beon gefed leahtras ac snotorlice 7 mid þare soðra
10 *nutriri vitia sed prudenter et cum karitate*

lufa þa he of acerfa swa swa hem þynce ænige gelettan
ea amputet. prout viderit cuique expedire.

ealswa we ær sædon 7 hogie he swyðor beon gelufon þænne
sicut jam diximus ; Et studeat plus amari. quam

beon ondrædod ne sy he adrefað 7 * anc sam ne sy he
timeri ; Non sit turbulentus et anxcius ; non sit

swiðlic 7 andan wille ne sy he nyð full 7 swiðe wenende
nimius et obstinatus non sit zelotipus et nimis suspiciosus :

for þy næfre he ne gesteð on þam sylfan bebodum
15 *quia numquam requiescit ; In ipsis imperiis suis*

forgleaw 7 forseone oððe æfter gode oððe æfter
*providus et consideratus : sive secundum deum. sive secundu*m

---

6. *det,* for *deþ;* influence of Latin ? 7. *upawyrtlian,* see note. *fæt* or *fæd*
in MS. ? 9. *w beon forlætanne beon gefed.* I think *w* is either a ' paving '
letter or the beginning of *we,* a dittography of the *we* going before, in which
case *beon* is attributable to the same cause, viz. to a dittography of *beon*
in l. 10. *forlætenne* is a mistake for *forlæte*=permittat. 11. *hem, e* or *o* ?
It is crossed out in the MS. 13. *anc sam,* corr. from or into *anx sum,*
probably — from a palæographical point of view — the former ; from an
etymological point of view, the latter. *anxius* is glossed as if it were
angustus. 14. *andan,* i. e. *anan.*

---

14. *obstinatus,* MS. *obstinandus. nimis,* MS. *in misu.*

wurulde   he sy   þa weorc   þe he   ge þeod   he gesỳndrige 7
seculum   sit;   Opera   que   injungit   discernat   et
gemetỳge þencende   gescad   þæs   halgan iacobes   secgende
temperet.   cogitans discretionem sancti   jacob   dicentis.

   mine heorde swiðor oððe   on gange   gif ic do   swingan
Si   greges meos   plus   in   ambulando   fecero   laborare:
hi swỳltað ealle   on anum dæge þas oðre gecỳðnỳssa gewitnessa
morientur   cuncti   una die;   Hec ergo   aliaque   testimonia
smæiunge   moder   mihta   nimende ealle þinc   gemetie   æt
159 b.) *discretionis   matris   virtutum   sumens: sic   omnia   temperet | ut* 5
he si strang   þæt þæt hi gewilniað 7 þa *uncruman hi na
et fortis   sit   quod cupiant: et   infirmi   non
forfleon   7 healicost þæt he andweardne   regol   on eallum
refugeant; Ét precipue   ut   presentem regulam in omni-
þingum gehealde þonne he   þenað   þæt he gehỳre
bus   conservet.   ut dum   bene ministraverit.   audiat

   þæt þe gehỳrde se goda þeowa seðe aspende
a domino   quod servus bonus   qui erogavit triticum
his efenþeowan on his tide   soðlice ic secge eow   sæde
conservis suis in tempore suo;   Amen dico vobis   ait. 10
ofor ealle   his godu   he geset
super omnia bona sua   constituet eum.

DE PREPOSITO MONASTERII. (CAP. LXV.)

oftrædlice witodlice hit belimpð þæt þurh   hadunge   prafostes
SEPIUS   QUIDEM   CONTINGIT   *ut per ordinationem prepositi*
hefilice ætswicunga on mỳnster   þonne bið sume
scandala gravia   in monasteriis oriantur.   dum sint aliqui
mid þam awỳridan gaste   modignesse *tobedde 7 wenende
maligno spiritu   superbie   inflati.   et estimantes 15
hine oðre   beon   nimende him   gewin
se secundos esse.   abbatis assumentes sibi tyrannidem.
æswicunga hi fedað 7 twỳrednysse on gegaderunga hi doð
scandala   nutriunt. et dissensiones in congregatione faciunt;
7 swiðost on þam stowum þær fram þam ỳlcan   oððe
Et maxime in illis locis.   ubi ab   eodem   sacerdote. vel

---

5. The *m* is indistinct in *gemetie*.   6. *uncruman,* read *untruman.*
14. *hefilice, l* corr. from *s.*   *tobedde,* read *tobrædde.*

2. *dicentis,* MS. *dicentes.*   3. *fecero,* MS. *fecere.   laborare,* MS. *baborare.*
4. *cuncti,* MS. *cuncta.   Hec,* MS. *Her.*   6. MS. *forte.   fortis,* for which
other MSS. have *fortes,* is postulated by gloss.   8. MS. *conservent.*
12. MONASTERII, MS. MONASTERIO.   14. *sint,* MS. *fuit.*

fram þam   abbotum   þa þa   abbod   hadiað   7
ab   eis   abbatibus   qui   abbatem   ordinant.   *ab ipsis etiam et*

se prafost   þe ær   bið gehadod   þæt bið hi   fullice hit is
prepositus   ordinatur ;   Quod quam sit absurdum

eþelice   undergiten   forþam þe býð   fram þam   sýlfan   anginne
facile   adfertitur.   quia   ab   ipso   initio   ordina-

hadunge   ontimber . geseald to motgenne   þonne hit bið getiht
*tionis :   materia ei   datur   super*biendi.   *dum ei suggeritur*

fram his geþohtum [m.] [m.]
5 *a   cogitationibus   suis   exutum   eum   esse   a   potestate*

his abbotes   forþam   þe he wæs * gehæle from þam
abbatis sui :   quia   ab ipsis   est ordinatus.   a   quibus

se   abbod   heonen   beoð astýrede   andan   geflit   * stalu
et *abbas ;   Hinc | suscitantur   invidie.   rixe.   detractionis* (160 a.)

efestes   twýrædnesse   unhadunge   7 hwænne þwýrnessa
emulationes   dissensiones.   exordinationes.   et   dum   contraria

heom betwýnan   7 se prafost geþafiað 7 heora neod is
*sibi   invicem   abbas   prepositus*que *sentiunt.* et *ipsorum necesse*

sawla   under heom
10 *est   sub   hac   disentione   animas   periclitari.* et *hi   qui   sub*

þænne hi lýfetað   dælmælum færað uton forspilled-
ipsis   sunt.   dum   adulantur   partibus   eunt in perdi-

nesse   þæs   frecednessa   ýfel   heom   * lucað   on   anginne
tionem ;   Cujus   periculi   malum.   illis   respicit   in   capite

[a.] ða swilcum on   hadunge   doð   ealdras   forþi
qui   talibus   in ordinatione   se   fecerunt   auctores ;   Ideo   nos

foresceawiað fremman   for   sibbe 7 þære soðre lufe hýrdræ-
*previdimus   expedire   propter pacis   karitatis*que   *custo-*

dene þæs abbo*des* standan on cýre   hadunge   minstres   his
15 *diam   in   abbatis   pendere   arbitrio   ordinationem monasterii sui;*

7 gif mæg beon   heora decanus si geendebýr   swa swa * weg
Et si potest fieri ;   per   decanos   ordinetur   sicut ante

bufòn   ælc   nýtwýrðnesse   mýnstres   be þam þe
disposuimus omnis   utilitas   monasterii.   prout   abba

---

6. *gehæle, æle* crossed out, and *hadod* (sic) has been substituted for it in
the margin.   12. *lucað*, read *luciað*.   16. *decanus*, copied from Latin?
weg, read *we ge*; the verb is left out.

---

2. *absurdum*, MS. *obsurdum*.   7. A hole in parchment before *rixe* ; it
does not affect the text at all, having evidently been there before the MS.
was written on.   11. MS. *perditione*.   12. *illis*, MS. *illi*.   13. *fecerunt*,
MS. *fecunt*, and *c* corrected from *r*.   17. *disposuimus*, MS. *disposimus*.

diht   þæt þænne   magon hit byð befæst   an   ne
disposuerit.   *ut dum   pluribus committitur.*   *unus   non*

modie   þæt gif oððe stow gyrnð oððe gegaderung
superbiat ;   *Quod si   aut locus expetit.   aut   congregatio.*

bit gescadwislice mid eadmodnesse [g.] se   demð
petierit rationabiliter cum humilitate.   et   *abba judicaverit*

gefremman swa hwænne swa geceost   mid geþeahte
expedire   quemcumque   elegerit   abba cum   consilio

        ondrædendra gode hadige hesylf   prafost   se
fratrum   timentium   deum ordinet ipse sibi prepositum ;   Qui 5

      se prafost   mid arwurðnessa þa þe fram his
tamen prepositus illa agat cum   reverentia   que   ab

      abbode   læhte   beoð naht ongen   wyllan   7 had-
(160 b.) *abbate suo ei injuncta fuerint nihil contra volun | tatem et ordina-*

ung þæs donde forðam þe   oðrum
tionem abbati faciens   quia   quanto prelatus est ceteris. tanto eum

gedafenað carfullicor healden beboda regoles se pra
oportet   sollicitus   observare precepta regule ; Qui prepositus

gif he bið gemet   leahtres oððe upahafennes beswicen
si   repertus   fuerit vitiosus   aut   elatione   deceptus 10

modignes   forhicge   þæs haligan byð   fandod
superbie aut   contemptor sancte regule fuerit approbatus

si geminegod mid wordum   oð feowersiðan gif he hit na
ammoneatur   verbis   usque   quater ;   Si non emenda-

gebet si gegearcod   þræiung regolicere styre
verit   adhibeatur   ei   correptio   discipline   regularis ;

                            he si adræfed of endebyrd-
Quod si neque sic correxerit ; tunc   deiciatur   de   or-

nesse pravostscire   seðe   is   stete his
dine prepositure.   et alius qui dignus est in loco eius subro- 15

                                            7 gehyrsum
getur ; Quod si postea in congregatione quietus et oboediens

---

9. *pra*, for *prafost* or *pravost*.   10. *leahtres*, should have been *leahterful*,
but either the scribe's eye was caught by the *s* of Latin ending, or by the
ending of *upahafennes*.   15. *stete*, i. e. *stede*.

---

3. *petierit*, MS. *petitierit*.   4. *quemcumque*, MS. *quecumque*.   6. *ab*
omitted by Latin scribe.   7. *ordinationem*. Between *r* and *d* the same hole in
parchment obtains, as spoken of before (see note to p. 110. 7).   8. *prelatus*,
MS. *relatus*.   13. *ei*, MS. *que*.   15. *alius*, MS. *aliter*.

he na byð   of mynstre   he si utadræfed þence
non fuerit: etiam de monasterio   expellatur ;   Cogitet tamen

                        to iyldenne
abbas se de omnibus judicis suis deo redditurum rationem : ne
    andan   æfestes lig forbærnde sawla
forte zeli   aut invidie flamma urat animam ;

DE OSTIARIIS MONASTERII.   (CAP. LXVI.)

  æt geate   mynstres   si geset   eald   wita   se   wite cunne
5 Ad portam monasterii   ponatur senex sapiens qui sciat acci-
underfon andswore 7 agifan þæs geþungennes hine   ne
pere   responsum et reddere.   cuius maturitas   eum   non
geþafige worian se geatweard hus scyll habban wið þæt
sinat   vagari ; Qui porterius cellam debet habere juxta por-
geat þæt cumende   andweardne gemeton from hwam
tam   ut venientes semper presentem inveniant. a   quo
andswore underfon 7 sona þænne cnucað oððe þearfa
responsum acipiant ; Et mox ut aliquis pulsaverit | aut pauper (161 a.)
   clypað goda þanc he andsware oððe bletsige 7 mid
10 clamaverit. deo gratias respondeat aut benedicat. et cum
ealre manþwærnesse godes eges heagilde andsware   ofstlice
omni mansuetudine timoris dei reddat responsum festinanter :
mid wylme þæresoðre lufe se geatweard   helpe
cum fervore karitatis ;   Qui portarius si indiget solacio :
ginran broðran underfo   mynster soðlice gif hit mæig
juniorem fratrem accipiat. Monasterium autem si   possit
beon   sceall beon gesett þæt ealle neod behefness þæt is
fieri ita debet constitui. ut omnia necessaria. id est
wæter   myll   orceard bæcern oððe mistlice cræftes
15 aqua molendinum ortus pistrinum. vel artes diverse
wiðinnan   minstre beon geganne þæt nesig   neod
intra in monasterium exerceantur. ut non sit necessitas
munecum werigende wiðutan for þam
monachis vagandi foris quia omnino non expedit
heora sawlum   þysne   oft we wyllað
animabus eorum ; Hanc autem regulam sepius volumus

11. manþwærnesse, w corrected from another letter ?

2. se de, MS. sed.   4. MONASTERII, MS. MONASTERIIS.   7. juxta, MS.
juxtam.   11. timoris, MS. moris.   13. MS. accipiant.   14. fieri,
MS. fierii. id est, MS. idem.   15. (h)ortus, MS. ortu.   17. foris, a non-
contemporary a has been put over the i in the MS.

beon geræd　ænig　gebroðra　be nýtennýssa
in congregatione　*legi :*　*ne quis　fratrum　se de ignorantia*
þæt na belædie
excuset ;

DE FRATRIBUS IN VIAM DIRECTIS.　(CAP. LXVII.)

þa sendlican gebroðra　on　wege　ealra gebroðra　　　[h.]
DIRIGENDI　FR*ATRES*　IN　VIAM.　OMNIUM　FRATRUM　*vel*

[b.]　[e.] gebed　befæstan　7　æfre　æt þam æfteme-
abbatis　se orationi commendent ; Et *semper ad*　　ora-　5

stan gebede　godes　weorces　gemýnd　ealra　and
tionem　ultimam　operis　dei.　commemoratio　omniu m ab-

weardra　7 beo　þagencýrrendan　gebroþra　of　wege
sentium　fiat ;　Revertentes　autem　*de　via fratres ;*

on þam dæge　on þam þe gehweorfað geond　ealle　minsterlice
ipso　die　quo redeunt.　　*per　omnes canonicas*

tida　þonne　bið gefýlled　godes weorc　astrehð　moldan
horas　dum　expletur　opus dei　prostrati　solo

oððe eorðan fram　eallum gebroðrum biddan　gebed　forgime-
oratorii :　ab　omnibus petant　orationem propter 10

leaste　þæt ænig þinc ne undersmuge on wege gesýhðe oððe
(161 b.) *excessum :　ne quid forte | subripuerit　in　via visus.　aut*

lýst　þinces　oððe idelre　spræce　ne ne gedýrstlæce
auditus　male　rei aut　otiosi sermonis ;　Nec presumat

ænig　oðrum gereccan swa hwýlce þinc swa he gesýhð wið-
quisquam　aliis　referre　quecumque

utan　on mýnstre　oððe　he gehýrað forþam þe hit is
foris　monasterio viderit. aut　audierit　quia

mænifealt　towurpon　[a.]　　　rego-
plurima　destructio　est ; Quod si quis presumpserit vin- 15

licre waclicre oððe stire he underþeodde swa gelice 7 se ðe
dicte　regulari　subjaceat :　Similiter et　qui

---

7. *þagencýrrendan,* read *þa agencýrrendan.*　8. *gehweorfað, g* corr. from
some other letter.　15. *towurpon,* for *towurponnesse?　regolicre, r* corr.
from *a.*　16. *waclicre?* see note.

---

3. DIRECTIS, MS. DIRECTUS.　4. *omnium fratrum,* MS. *omniam fratres,*
but *ũ* above *res,* as if to indicate the correction.　9. *prostrati,* MS.
prostratu.

I

gedýrstlæcð clýsunga minstres utgan oððe awýder faren oððe
presumpserit claustra monasterii egredi : vel quoque ire vel
ænig þing þeh þe litel buton . hæse þæs abbotes
quippiam quamvis parvum sine jussione abbatis
don
facere ;

SI FRATRI INPOSSIBILIA JUBENTUR.　(CAP. LXVIII.)

gif hwilcum breðer ænig hefines oððe * unacumendalice
5 SI CUI FRATRI ALIQUA *forte gravia aut inpossibilia*
beoð geþeodde he underfo witodlice bebeodendes bebod
injunguntur suscipiat quidem jubentis imperium
mid ealre manþwærnesse ⁊ gehirsumnesse þæt eallunga
cum omni mansuetudine. et obedientia ; Quod si omnino
heora mægena gemet gif he gesýhð began
virium suarum mensuram viderit pondus oneris excedere
his unacumenlicnesse se þe gewis
inpossibilitatis sue causas ei qui sibi preest
⁊ gedafenlice na modigenne oððe wið-
10 *patienter et oportune suggerat ; non superbiendo : aut resis-*
standende æfter his tihtinge
tendo : vel contradicendo ; Quod si post suggestionem suam
on his cwýde bebod þæt gif þurhwunað
in sua sententia prioris imperium perduraverit :
wite se gingra swa him selfan gefremman ⁊ of soðre lufe
sciat junior ita sibi expedire : et ex karitate
getruwigende be godes fýlste gehýrsume |
confidens de adjutorio dei obediat : |　　　　　　　(162 a.)

15　UT IN MONASTERIO NON PRESUMAT ALTER ALTERUM
DEFENDERE.　(CAP. LXVIII.)

mid ænigum intingan ne gedýrstlæce oðer
Precavendum est ne quavis occasione presumat alius
oðerne bewerian oððe swýlce gescýldan
alium defendere monachum in monasterio. aut quasi tueri

---

5. unacumendalice, read unacumendlice ?　7. manþwærnesse, æ or a ?
9. þe, þ corrected from g.

---

2. parvum, MS. parvium, but i underdotted.　6. imperium (= imprum),
MS. impium.　　　15, 16. Heading not in the MS. ; supplied from the list of
chapters.

þeah þe hig mid ænigre mæg sibbe blodes   sibbe   beon ge
etiamsi   qualibet consanguinitatis   propinquitate   jun-
þeodde ne ne mid ænigum gemete   fram munecum
gantur ;   Nec   quolibet modo   id   a   monachis
si gedýrstlæcð forþam þe mæg þanon seo hefegoste intinga
*presumat*ur :   *quia exinde gravissima   occasio*
æswicunga unaspringon þæt gif for ænig   gemeleasað
scandalorum oriri potest ; Quod si   quis   hec transgressus

   * arlicor hi si geþread
fuerit : acrius   coerceatur.   5

UT NON PRESUMAT ALIQUIS ALIUM CEDERE. (CAP. LXX.)

forboden   ælc dýrstignýsse   intinga we ge-
VETETUR IN MONASTERIO OMNIS PRESUMPTIO*nis occasio ;   Or-*
endebýrdað 7 we gesettað   alýfed ænigne heora
*dinamus atque constituim*us *ut nulli liceat quemquam fratrum*
gebroðra amansumian oððe slean buton þam þe mihte
suorum excommunicare. aut cedere. nisi   cui potestas ab
   biðgeseald ða sýngendan   ætforan eallum gebro-
abbate data fuerit ; Peccatores autem coram   omni-   10
ðrum beon geþreade   oðre ogan þæt habban   cildum
bus arguantur : ut ceteri metum habeant ; Infantibus
       oð þone fifteoðan   gear ýlde lare oððe
*vero usq*ue *ad quintum decimum annum aetatis disci-*
stýre geornfulnessa   si gegearcod hýrdrædene
pline diligentia ab omnibus adhibeatur. et custodia sit :
ac eac swýlce mid eallum gemete 7 gesceade soðes   strangran
sed et hoc cum omni mensura et ratione ; Nam in fortiori
ýlde se de gedýrstlæcð æthwega butan bebode þæs abbodes oððe
aetate qui presumpserit aliquatenus sine precepto abbatis :   vel 15
   on þam sýlfan cildan butan smegunge onstingð regolicre
(162 b.) *in ipsis   infantibus sine discretione exarserit : | disci-*
stýre   he underhnige   þe
pline regulari subjaceat : quia scriptum est ; Quod tibi
sýlfan þu nelt beon ne oðrum ne do þu
    non vis fieri : alii ne feceris ;

---

3. *mæg*, gloss to *potest*, in l. 4.   4. *for œnig gemeleasað*, read *œnig for-
gemeleasað*.   5. *arlicor*, read *tearlicor*.

---

2. *id*, supplied by glossator. *a*, MS. *ad*.   3. *quia*, MS. *qui*.   4. *hec*,
MS. *hic*.   6. Heading not in the MS.; supplied from the list of chapters.
13. *custodia sit*, MS. *custodiat se*.

UT OBEDIENTES SIBI SINT INVICEM FRATRES.　(CAP. LXXI.)

gehýrsumnesse god　na þæt an　þam abbade is togearcienne
OBEDIENTIAE BONUM NON SOLUM.　ABBATI　EXHIbendum　est

　　　　heom * betwýnanan　　hi gehýrsumian
ab omnibus.　sed etiam sibi　invicem　ita　oboediant

　　witende for þisne gehýrsumnesse weg　him sýlfne to
fratres : scientes per hanc　obedientiae　viam : se

farenne to　gode on ðam fore sædon　　　　prafosta
5 ituros ad deum ;　Premisso ergo　abbatis atque prepositorum

þa þa fram him beon gesette　bebode þam　we ne geþafiað
qui ab eo　constituuntur imperio.　cui　non permittimus

asindrodum beboda beon foreset þær to eacan ealle þa gingran
privata imperia　preponi :　de cetero　omnes juniores

heora ýldrum　　on ealre soðre　lufe hohfulnesse
prioribus　suis　omni karitate.　et　sollicitudine

hi gehirsumian þæt gif ænig　　sacful　fuerit byð gemet
obediant ;　Quod si　quis contentiosus,　repperitur :

he si geþread gif hwýlc broðor　for ænigum gehwædum intinga
10 corripiatur ; Si quis autem frater pro quavis minima causa

　　 oððe for gehwýlcum ealdre his beoð geþread
ab abbate vel a　quocumque priore suo　corripitur

mid ænigum mete oððe gif he leohtlice undergit　mod ealdres
quolibet modo : vel si　leviter　senserit animum prioris

　　ongen him wrað oððe astiredne þeah þe
cujuscumque　contra se iratum vel commotum quamvis

æthwega　sona buton ýldinge swa lange astreht on eorðan
modice :　mox sine　mora　tamdiu prostratus in terra

toforan his fotum　ac he licge gebetende oððe þæt bið
15 ante pedes ejus jaceat satisfaciens : usque dum

bletsunge gehæled seo stýrung　gif he forhogað don
benedictione sanetur illa commotio ; Quod si contempserit facere :

oððe he lichamlicere wrace þæt gif forsihð oððe gif anmod
aut　corporali vindicte　subjaceat :　aut si contumax

he bið of minstre he si utadræfæd
fuerit de monasterio　expellatur. |　　　　　　(163 a.)

　3. betwýnanan, read betwýnan.　7. asindrodum beboda, see note.　9. fuerit,
added by glossator.　11. for, read from.　17. þæt gif forsihð, I suggest
that this was originally written in the margin as supplementary gloss to gif
he forhogað. It was then copied into the text in the wrong place.

17. vindicte, MS. vindincte.

DE ZELO BONO QUEM DEBENT MONACHI HABERE. (CAP. LXXII.)

swa is [h.] se ẏfela   biternesse   anda   7
Sicut   est zelus   amaritudinis   malus qui separat a deo et

læd to   helle   is se goda anda se ðe sẏndrað fram
ducit ad infernum ita est   zelus   bonus qui separat   a

leahtre 7 læt to gode   þẏsne   andan
vitio et ducit ad deum et ad vitam aeternam ; Hunc ergo zelum

mid þære wealdestan   .   began   mid
ferventissimo   amore   exerceant monachi id est   ut 5

wẏrðmente   forhradian heora untrumnessa oððe
honore se invicem   preveniant ;   Infirmitates suas   sive

lichama oððe þeawa gepẏldelicost forþẏldian gehirsumnesse
corporum sive morum patientissime   tollerent   obedientiam

him sẏlf geflitmælum   hi beodan   na ænig þæt þe he
sibi certatim   impendant ;   Nullus quod sibi

nẏtwẏrdlice deme   folgie   swiðor oðrum þa soðe
utile   judicat sequatur ; sed quod magis   alio ;   Carita-

lufe broðor rædene mid clænre hi beodan   lufe   hi on
tem fraternitatis   casto   impendant amore ;   Deum 10

drædan heora abbud   mid sifre 7 eadmodre soðre *lare
timeant. abbatem   suum sincera et humili   caritate

hi lufian cristes eallunga naht hi forasettan sege   ætgædere
diligant ; Christo omnino nihil preponant. qui nos pariter

[g.]   [g.]   bringe
ad vitam aeternam perducat ;

DE HOC QUOD NON OMNIS JUSTITIE OBSERVATIO IN HAC SIT
REGULA CONSTITUTA. (CAP. LXXIII.)   15

þẏsne regol   we awriton   healdende on
Regulam   autem hanc discripsimus, ut hanc observantes in

minstre   æthwega oððe arwurðnesse þeawa oððe anginn
monasteriis. aliquatenus vel honestatem morum aut initium

drohtnunge us *þe geswutelian habban oðrą haligra to ful-
conversationis nos demonstremus habere ; Ceterum ad per-

fremednessa drohtnunge   sẏnd laræ
fectionem conversationis qui festinat. sunt doctrine sanctorum

---

11. *lare*, a misreading for *lufe*.   18. *þe*, read *we*.

6. *Inflrmitates*, MS. *Infirmites*.   14. QUOD, MS. QUO.   OMNIS, MS.
OMNES.

fædera   þara gehealdsum gehealdsum ne gelæd   mannan   to
patrum.   *quar*um | *observatio*   *perducit* *hominem   ad* (163 b.)

healdsumnessa fulfremednessa la hwylc . tramod   oððe hwylc
celsitudinem   *perfectionis;   Que enim pagina   aut   quis*

spræc godcundlice ealdordomes ealdre 7 niwe gecyðnesse nis
sermo   divine   auctoritatis   veteris ac novi testamenti non

se rihtoste   bysen lifes mennisces oððe la hwilc boc   haligra
est rectissima norma vite humane: Aut   quis   liber sanctorum

rihte   fædera   þæt   na sweg   mid rihtum rine
ç *catholicorum patrum   hoc non   resonat   ut   recto cursu*

we becumende to urum scyppende   eac swilce 7
perveniamus   ad   creatorem   nostrum ; Nec   non   et

þurhtogenessa   7 gesetnessa heora lifes   ac eac
conlationes   patrum et instituta   vite eorum. sed   et

swylce regol   basilius hwæt   elles sind
regula   sancti patris nostri basilii : quid aliud sunt.

butan wel libbendra 7 gehirsumera   muneca   7 gesetnessa
nisi bene viventium et obedientium   monachorum   instituta

mihta   us   asolcenum 7 yfel   lybbendum 7 gime-
10 *virtutum. nobis autem desidiosis et male viventibus atque neg-*

leasum   scame   gescyndnysse   swa hwilc
legentibus rubor. confusionis est ; Quisquis   ergo ad patriam

þu efast þysne þane læstan *acunnednesse regol awri-
celestem festinas. hanc minimam   inchoationis regulam dis-

tenne fylstendum criste þu gefremme 7 þu ætnyxtan to
criptam adjuvante christo perficias : ct tunc demum   ad

maran þe wiðufan we gemundon lare   lare   7 mihta
majora que   supra commemoravimus   doctrine   virtutumque

geþincðe godes scildendum becimð wyrcendum þas þinc
15 *culmina deo protegente pervenies; Facientibus hec   regna*

geopenað þa ecan.
patebunt aeterna ;

FINIT REGULA SANCTI BENEDICTI.

1, 2. *gehealdsumnessa* in l. 2 is the proper gloss to *observatio* in l. 1, and
the *gehealdsum, gehealdsum* in this line, I am unable to explain except as a
double dittography.   2. *-sumnessa*, first stroke of *m* erased.   12. *acunncd-*
nesse, read *acennednesse*.   14. *lare* was first put over the ending of *com-*
memoravimus, then erased and written again over *doctrine.*

---

1. *quarum*, MS. *quorum.*   2. *Que enim*, MS. originally *Qu. fenim*, from
which *Que enim* has been corrected.   7. *patrum*, third stroke of *m* erased.
10. *desidiosis*, MS. *desidiosus.*   11. *rubor*, MS. *robur.*   12. *festinas*,
MS. *festinans.   regulam*, MS. *regula.*

NOTES.

1. 5. *fremfi.* After this word there is a gap in the MS., so that some letter or letters may have been there, which are now gone. Read *fremfullice.*

1. 8. *roluptatibus.* This reading, for which nearly all other codices have *roluntatibus,* is supported not only by two of the Latin MSS. (G. U.), but also by the gloss.

2. 8. Above *dicente,* a little to the right, ū is found in the MS. I presume it is the ending of *secgend,* which gloss was filled out by a copyist in its proper place, and thus written twice.

3. 3. *-eond,* as gloss to (*proh*)*ibe.* The other texts have *forhafa* (Schröer, Die Prosabearbeitungen, 2. 21), except S. (W. V. 5. 15), which gives *heald.* Neither of these suggests a reading for our text. Possibly the *e* is a misreading for a *t* (which suggestion is favoured by the palæographical evidence), and the gloss was *forstond.* I am happy to acknowledge my indebtedness to Professor Cosÿn, of Leiden, for this and other suggestions.

3. 11. *gebroht,* as gloss to *perducatum,* is in itself undoubtedly right. Only *per ducatum* was wrongly taken as one word; see context. Similar cases where a misreading of the MS. produced a wrong gloss— wrong so far as the context is concerned—are numerous. See e. g. *sægde,* as gloss to *ait,* which is wrong for *aut* (78. 1).

3. 16. *Habitavit=habitabit.* See Sweet, O. E. T., p. 185.

5. 10. *de habitatore* (MS. habitatorum), glossed by *be wunungum.* The other texts have '*be þæm bugendum* his *eardungstowe*' (Schröer, Die Prosabearbeitungen, 4. 22). But the Winteney Version, which is independent of our text, has '*be þam wuniunge his eardingstowe*' (7. 27). That the original also had *wunungum* is made (at least) likely by the MS. reading *habitatorum* for *habitatore,* which may be owing to the *-um* of the gloss. But whence the form *wunungum?* To read *wunigendum* (see ib., l. 11) is an easy way out of the difficulty, but scarcely the right one. We must have very good reasons indeed for assuming that a commoner form made room for a rarer one. Considering that the earliest examples given by *Koch* (I², p. 342, § 61), of participial forms in *-ing* are from the A-text of Layamon's Brut., i. e. about the year 1200 (see ib., p. 10), I should not dare to think that we had here an early instance of it, if this form stood alone in our text. But we also find *latens* glossed by *lettincg* (80. 10). There would not seem to be the shadow of a doubt concerning the ending *-incy* being that of a participle; but I would again not lay too much stress on this instance by itself, since I am not sure as to the meaning of the gloss itself. But if we find *monstrante* glossed by *swijtelunge* (35. 3), we may perhaps look upon the others too, as evidencing a participle in -*ing*[1].

I cannot leave the matter alone without going at some length into detail as to the origin of the form in -*ing*. I may at once state that I look upon it as a direct and phonetic representative of the A.-S. form in -*ende*. Whatever be the origin, whether the above view will prove to be the correct one, or whether we must continue to view it with Prof. Max Müller (Lectures on the Science of Language, II) as a 'corruption' of a verbal substantive in the dative, we are alike struck with the fact that for a long time, down to Gower and Chaucer, nay, to early in the fifteenth century[2], the forms -and, -end, -ing continue to be found parallel in the same authors. Now, though a hundred and eighty years more of parallelism may increase our wonder, they need not materially alter our view of the case.

Let us now turn to our text, and see what the frequent occurrence of -*enne* by the side of -*ende* for the pres. part., as well as for the gerund or participium necessitatis (Introd., V, § 89), gives us a right to conclude. If we may lay down anything, it will be this, that the ending -*ende* has dwindled down into a combination of a certain vowel (of no definite phonetic value) + the nasal which occurs before dentals, and, be it remembered, a *voiced* nasal before the voiced *d*. I denote this voiced nasal by ñ. This ñ was sometimes continued, i.e. lengthened; but sometimes the stop was undone with a jerk, occasioning the explosion which is symbolised by *d*. Now the only difference between this form eñe and -*inge* is that the dental nasal is replaced by the guttural nasal, which I denote by *ñ*, surely in itself no very great change, especially as analogues are by no means wanting. We must look to vulgar speech for some of these analogues. An *orphan* becomes an *orfling* (sometimes a *horfling*), etc. See *H. Baumann*, Londinismen, Slang und Cant. (Berlin, 1887), Introduction, § 5, sub 3 (p. xci), from which passage it must not, however, be supposed that this pronunciation is peculiar to London. I may also instance the 'peculiar' pronunciation of the French nasals in the mouths of badly taught Germans, and—what is more interesting at this conjunction— English children. I distinctly remember the contortions that some untrained pupils of mine in an English school had to make their mouths undergo, when they had to pronounce 'je demande, tu

---

[1] Cf. Bosw. in v. *wellicung*; also Cant. Ps. 149. 4. (See the forthcoming edition, by Mr. Fred. Harsley.) Reluctantly, I must draw attention to the ending, -*e*, which is not that of an A.-S. participle in the dative. Can the glossator have taken *monstrante* as a gerund, = *monstrando*?

[2] I was strengthened in my conviction by a correspondence on this subject with Mr. C. Stoffel, of Nymegen, the results of whose extensive reading are always so kindly placed at the disposal of his correspondents.

demandes,' etc. The words invariably became je demangde, tu demangdes, nous demángdons, etc., no doubt in all respects a fit analogue.

6. 3. *we hihtaᷤ.* Evidently a marginal gloss got in the wrong place, instead of over *speramus.* See note to l. 5 on page 6.

9. 18. *dan. orseclena,* as gloss to *anachoritarum.* Read *onsetlena.* But what does *dan.* mean? I suspect that *d* is a paving or sequence letter, and that *an* indicates that instead of *onsetlena* we may also read *ansetlena.* Thus interpreted, *-an* would be another case of merography, a part put for a whole (Introd., V, § 4).

9. 19. *conversationis,* MS. *conversionis.* The same corruption obtains in six other MSS., but both context and gloss show *conversationis* to have been the original reading.

10. 1. *frore* for *frofre.* The dropping of the *f* (after it had become voiced), i.e. the merging of it into the *o,* may very well be a phonetic process. See also *Ellis,* E. E. P., II, pp. 513, 514.

10. 7. *vel oðđe.* I think that originally the gloss to *experientia* was *ꝥ afundennessa.* (For this use of ꝥ = id est, see Skeat's ed. of Matthew passim, and l. 1 on p. 25 where *oðđe* = ꝥ occurs after the word; see note to 29. 15 ; 55. 2.) A second glossator, who did not see that ꝥ meant the same as .i. (=id est), or as 7 (cf. 20, 2 ; 20, 3 ; 84. 9, etc.), added the lemma *vel.* For other cases where part of the gloss was wrongly translated into Latin, I refer to (92. 1). *Colore* was here glossed by *be bleo* ; a second glossator adds *de,* as supposed lemma to *be.* Cf. also (93. 3) *et sagum.* where *et* may have a similar origin.

12. 1. *geondsprecend.* If it means anything, *geondsprecan* = to address or to make anyone hear, which in this place has no meaning. Read *geondsprēcend* = *geondsprencend.* See Introd., V, § 70.

15. 5. *bennᷤe* stands over *ne he,* and *ne he* over *Neque. bennđe,* as gloss to *neque* is unintelligible ; read *bemiᷤe,* and take it as gloss to *dissimulet.* Cf. Corpus gl. 681, and Wright-Wülker, 388. 31, 32 (Dissimulare, bemiþan oᷤᷤe yldan).

16. 9. *for forht taliendre,* as gloss to *parvi pendens,* is corrupt ; it is very likely that *forht* was misread for *nawht,* which is a not infrequently occurring form of *nawiht.*

17. 15. *est,* a little erased. The fact is that *faciat* is found in other MSS. in this place, but in our MS. lower down (l. 16) erased. Someone who did not understand the words *et quod utilius judicaverit* in the context tried to restore sense by adding *est.*

18. 4. *hwonlicor,* as gloss to *salubrius?* Read *halwendlicor.*

20. 10. *factam,* MS. *factum.* Of the other texts (Schmidt, p. 13), none has *factum* (but the collation of our text is very imperfect, our reading *i.a.* not being given ; see Schröer, Die Prosabearbeitungen, p. xxvii): they read *factam, factas,* or *facta.* Originally, I suppose, our text had *factam,* agreeing with *injuriam.* Hence the gloss *gedonne,* agreeing with *tregan.* In this state our text must have been copied out, and the copyist, by an absolute blunder, or mislead by the masc.

termination of the gloss, wrote *factum*. After that, some one added the gloss *dæde* to the new lemma *factum*.

20. 13. *c̃e modig*, as gloss to *desuperbum*, đ=*debere*, must have been copied into the Latin as though it were part of *superbum*.

21. 13. *frœdlice*. *Rœdlice* (=hrædlice) (cf. Wright-Wülker, 243. I : frequenter, celer) must have been there first, and *f* added by the influence of the Latin. Or we must take *o* to be no paving letter, and read ofrædlice=oftrædlice.

26. 6. *sӯlfsӯne*, as gloss to *rara*. *seldsӯne* was probably there originally. The corruption is easy to understand if we suppose *selƥsyne* (cf. Introd., V, § 55) to have been there.

27. 2. *c. us. ӯ.*, as gloss to *nobis*. Do *c, y* perhaps form part of the gloss to *nobis*; and must we consequently look upon it as a misreading for *us. y. c.*, i.e. *usic*? It would be quite in accordance with the usual practice if more or less uncommon forms were misunderstood, and consequently mutilated. It is true that forms in -*ic* are found only in the accusative, whilst a dative form is postulated by the lemma; but first, this rule holds good only for the classical periods of Anglo-Saxon (cf. Sievers², § 81, Anm. 2), and secondly, the acc. may be explained as dependent upon *clӯpaƌ*.

28. 12. *a, an*, over *inseruit*. *a* may of course be a gloss-letter, but *an*? I have thought of the following explanation : that *a, an*, as indicating the weak nom. and gen. ending (or acc. plural) were put over *ascendendos*. Afterwards the full gloss was added. A case in point may be adduced here from a Leiden MS., where we find *lucubro* glossed by *brasbrat*. The explanation—see *Goetz-Loewe*, Glossae Nominum, Leipzig, 1884, p. 161—is given by *Vossius* as lucubro, (lucu)bras, (lucu)brat. The gloss to *inseruit* is *gesætt* in l. 10.

29. 11. *asmaidan*. Is this a corruption of *asmaiand=asmeagend*?

29. 15. *soƌes oƌƌe secge*, as gloss to *dicat*. *soƌes* may be a mere repetition of the *soƌes* in l. 14, and then *oƌƌe (secge)* simply means the same as the .i. or the 7 found over Latin words to introduce the gloss. But there is also the possibility that in *soƌes* we have a remnant of the verb *seƌan*, to affirm.

30. 9. *insint*? Must we read 7 *sint gewordene* as gloss to *facti sunt*, and *in* as gloss to (or repetition of?) Latin *in*?

30. 17. *ƥæt he oseo*. Read, as pointed out in the foot-note, *ƥæt he seo*. If the *o* is not a solitary paving letter—which, see above, p. xxxiii, is not altogether a contradiction in terms—the only explanation to fall back upon is, that an original had *heo seo* ; *heo* under the influence of the following *seo*.

31. 14. *under* should stand over *ƥæt*; it is part of the gloss to *subdat* in l. 15.

34. 7. *wursan*, gloss to *vermis*. How *wurm* can be corrupted into *wursan* I fail to understand. The unfortunate *s* makes it alike impossible to assume either a mistake of the eye or of the ear.

54. 4. *swӯrige*? The only way out of the difficulty I know is

to assume that *swýrige* is somehow or other misread for *scýrige*, and that this should be gloss to *partiat* as well as *todæld*.

55. 2. *þelæs þe hi wýrðan oððe gewundode.* The first glossator put ł *gewundode* over *vulnerentur* (cf. note to 10. 7). Another added the auxiliary, and wrote *oððe* for ł.

56. 8. *gemedemod*, read *gemet*. Probably *med* (for *met*) was found there first by a copyist, who, not understanding this, or not deeming it sufficient, put *gemed* before it. This *gemed med* was copied out as *gemedemod* = temperatur.

58. 4. *gesewene*. I think we have a remnant here of the rare verb *geseon*, for which see Grein, in voce. Also in v. *séon*, and Bosworth, ed. 1838, in v. *seon*.

59. 14. *for* belongs to *swýrian* (= swyÿrian, cf. Introd., V, § 57), and *an* is possibly a wrongly transcribed dittography for *na* of naht.

61. 2. *gehealdenne*, gloss to *sanentur*. Either a copyist found *gehealde* = *gehælde* (Introd., V, § 17) or *sanentur* was glossed by *salrentur*, and this by *gehealdenne*. Subsequently this middle gloss was omitted. This kind of double glossing occurs very frequently, e. g. in Bouterwek's Aldhelmglosses (H. Z. 9).

64. 1. *anwealde* is gloss to *potestate*, and not to *voluntate*; and in no way can I suppose *anwealde* to be corrupted from any word meaning *potestas*. And the Latin texts T. U. G., i. e. exactly those that agree most in particulars with our own Latin text, also have *voluntate*, whence it is likely that our text must have originally presented this reading. Otherwise we might suppose our text to have been corrected by another (which had *voluntate*), after the original *potestate* had been glossed by *anwealde*. Cf. note to 88. 6.

69. 9. *frum anginne*, as gloss to *incipiente*. I cannot quite make this out; we must expect a dative or a nominative (Introd., V, § 3) of the present participle. Professor Cosÿn suggests *fruman anginne*, which is certainly the best I can think of, although it is not entirely satisfactory.

69. 12. *drenc* as gloss to *musitatio*? Several explanations suggest themselves. *d* may be a paving letter, in which case *rene* may stand for *ryne* = mysterium, or better still *rene* = *ryne*. Cf. Grein in v. *rýn*. Cf. Introd., V, § 27. If we take *d* to be part of the word we may think of *drem* = *dream*. Cf. Introd., V, § 30.

70. 4. *seo wuca þen*. If we had not Sievers, § 337, Anm. 2, and supra, § 84, to refer to, where other instances from the above text are given, we might possibly be induced to look upon *seo* here as a solitary proof of a feminine origin of our text, which would then be in the same plight as Schröer's texts (cf. Die Prosabearbeitungen, p. xxix). But by these references this phantom vanishes into thin air.

73. 11. *belippendan* = *continuanda*. If we may suppose *continuanda* to have been misread for *concernanda*. *belippendan* would stand for *belimpendan* (cf. Introd., V, § 39). But this explanation does not seem entirely satisfactory.

82. 3. This word cannot be otherwise explained as *gif forcrafað* (cf. Introd., V, § 70); *gif*, as gloss to *si*, in l. 2.

86. 3. I had thought *bigænge* to be a dittographical gloss to *in itinere*, which had got into the wrong place. However, Professor Cosÿn suggests that *m. g. bigænge*=under religious worship, should here be understood. I suspect that we shall have to combine the two explanations, because there is no lemma, which, taken by itself, could occasion the gloss *under religious worship* (unless it be cum *tremore* divino ?). A copyist put *bi gænge* in the margin, and another, misled by the frequency of the occurrence of the expression, mid godcundum bigænge, put this over *divino*. It must, however, be admitted that the train of thought, the association of ideas, may very well have given rise to the error of mistaking these two words (*b. g.*) for one.

86. 17. *egelod*, as gloss to *condatur*. This is the reading of the MS., but we may detach *e* as a ' paving letter' from the body of the word, and thus *gelod* remains to be explained. The lemma suggests a connection with *gelogian* (cf. e. g. 98. 15), of which the past part. would be *gelogod*. This might easily become *gelowod* (cf. Introd., V, § 68), and this could be contracted into *gelod*. But since I have no other instances of such ' contractions' I prefer to look upon it as a mere scribal error.

88. 6. *mæð*=humilitas, which is in the other texts. Compare for the probable origin the notes to 64, 1 ; 99, 13.

91. 17. *fiand reaf*? Perhaps corrupted from *færeld reaf*? or from *fierdreaf*? But, writes Professor Cosÿn, what would monks do with those? To add another possibility, I suggest that it is from *fot reaf*. Cf. the reading of the other texts *fotgewadum*.

97. 2. *habban ðretioðinge*, as gloss to *habita . . . . deliberatione.* We may perhaps assume *habban* to be an infinitival gloss (cf. Introd., V, § 3) to a verbal inflection, which would seem to be of rare occurrence, and therefore liable to corruption, and then *ðretioðinge* would be a corruption of *ymbðriodunge*. This can be more easily accounted for if we think of the phenomenon which I discussed in the Introduction (V, § 4).

98. 15, and **100. 1, 2.** I have stated, Introd., V, § 93, that I fail to understand these forms. The first *o* in *gelogodre* is indistinct; for the verb, cf. note to 86. 17. The only explanation I can think of is, that in each case the *r* was misread from an original *n*. This would yield perfectly intelligible forms ; and palæographically speaking, the corruptions are very likely to occur. The puzzling *mæssepreostra* for *mæssepreostrum* (see note to 100. 10) may be in the same plight.

99. 4. MS. 'Offerunt de filiis nobilium aut pauperum qui.' The original must have read,

Offerunt '

De filiis nobilium aut pauperum qui.

The copyist read *offerunt* ' first, although it was meant for the last word, and not seeing the MS. sign for *ur*, he copied the word as *offerunt*.

99. 13. *suffectam* would seem to be the right reading, although as many as nine other texts have *suspectam* (C. D. G. H. K. L. S. T. U). At one time or another this must also have been in our text (cf. note to 64. 1), or *suffectam* must have been misread as *suspectam*. With this word the gloss corresponds. How little *suffectam* was understood is proved by the fact that our text would seem to be the only one that had preserved it, since A. O. P. Q. R. have *subjectam*.

100. 10. *mæssepreostrum*. In § 36 of the Introd. (V) I have stated that the *r* was inserted. Professor Gallée, of Utrecht, suggests that the word **preostr* may have existed, in which case I should have to cancel the above statement. I can only add that, although I have not found any traces of it, it is extremely likely, considering the Greek origin, and the analogue of the Dutch and German form *priester*. But see note to (98. 15).

108. 7. *awyrtlian*, a legitimate form for *awyrtwalian*? The gloss reads as if the lemma were *eradicare*.

113. 16. *waclicre oððe styre*. Cp. 115, 12, 17; and 116, 17, and read *regolicre wrace, lare oððe styre*.

116. 7. *asindrodum beboda*. As it is not likely that we can look upon *beboda* as a crude form in the plural (cf. Introd., V, § 3), I suspect that *beboda* was misread for *bebodū* = bebodum.

ISBN 0859918483